Waterloo

To Uncle Ken & Aunt Bodie
With all best wishes,
Ken
Waterloo, 1990

Waterloo

An Illustrated History
by Kenneth McLaughlin

"Partners in Progress"
by Richard Pearce

Produced in Cooperation with
the Waterloo Chamber of
Commerce

Windsor Publications (Canada)
Ltd.—History Books Division

Managing Editor: Karen Story
Design Director: Alexander D'Anca
Executive Editor: Pamela Schroeder

Staff for *Waterloo: An Illustrated
History*
Manuscript Editor: Teri Davis
Greenberg
Photo Director: Susan L. Wells
Senior Editor, Corporate Biographies:
Judith L. Hunter
Senior Production Editor, Corporate
Biographies: Phyllis Gray
Co-ordinator, Corporate Biographies:
Gladys McKnight
Editorial Assistants:
Phyllis Feldman-Schroeder,
Kim Kievman, Michael
Nugwynne, Kathy B. Peyser,
Susan Schlanger, Theresa J. Solis
Publisher's Representatives,
Corporate Biographies:
Maya Hart, Eric Cairns
Layout Artist. Corporate Biographies:
Chris Murray
Designer: Tom McTighe

ISBN: 0-89781-416-9

Windsor Publications, Ltd.
Elliot Martin, Chairman of the Board
James L. Fish III, Chief Operating
Officer
Michele Sylvestro, Vice
President/Sales-Marketing
Mac Buhler, Vice President/Sponsor
Acquisitions

*Pages 2-3: Woldemar Neufeld's
painting of Snider's Mill and the
Bank of Montreal provides a vivid
depiction of Waterloo's central
business district in an earlier era.
Courtesy, Woldemar Neufeld and
Sand Hill Books*

Right: The Procession, *a nine-
teenth-century wood engraving by
F.M. Bell Smith, captures the fes-
tive aura surrounding the great
Saengerfest. Courtesy, Kitchener
Public Library*

Contents

Acknowledgments

The Waterloo Chamber of Commerce's Centenary celebration, of which this book is part, commemorates 100 years of progress.

The Chamber has played an important role in this city, including the development of Waterloo Park, securing Waterloo Lutheran University (Wilfrid Laurier University) and assisting our membership, the City, and community to grow and prosper. We continue this role and look forward to serving the interests of our community during the next 100 years.

We are blessed with a community with a solid future. Waterloo possesses the same qualities that fueled a diverse and healthy town 100 years ago: citizens with vision and fortitude who strive to enhance our community's quality of life.

The culmination of this book and the Chamber's 100th Anniversary Celebration are the result of a vision made reality by a group of dedicated individuals. We thank Dave Sandrock, Centennial Committee chairman, for his leadership role and foresight in making our centenary larger than our dreams. His committee spent more than two years planning this celebration. Many thanks for an outstanding contribution.

We also recognize our Chamber members, volunteers, staff, Waterloo citizens, and city staff, past and present, for their contributions to our city. Their efforts mirror the success of our Waterloo.

Tom Burns
President
Waterloo Chamber
of Commerce

Jane Falconer
General Manager
Waterloo Chamber
of Commerce

This book represents the culmination of many people's efforts to produce a history of the life of a city—Waterloo. A reflection of progress, focus, and commitment by citizens aspiring to create an industrious place smitten with "quality of life, prosperity . . . a future."

The Waterloo Chamber of Commerce initiated a committee to celebrate its centenary early in 1988. This committee focused its efforts on "giving something back to the community" in commemorating this organization's 100th anniversary in 1990—an opportunity for all to share in the experiences of our city's past.

We searched for those willing to contribute to this project with the same determination our city forefathers demonstrated in creating our Waterloo.

The task proved simple. Author Ken McLaughlin lent his expertise, enthusiasm, and love for his city in compiling an "urban biography." His inspiration, knowledge, and constant search for the facts is enviable and appreciated. Local artist Peter Goetz kindly donated his time and talent to paint our city's former City Hall, which graces our book cover. A heartfelt thank you for your generosity.

Our desire to create a quality, historical keepsake adorned by local artists' talents that make "history come alive," inspired us to gain permission for paintings that reflect our city's past. We recognize Woldemar Neufeld for his generosity in permitting us to use his works. Many of the black and white photos included in this book were originally gathered by Joye Krauvel and her committee for the city's 125th anniversary.

We acknowledge the many citizens who contributed to our city's "life," past and present, and to our youth who will fulfill the promise of our future.

Michael Voisin
Centennial Book Chairman
Centennial Committee

Dave Sandrock
Centennial Committee
Chairman

WATERLOO CHAMBER OF COMMERCE PAST PRESIDENTS

Year	President	Year	President	Year	President	Year	President
1890	C. Kumpf	1908	J.B. Hughes	1935	W. Uffelman	1964-1965	W.W. Timmis
1891	J. Shuh	1909	T. Hilliard	1936	W.P. Kress	1966-1967	D. Meyer
1892	R. Y. Fish	1910	S.B. Bricker	1937-1939	J.R. Beaton	1968-1969	J.R. Coghill
1893	H. Grasset	1911-1912	J.C. Mueller	1940-1941	H.A. Moyer	1970-1971	A.P. Schendel
1894	R. Roschman	1913-1916	A. Bauer	1942-1943	W.J. McGibbon	1972-1973	Dr. C.R. Buck
1895	J. W. Fear	1916-1918	P.V. Wilson	1944	W.H. Carlisle	1974-1975	R.R. Kleinschmid
1896	G. Diebol	1919-1920	A. Bechtel	1945-1946	E.H. Sipple	1976-1977	J.B. Forbes
1897	W.H. Riddel	1921	E. Bauer	1947	A.J. Thom	1978-1979	W.B. Pernfuss
1898	S. Snyder	1922-1923	C.W. Wells	1948-1950	H.J. Heasley	1980	K. Tyers
1899	Dr. J.H. Webb	1924-1926	A.K. Cressman	1951	A.M. Snider	1981-1982	J. Duffy
1900-1901	J. Roos	1927-1928	A. Foster	1952	M.J. Smith	1983-1984	J. Robertson
1902-1903	R. Roschman	1929	W. Henderson	1953-1954	J.O. Beynon	1985-1986	D. Sandrock
1904	L. Stauffer	1930-1931	A.M. Snider	1955-1956	H.C. Gerster	1987-1988	J. Harper
1905	G. Moore	1932	W. Henderson	1957-1958	D.A. Roberts		
1906	J. Muir	1933	L. Henhoeffer	1959-1961	N.W. Parker		
1907	W.G. Weichel	1934	C.C. Parsons	1962-1963	J.M. Harper		

This is not a conventional local history. Missing are the lists of facts and dates as well as the names of many local notables and their achievements. Instead, this is a history of the life of a city, an "urban biography" rather than a "local history." For me, this book also completes a trilogy of urban histories that began in 1983 with *Kitchener: An Illustrated History*, co-authored with my good friend and colleague, Professor John English, followed in 1987 by *Cambridge: The Making of a Canadian City*.

I have been fortunate once again to have had an excuse to spend time in the Grace Schmidt Room at the Kitchener Public Library, which is a model throughout the province of what a local history library can be. At the University of Waterloo, Susan Saunders Bellingham, Head of Special Collections at the Dana Porter Library, was also extremely helpful. Not only has she established a wonderful collection, but she has also succeeded in making the University Library an attractive centre for the larger community. Nancy Saunders Maitland, the Corporate Archivist at Mutual Life, and Sandra Lowman, Archivist at the Seagram Museum, provided generous access to their collections. In keeping with a longstanding family tradition, Sue Mansell gave information from her personal files as well as help with the records of the Local Architectural Conservation Advisory Committee. Staff at the City of Waterloo endured countless interruptions with equanimity. Mike Voisin, my contact with the Centenary Committee of the Chamber of Commerce, shared his enthusiasm, support and friendship.

Historical photos are from the local collections named above and also from those in the Waterloo Public Library and the Joseph Schneider Haus as well as from the National Archives in Ottawa and the Public Archives of Ontario. John Bell and Ann Martin expedited the gathering of photographs in Ottawa while John Shewchuk, a former student and now a practising public historian, assisted me in Waterloo with both the text and the illustrations. In this as in the history of Cambridge, James Stevenson of Photo X in Waterloo was generous with his time, his advice, his considerable photographic talents, and with many of his photos. Two prominent artists, Peter Goetz and Woldemar Neufeld, made possible the reproduction of their paintings for which I am especially grateful. In this regard I would also like to thank Paul and Hildi Tiessen who have kindly allowed me to reproduce paintings by Peter Goetz and Woldemar Neufeld previously published in two of their books.

In the preparation of this book I have benefited from the research in local topics done by students at St. Jerome's College and in the history department at the University of Waterloo, especially Wayne Allen, Jeannie-Anne Boyes, Cindy Day, Mark Epp, Richard Haigh, David Plouffe, Patti Shea, John Theiss and Christine Veale.

I am most pleased once again to have persuaded Rita Racanelli to input my manuscript. Her unfailing care and commitment to excellence has proven invaluable. The President of St. Jerome's College, Douglas Letson, the Assistant Dean, Michael Higgins, and the Registrar, Kevin Donelson, carried a disproportionate share of the administrative duties while I completed this book. I want to thank them and my colleagues in the history department for their continuing encouragement and support.

Three men who unfortunately will not see this book but who influenced the development of both its author and the city merit special mention. Charles Voelker, longtime alderman and civic leader was instrumental in shaping the look of the present City of Waterloo and in keeping alive a sense of its past; Dr. J. G. Hagey, former President Emeritus of the University of Waterloo, and Rev. C.L. Siegfried, C.R., former President Emeritus of the University of St. Jerome's College, led in the development of the University and were a visible sign of its presence in the community.

Lastly, I would like to express my gratitude and heartfelt thanks to my wife, Elizabeth, and to my two daughters, Nicola and Janet, whose continuing and uncomplaining support throughout the research and the writing of this book has made my task a great deal easier and the book a great deal better.

Kenneth McLaughlin

Valley of
the Grand

O n June 18, 1815, the combined
forces of the Duke of Wellington, leading an allied army of
British, Dutch, Belgian, and
German soldiers, along with the Prussian
army led by Gebhard Leberecht von
Blucher, overwhelmingly defeated
Napoleon Bonaparte on a battlefield three
miles south of the Belgian village of
Waterloo. Thus ended 23 years of almost
constant warfare that had raged across
Europe. The peace that ensued was felt
not only in Europe, but also in the far
reaches of the British colonies in North
America. In the province of Upper Canada
the influx of settlement led to the creation
of new townships throughout the
province. It was no small irony that in
1816 the area along the Grand River,
known originally as the German Company
Tract and settled primarily by pacifist
Mennonites, would be elevated to the status of a township and named Waterloo
after the famous victory of Wellington and
von Blucher. In a way this was not inappropriate, for Waterloo township was to
develop as one of the foremost areas in
Ontario in which German and British settlers would co-mingle.

All of this, however, was far in the
future when Sir Frederick Haldimand, the
Governor of Quebec at the time of the
American Revolution in 1784, had first
sought to establish the United Empire
Loyalists in the virtually uninhabited

This sketch of a pioneer wagon crossing one of the many waterways that impeded settlement in the early years illustrates the rigors of frontier life. Courtesy, Public Archives of Canada

territory of what is now the Province of Ontario. But, for Haldimand, too, these lands bordering on the Grand River, or Tintaatuoa as the Indians had called it, would have a central importance, and the village of Waterloo, which came to be located on a small tributary of the Grand River known simply as Beaver Creek, would share in the remarkable destiny of these new lands.

As the British Governor of the old Province of Quebec and its adjoining territories, Haldimand was responsible for creating an independent colony that would be economically self-sufficient. In addition to organizing the rapid improvement of the colony's defences against an American attack, he had ordered his surveyors to take steps to assure the economic survival of the colonies. In particular he was anxious to identify and locate potential sites for grist and sawmills, for mill sites could often determine the success or failure of any new settlement. Governor Haldimand had already been warned that some "evil and designing persons" hoped to dissuade the United Empire Loyalists from taking out land in Canada by luring them with the promise that better terms could be found in the neighbouring American states where they "were not prohibited from erecting mills."

Under the earlier French regime, mill sites in Canada were considered to be so important that they were retained either by the seigneur or by the governor. Haldimand was quick to recognize the need to amend this practice and in September 1788, "after much uneasiness ... and discontent among the inhabitants," mill sites were allowed to be considered as part of the land grant. With this reassurance along with generous assistance by the British government for those who had taken an active part in resisting the rebellion in the American colonies, the rapid settlement of the new British territories seemed assured.

The influx of the United Empire Loyalists led almost immediately to demands for the creation of a separate "British" province out of the former French territories. In 1791 the Province of Upper Canada was officially established with Lieutenant-Colonel John Graves Simcoe as its first lieutenant governor. As he prepared to leave London on his way to chart the destiny of Upper Canada, Simcoe gave a great deal of thought to the colony's needs. Among his well-known steps to develop the colony would be the removal of the capital from Niagara-on-the-Lake to York and the commencement of major roads, including Yonge Street, to help open the province for settlement. Even before arriving in Upper Canada, however, Simcoe had written to Britain's already troubled foreign secretary, Lord Grenville, urgently requesting that the British government "furnish the necessary materials for grist and sawmills to be erected in spots carefully chosen for that purpose." Grist mills especially, Simcoe had advised, "are universally necessary and will be a great inducement to speedy settlement of lands in their area." Like Haldimand in Quebec, Simcoe quickly removed the former restrictions on mill sites so that "all proprietors of land with mill seats were authorized to make use of mill sites provided fish and navigation were not blocked." To further encourage the early construction of grist mills, the legislature of Upper Canada had passed a new regulation effective January 1, 1793, which increased the miller's toll from one-fourteenth to one-twelfth of the grain brought to be milled, making an already good business venture even more profitable.

It was not surprising when Abraham Erb, a young Pennsylvanian Mennonite who arrived in Upper Canada in 1806, holding title to nearly 4,000 acres of land in the newly surveyed German Company Tract, chose to settle where there was promise of adequate water power to operate both grist and sawmills. At the time of Erb's death in 1830, his mill site, which had laid the basis for the subsequent establishment of the village of Waterloo, was regarded as the best mill site west of the Grand River. Situated in the heart of a Mennonite colony in Upper Canada that came to contain more than 100,000 acres of the province's richest agricultural land, Abraham Erb knew well the wisdom of his decision to establish both a grist mill and a sawmill in so central a location. Erb, too, had well understood the land hunger and the agricultural prowess of his fellow Mennonite co-religionists in Pennsylvania for whom the convenient location of his Union Mills could only redound to his success.

Propelled by water with an overshot wheel, Erb's mills had led to the creation of a large dam on what was then known as Beaver Creek. For many years this dam would be known as Waterloo Dam and later as Silver Lake when it became incorporated into the Waterloo Park system. The low-lying swamp land on which a village and later the City of Waterloo would be developed, however, would pose problems for years to come as sand would have to be hauled from the nearby "hills" to raise lots to a level where they could be drained for residential and commercial development. In the early years buildings were mounted on foundations of oak planks, resting on "quicksand" and "black swamp muck."

John Graves Simcoe, commander of the Queen's Rangers during the American Revolution, became the first lieutenant governor of Upper Canada in 1791. He began the policy of granting land to American settlers, including Mennonites, confident that they would be loyal to the Crown. Courtesy, National Archives of Canada

Snider's Grist and Flouring Mills had been a Waterloo landmark since Abraham Erb had located the first grist mill on this site in 1816. Only the railway tracks across King Street now remind Waterloo's citizens of its presence. Courtesy, Waterloo Public Library

King Street, which became Waterloo's main business thoroughfare, built as a corduroy road made of elm logs, was originally 8 to 10 feet below the present level. Cedar stumps and large chunks of elm wood can still be found below the present surface. All of this mattered little to Abraham Erb, who had no intention of establishing a village plan. At the time of his death in 1830, Erb had consistently refused to subdivide his land. His mills, however, had prospered as the surrounding townships became one of the richest and most densely populated agricultural areas in the province. John Graves Simcoe, one suspects, would have approved.

Abraham Erb's sawmill had begun operations in 1808 and his grist mill in 1816. The grist mill was considerably larger than might have seemed necessary for it also contained a massive brick-and-stone fireplace built into the foundation to warm the weary farmers who brought their grain to be milled. An early historical account explains the central importance of Erb's grist mill and of its rudimentary accommodations:

As this mill was one of the first in this section of the country, farmers had to bring their grain long distances to be ground into flour. Even if the distance was not great, a trip over poor trails and over corduroy roads through swamps was a difficult one and slow as well, for oxen were used for teaming. Consequently, a trip to the mill was often a matter of two or three days.

In addition to the duration of the trip, farmers in early Upper Canada often suffered

from a sense of isolation. Erb's mill also provided a welcome break from the round of endless chores and backbreaking labour:

While waiting for his grist the farmer lounged about the basement where it was warm and comfortable, and where he met his friends, the other farmers, so that it became a social centre and a business mart as well . . . They warmed their victuals and made coffee at the fireplace, and at night wrapped themselves in their blankets and slept on the floor, or on the bags of bran, or anywhere so long as they received the warmth of the fireplace.

Business at Erb's mill had continued to flourish, so much so that it would soon be necessary to add steam power to supplement the original water course.

When he died at the age of 57 on September 6, 1830, Abraham Erb, the man whom many would call the founder of the Village of Waterloo, had witnessed remarkable changes to the world he had known. He had been born into a prosperous Mennonite family in Pennsylvania in 1772 at a time when the 13 American colonies were still the centrepiece of Britain's empire. Dominated by a Quaker-led government in Pennsylvania, life for the Mennonites and other pacifist religious sects seemed stable and assured. Even the early rumblings of discontent against the administration of Lord North in faraway England seemed to have little effect on their life. Grievances like the famous Stamp Act and the new Townshend Duties seemed of more concern in New England's seaports and among the merchant class. The Boston Tea Party on December 16, 1773, when a group of young Bostonians, thinly disguised as Mohawk Indians, boarded three British ships and threw their cargo of tea overboard, may have caused a sense of glee in Boston, but was less popular among the law-abiding Mennonites in Pennsylvania.

The beginning of armed hostilities in

Massachusetts in April 1775, however, brought the likelihood of war much closer and with it the fear that Pennsylvania's pacifist religious sects, the Tunkers, Quakers, and Mennonites, including Abraham Erb's parents and their relatives, would be faced with a profound crisis of conscience. Although the Continental Congress of 1775 and 1776 had determined that Quakers, Mennonites, and other similar sects could continue to practice freedom of religion and be exempt from bearing arms, rights similar to those they had under the British Crown, many Mennonites found themselves impressed into non-combatant roles both by the Patriots and the British.

Abraham Erb, however, was only 3 years old when the war began and 11 when peace was finally declared. His generation had been spared much of the great trauma of the Revolutionary War. It would be another 23 years before Erb and his fellow Mennonites would set out for Upper Canada. Nonetheless, their destiny and that of the new lands they would acquire was inextricably caught up in the land hunger created by that long drawn out war and in Britain's policies for her new colonies to the north.

At the end of the Revolutionary War life had to begin anew for another group of colonists. Those who had remained loyal to Great Britain or who had fought on her behalf now found themselves as outcasts from the American states. Prominent among those seeking special redress from the British government were Joseph Brant (Thayendanegea) and the Six Nation Indians who had fought ruthlessly and valiantly for the British cause. Commissioned as a captain by the British in 1780, Brant retained his position as a war chief in an Indian-loyalist band throughout the duration of the Revolutionary War.

The Six Nations sought new lands both for the loss of their hunting grounds as well as for a reward for their loyalty to the British Crown. It would be no small irony that a group of pacifist Mennonite farmers, led by the Erb family, would ultimately acquire title to a large part of the lands won by the Indians for their wartime prowess. Between the ultimate resolution of the ownership of these lands in 1805 and the original creation of an Indian Reserve in 1784 lies one of the most complex and fascinating accounts ever to unfold in the early years of Upper Canada.

Even before Upper Canada had been formally established as a province, Brant had urged the British governor of Quebec, Sir Frederick Haldimand, to purchase "from the Mississaugas or proprietors" a tract of land "consisting of about six miles on either side of the Grand River . . . running from the River la Tranche [the Thames] into Lake Erie, for the use of the Mohawks and such of the Six Nations as are inclined to join them in that settlement."

Recognizing the validity of their claim while also fearing further unrest and not entirely trusting the motives of Joseph Brant, Governor Haldimand acted with despatch. In the famous "Haldimand deed" of October 25, 1784, he set out the terms of what was surely one of the most unusual loyalist land grants:

I do hereby in His Majesty's Name authorize and permit the said Mohawk Nation and such others of the Six Nation Indians as wish to settle in that quarter to take possession of and settle upon the banks of the river commonly called Ouse or Grand River, running into Lake Erie, allotting to them for that purpose six miles deep from either side of the river beginning at Lake Erie and extending in that proportion to the very head of the said river, which them and their posterity are to enjoy forever.

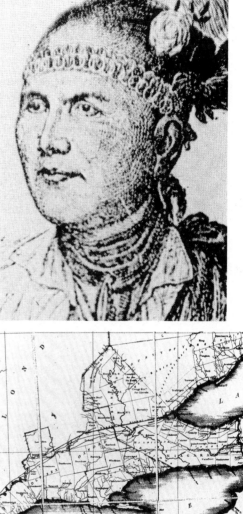

Top: Joseph Brant, or Thayendanegea, was a Mohawk war chief who rallied to the British cause during the American Revolution. He led his people to settle peacefully on a large tract of land along the Grand River and was a formidable figure in the life of Upper Canada in its early years. Courtesy, Provincial Archives of Ontario

Bottom: This detail of a map drawn by William Chewitt, senior surveyor and draughtsman in Upper Canada, illustrates the lands of the Indian Reserve along the Grand River. Courtesy, Public Archives of Ontario

This description left the precise boundaries somewhat obscured owing to a very ill-defined sense of Upper Canadian geography. It was not the size of the grant that would lead to problems, although this, too, was not without complication. Rather, it was the last phrase that Governor Haldimand had added that would bedevil Canadian politics. Haldimand had clearly implied that this land was to be retained by the Six Nation Indians "and their posterity" which they are "to enjoy forever." These terms, however, would prove to be extremely contentious. The man who would make them so was Joseph Brant, the strong-willed and tempestuous Mohawk warrior.

Brant's life and his career deserve fuller study than can be attempted here, and the historical assessment of him is by no means unanimous. To many he has been a great leader and a hero of his people; for others he has been a crass and spiteful manipulator whose personal interests and ego seemed always to take precedence. Whatever view one takes, Joseph Brant came to play a central role in the future of the lands along the Grand River and in the negotiations that made possible the development of Abraham Erb's mill site in Waterloo.

The official survey of the boundaries of the Six Nation's lands was conducted in January 1791 by Augustus Jones, the newly appointed deputy surveyor for Upper Canada. His completed plan (submitted on 24 August 1791) outlined 674,910 acres that carved a great swath through the very centre of the new province. The implications of controlling so important a land area were not lost on the government of Upper Canada nor on the Mohawk leader, Joseph Brant. Almost from the beginning a controversy developed over the right of the Six Nations to dispose of parts of their land.

Brant's reasons for wishing to sell or lease large parts of the Indian lands are not particularly convincing. He alleged that incursions of white settlement had adversely affected the Indian hunt and,

The Indian hunts being worn out and their people fallen into disuse of that method of subsistence, and, it not being sufficiently advanced in agricultural arts to maintain themselves, the Letting of the Lands appears [to him] the most reasonable mode of making provision for their Women, Old Men and Children.

It is not without a little irony that the lands Brant sought to dispose of were the most distant from the settlers along the lakefront. His attempts to sell parts of these lands were immediately blocked by Lieutenant-Governor Simcoe, who did not believe that this would be in accord with the intent of the original land grant set out by Governor Haldimand. For his part, Brant saw this as a slight against the native peoples' right to control their own destiny.

With ill-disguised hostility, Simcoe and Brant threatened, cajoled, and attempted to intimidate each other. When Simcoe left Upper Canada in 1796 little had been achieved. His successor as administrator of the province, Peter Russell, was soon confronted with Brant's determination to sell the Indian lands. Russell lamented to Simcoe that:

Application has been repeatedly of late made by that Chief to the Attorney General for deeds to sundry persons subjects of the United States (some of them Officers in their army) to whom he has sold considerable tracts of it.

Russell feared the consequences of the disposal of this land without government control:

The King's interest and the safety of this province (would be endangered) by thus permitting considerable bodies of Aliens (of whose fidelity I have every reason to be suspicious) to obtain so large a property in the very heart of it, to which they may throw open a wide door by the mouth of that River to the introduction of their countrymen, whenever they shall form the design of wresting this country from us.

Russell's apprehensions were intensified by the fact that Britain was already at war with France and that many Americans made no secret of their hope for a French victory. Russell reminded Simcoe of the delicacy of his situation when he speculated that if Brant was determined

to convey this land in his own way to those people and settle them upon it, I am sorry to say I have not the means of preventing him without risking the chance of involving this Province in an Indian and perhaps an American war to which Your Excellency too well knows our present strength and resources are very inadequate.

The prescience of Russell's arguments would undoubtedly be recalled at a later date in 1812 when war between the British and American colonies was once again imminent, and it was a forcible reminder of the continued tension and fear of American ill will ever present in the minds of many Upper Canadian leaders at this time. As Russell candidly warned Simcoe, if Brant were to have his way, "We may soon expect to see an inundation of Americans pouring in upon us."

Brant had come to have a strong dislike for Peter Russell because of his unwillingness to grant his requests. Perhaps out of frustration, perhaps with a sense of vindictiveness, or perhaps with a feeling of a real politique, Brant journeyed to Philadelphia to meet with the British consul, Robert Lisbon. The report to Lord Grenville sent by

Lisbon reveals the intensity of Brant's emotion and also something of his chicanery:

Before I had an Opportunity of seeing him (Brant) however, I heard with surprise and concern, through Persons that frequented the Inn where he took up his Quarters, that

he talked with great resentment of the treatment he had met with from the King's Government of Canada, and threatened, if he did not obtain redress through me, that he would offer his assistance to the French Minister Adet, and march his Mohawk's [sic] to assist in effecting a Revolution, and overturning the British Government in the Province (of Upper Canada) . . .

In the end, it was finally determined that the land would be surveyed and sold by the government on behalf of the Indians. This would provide the government with some control over the loyalty and integrity

This 1820 survey map clearly indicates the central importance of the Grand River as it crosses the townships of Waterloo and Woolwich, formerly Blocks 2 and 3 of the Six Nation's Reserve. Courtesy, National Archives of Canada

of the purchasers of such a major tract of land as well as over the disposition of the funds. Far from resolving the problems, this arrangement led to incredible rancour and for a time again threatened the future of the land and its new settlers.

On November 25, 1796, Joseph Brant drew a deed for 93,160 acres on Block 2 of the Indian lands in favour of three prominent Upper Canada businessmen—Richard Beasley, John Baptiste Rousseau, and James Wilson. Their deed was recorded at Newark (Niagara-on-the-Lake) at the seat of the government of Upper Canada. Under its new policies, the government halted the sale. Two years later, however, on February 5, 1798, a Crown Grant was finally drawn for this block of land and the title registered. Richard Beasley, who had assumed the interest of his partners, signed a new mortgage, this time not to Joseph Brant, but, rather, in favour of the trustees for the Indians, for £8,887 provincial currency.

Influential and energetic, Richard Beasley, the new proprietor of these lands, had become well-known throughout Upper Canada. Arriving in Upper Canada in 1777 as a "refugee loyalist," he had quickly become involved in a number of commercial projects particularly near his home at Barton on a commanding site overlooking Burlington Bay. He was also well-connected socially in the small society of Upper Canada. A cousin of Richard Cartwright, one of the province's wealthiest businessmen, Beasley had also entertained Lieutenant-Governor Simcoe and his wife Elizabeth. At the time of his purchase of the Indian lands, Beasley was also sitting as a Member of the Legislative Assembly. Joseph Brant undoubtedly felt assured that if anyone could open these lands for settlement and could assure the provincial leaders of his loyalty to the Crown, it would be Richard Beasley.

The land that Beasley had purchased was 30 miles from the lakefront at Dundas and even further removed from the capital at York. While not appealing to some set-tlers, its isolation and the quality of the soil was especially attractive to a number of farmers from Pennsylvania. Although not considered to be United Empire Loyalists, many of the early Mennonites and other pacifist sects from Pennsylvania had taken no part in the American Revolution. Indeed, even that ardent imperialist Lieutenant-Governor John Graves Simcoe had encouraged their immigration to this new province by recognizing their religious rights and assuring them that they would have "a just right to such exemptions from bearing arms as they have hitherto met with under the ancient Government of the British States." In 1793 he went further, specifically outlining the means by which "Quakers, Mennonites and Tunkers would be exempted from military service." Mennonites had been arriving from Pennsylvania since 1786 and settling along the shores of Lake Ontario. Simcoe's assurances had made Upper Canada even more attractive to them as had the liberal terms of sale offered by Richard Beasley on his new lands.

In 1800 some of these Mennonites had travelled to the Grand River with an Indian guide and a surveyor provided by Beasley, choosing a homestead site and acquiring a deed for their property from him. Within two years 25 families had settled on Block 2 of the former Indian lands. It came as a painful shock to them in 1803 when Samuel Bricker, one of the Pennsylvania farmers, learned in York that some of Beasley's creditors had called his land dealings into question and that, despite the back-breaking work clearing their lands, the Mennonites in Block 2 did not hold a clear title to their property.

Land speculation had clearly burdened Beasley with a heavy debt on which he had not been able to pay the annual interest on his new purchase. He had, however, paid significant sums to Joseph Brant as the duly accredited agent of the Six Nations Indians, and Brant, in light of his past relationship with the Executive Council, was in no mood to turn these funds over to the government. Beasley also seemed to have aroused the jealousy and ire of some of his political and business rivals. Popular accounts have attempted to impugn Beasley's motives and his character for selling some of the lands in Block 2 before he had retired the entire mortgage on his purchase. This interpretation has become enshrined in local legend, but there is no primary evidence to suggest that Beasley had either gulled or misled the early Mennonite settlers. It is more likely that both Beasley and the Mennonites were caught up in the longstanding rivalry between Joseph Brant and the members of the Executive Council of Upper Canada.

When the Executive Council prepared to take action against Beasley, Joseph Brant entered the fray, leading the Indians to Beasley's defence. Writing on behalf of the chiefs, Aaron Hill, Jr., warned the council:

(The Chiefs) are surprised to have heard (the executive council) were about to sue Mr. Beasley & Co. respecting the Township, particularly as they had understood that you had refused to act as a Trustee when your aid was wanted to forward the business. They cannot consent to have Mr. Beasley distressed wantonly as they are convinced he has done his endeavour to pay them, and had separate Mortgages taken place, they have every reason to believe that he would not have been the least behind in the performance of his Contracts, they therefore request that time may be given to him.

In fact Brant was quite blunt about his support for Beasley and his distrust of the motives of the Executive Council. Beasley, he said,

has done everything in his power to fulfill his Contract, and more than probably could he have obtained separate Mortgages as prayed for, in that case by his Manly and strenuous exertions, We rather think he would then have been enabled to have done

us every justice. And separate Mortgages were faithfully promised him by our Trustees, and we again repeat, had this promise been complied with on the part of the Trustees, that we cannot think otherwise, but that Mr. Beasley would have paid us to the uttermost fraction.

This stirring testimonial on Beasley's behalf led the Executive Council to extend his title for another year in order for him to raise new funds to pay off the mortgage.

For their part, the Mennonite settlers had at first been despondent over the lack of clear title to their lands. Soon, however, they realized that Richard Beasley's predicament could work to their advantage. Two of them, Samuel Bricker and Daniel Erb, offered to purchase all of the unsettled portion of Beasley's land (some 60,000 acres), hoping to arrange for financing within their families in Pennsylvania. In keeping with a tradition that had been established among some Mennonites, Erb had in fact been sent to Canada hoping to find "a large enough tract to accommodate a group settlement." Beasley's land problems seemed to offer a unique opportunity.

Land in Pennsylvania had become far too expensive for the younger Mennonite families. By contrast, Beasley's land was inexpensive. From the Executive Council's point of view, the Mennonites, while not considered to be United Empire Loyalists, were also not rabid republicans or revolutionaries, and their reputation as skilled agriculturalists had preceded them. In November 1803 an agreement between Richard Beasley, Daniel Erb, and Samuel Bricker was filed with the Executive Council and in May 1804 the Mennonites paid a first instalment of £4,602.10 to Colonel Claus, chairman of the trustees for the Six Nation Indians. A bond was given at that time for the balance of the purchase—£6,102.10—to be paid on May 23, 1805.

Ironically, the new purchasers soon found themselves in a position remarkably

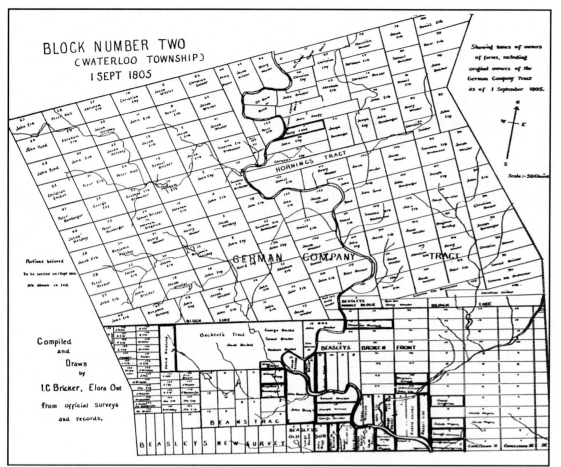

This map shows Block 2 (the future Waterloo township), as of September 1, 1805, including the names of the original purchasers. Abraham Erb's lots 14 and 15 would become the nucleus of the village of Waterloo. The stream used to power his grist mill is clearly visible in the upper section of the map. Courtesy, Waterloo Historical Society

similar to that which had confounded Beasley. They had failed to raise the necessary funds and, like Beasley, Bricker, and the Erbs, could not make full payment on the date the bond came due.

According to one author,

this small group of men (Samuel Bricker and his in-laws and John, Jacob, and Daniel Erb) hoped to secure title to the tract in their own names. It is believed that they hoped to secure an extension of the time limit to enable them gradually to dispose of the property to incoming settlers and pay off the balance with the proceeds, with resultant profit to themselves.

Although Claus may have been impressed by the earnestness and sincerity of these young Pennsylvania farmers, he would not make allowances for them to grant separate title to the land any more than he would have for Beasley. His reasoning was simple enough: if separate title or partial

discharge could be permitted, the best lands would be taken up and the remainder left as waste. Claus insisted that the terms for final payment would be extended for not longer than one year plus one week.

Returning to Pennsylvania with a plea combining a sense of religious duty and economic motivation, the farmers raised the remainder of the money to clear the title and to create a Mennonite colony where religious ideals could be practised. A group of 26 individuals contributed funds and, in order to divide the 60,000 acres in an equitable way, formed an organization that has come to be known as the German Company. This name was used to describe their portion of the Indian land now officially referred to as the German Company Tract. Augustus Jones was commissioned to survey the holdings and divide them into equal-sized farm lots. Lots 1 through 128 were 448 acres each, while the remainder were 83-acre lots. The lots were then numbered and awarded by random drawing so that lot selection would be fair and equitable for each shareholder.

The arrival of these young Mennonites with such large sums of money had caused more than a little discussion in the capital of Upper Canada. The trip from Pennsylvania, arduous at the best of times, was no small feat with this amount of currency. The initial payment of $4,692 was brought to Canada by horseback with the money—made up of American silver dollars—sewn into small leather bags. The second and larger payment of £6,102.10 was packed into an oak keg (or kegs) and then fastened onto a wagon driven by Samuel Bricker. His brother John, along with Daniel, Jacob, and John Erb, armed with muzzle-loaders, served as outriders to discourage any would-be robbers.

On June 29, 1805, the original mortgage was discharged and title to the property was given to Daniel and Jacob Erb as representatives of the Mennonite community. Members of the extended Erb family were in fact some of the largest landowners in the new German Company Tract. John Erb, who would immediately commence to establish a grist mill and sawmill at the future site of Preston, had purchased 20 lots totalling 7,500 acres. His brother Jacob acquired 8 lots, each containing 448 acres, while their other brother, Abraham, held title to lots 14, 15, 27, 29, 55, 69, 77, 102, 135, and 152. Of all of this land, it would be lots 14 and 15 that Abraham would choose for himself and from which the nucleus of the Village of Waterloo would ultimately be formed. The wisdom of Abraham Erb's decision was confirmed almost immediately when a second group of Mennonites from Lancaster County decided to emulate the experience of their co-religionists by purchasing another block of Indian lands containing 45,195 acres adjoining the original Block 2.

The agents of this new "German Land Company" were Abraham Erb's two brothers, John and Jacob. Along with solicitor William Dickson from Niagara, who would himself soon purchase Block 1 of the Indian lands, and the deputy-surveyor, Augustus Jones, personal friend of Chief Joseph Brant and son-in-law of another Mohawk chief, they completed the arrangements. Although Abraham Erb did not purchase additional lands in Block 3, he would stand to gain the most when the new area was opened for settlement. His sawmill and, after 1816, his grist mill would occupy a central position in this

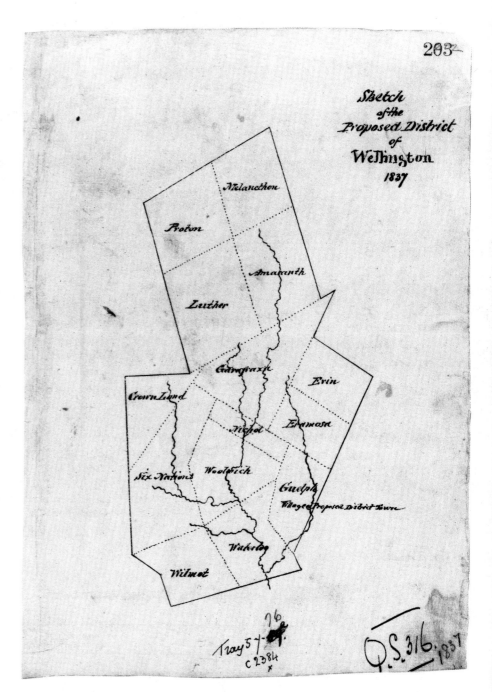

extended area. As new roads were opened and new lands cleared, the wisdom of Abraham Erb's choice of the mill seat on Beaver, or as it was later called, Laurel Creek, would be even more evident. Union Mills was an apt choice as the roads, laden with settlers opening up these new lands, all converged directly at Erb's mill.

This sketch of the proposed District of Wellington in 1837 outlines the path of the Grand River and of Waterloo's central position in the German-speaking townships. Courtesy, National Archives of Canada

CHAPTER 2

New Beginnings

The existence of the German Company Tract had created a situation unique in Upper Canada. The purchase by the "German Companies" in Pennsylvania of the future Waterloo and Woolwich townships had made possible the establishment of a Pennsylvania Mennonite colony markedly at variance with the rest of the province. This was a unique opportunity to create a colony where religious ideals could be put into practice. Isolated from the commerce and development along the lakefront, the colony contained no Crown reserves, no clergy reserves, and no large Loyalist land grants through which to establish an Anglo-Saxon elite or presence in the community. Even the land surveys were not done in lots and concessions, but, rather, simply divided into equal-sized farmsteads without the customary road allowance.

The idea of a Mennonite colony within Upper Canada set apart from the intended Anglo-Saxon values of the rest of the province had developed naturally from the Mennonites' past. With a religion based on a literal interpretation of the Bible, emphasizing a pattern of "simple life," an independent social system, and a sense of spirituality that was enhanced by an agricultural life, many Mennonites had become accustomed to a lifestyle that differed from the existing religious, political, and social values of the surrounding

An early illustration of Niagara Falls depicts the falls as they may have looked to the Mennonites and other settlers as they travelled past its shores in the early years of the nineteenth century. Courtesy, National Archives of Canada

areas. Marriage outside their faith was discouraged, large families were common, and close ties of kinship and the use of the German language strengthened their social system.

While a few of the Mennonites, like Abraham Erb, owned mills or were teachers, craftsmen, and shopkeepers, the majority remained as farmers. Settlement in "blocks" made possible the retention of their unique church and social life at the same time as it ensured large amounts of land for the families of the next two or three generations. The isolation of their townships from the other settlements did not trouble them. Nor did it trouble Abraham Erb. His grist mill would continue to flourish with each new wave of Mennonite settlers.

The lands surrounding his mills would change very little during the next half-century. Only after the railway from Toronto had made its inroad into the nearby community and the ownership of the land had passed out of Mennonite hands would a village begin to grow. Even then, its orientation would remain directed toward the surrounding agricultural lands rather than as a major competitor for urban development.

In the beginning, lands in the new settlement were purchased in Pennsylvania rather than in York, the capital of Upper Canada. It was in Pennsylvania, too, that the settlers began the weary trek to their new lands. Often lasting as long as 10 weeks, the journey was difficult and dangerous over unmarked roads and along half-finished trails. Travelling by means of a Conestoga wagon drawn by a team of four or six horses (and sometimes by oxen), these early pioneers must have been a curious sight. The wagons with their high box and heavy running gear surmounted by stout ash or elm hoops over which was stretched a canvas top lumbered, heavily laden, followed by an array of cows, sheep, goats, and pack horses.

Most of the pioneers brought household furniture and farming implements with them. Children were carried inside the wagons. The men drove the teams while the women and older children were assigned the duty of driving and watching the cattle and other livestock. Of the 500 miles, it would be fortunate if the women would ride more than a few miles. Mostly they walked. The route to Upper Canada passed directly across the Allegheny mountains through which there were only the poorest of roads. The journey over the mountains was an unforgettable experience for even the hardiest of travellers. As one early account notes,

the difficulties and at times dangers attending upon the travellers were sufficient to appal even the stoutest hearted and most persevering.

The pass over the Allegheny mountains was particularly treacherous:

"Climbing" is almost the only idea which can express the methods adopted to surmount these hills of tribulation. Six to eight horses would generally be "hitched" to one wagon, and it was only by great exertions that the loads were drawn up to a level spot, where the wagon would be left while the horses returned for the others.

Often too, the women would move alongside of the wagon, holding on to ropes attempting to keep the wagon and its contents upright while they themselves struggled for a precarious balance. "Sometimes we advanced only a few miles a day," one traveller recalled. "Often a wagon would upset, sometimes in a pool of mud, once or twice a dog was buried in the debris and the howling that followed for a short time was woeful music . . . Mud, mud, mud," she lamented. "The roads were awful!"

The mountains were not the only problem. Still awaiting was the famous Niagara River and its mighty waterfalls. The crossing was at a point called the Black

Rock, which was a natural landing place above the falls. The Conestoga wagons, livestock, and passengers were loaded onto scows propelled by men operating large "sweeps" or oars. The wagon body, with its load, was placed crosswise on the float, which "wiggled and wobbled," requiring "the utmost exertion on the part of the driver to prevent it from capsizing."

Once in British territory, the weary travellers disembarked at Fort Erie, a British military port on the Niagara River opposite Black Rock. The land was well travelled and cleared past Niagara Falls and Queenston. Heading west toward the head of Lake Ontario at Dundas, most immigrants chose the easier and shorter route along the crest of the Niagara escarpment, rather than along the lakeshore to Burlington inlet and back to Dundas. Elizabeth Simcoe, wife of the lieutenant governor, noted about the upper road, opened shortly after 1796: "The Governor intends to open a road from Niagara to the head of the lake, instead of travelling on a most terrible road below which . . . is full of swamps, fallen trees, etc." Most the immigrants coming to the German Company lands followed this route to Coote's Paradise, later known as Dundas, where there was a small hamlet with several stores. From here the route was either through the tortuous and almost impassable Beverly Swamp or along the Governor's Road to the junction of the Grand and Nith rivers (the present site of Paris). From this point onward the road was merely an Indian trail that skirted the east bank of the Grand River.

The Beverly Swamp between Dundas and Galt was ever to be remembered as perhaps the most difficult part of the journey. One early account paints a vivid picture both of the swamp and its role in the folklore of the Mennonite colony:

All the trials and difficulties of the former part of the journey were insignificant compared to what stared them in the face at this point and a description utterly fails to give an idea of the "passage" through this Slough of Despond. A road there was, but it was scarcely an apology for one. An attempt had been made to fill the innumerable mud holes with logs and brushwood, but to dignify it with even the name of "corduroy" would be a sacrilege . . . half a load was generally taken at a time, and through the conglomeration of rural and brush the horses would flounder and scramble while the wagons were sunk to the hubs. When a more favourable piece of road was reached three or more teams would be "hitched" and the whole load dragged through and thus after days of the most arduous labour the caravan was conveyed to dry land on the west side of that dismal swamp.

The shared experience caused by these hardships created a common folklore that further united the colony. The administrative decision in 1816 that elevated the German Company Tract into Waterloo Township merely enhanced the feeling of separateness. These traditions would endure long after the major Mennonite migrations ended in 1828.

The first group of what would become an annual pattern of migration from Pennsylvania arrived on the German Company lands in October 1804. Included among them were a large number of the Eby family and their relatives, who chose lot 1 as the location for establishing their new life in Upper Canada. In May 1806 another large convoy arrived, including the future Mennonite bishop, Benjamin Eby, as well as Abraham Erb and his wife, Magdalana (Erb) Erb. The close family ties of the Mennonite settlement is obvious not only in the repetition of prominent surnames, but also in the close proximity of the establishment of their first farms. Benjamin Eby, for example, "decided to settle on the southeastern part of lot 1, just across the property line of his cousin, Joseph Eby." Other relatives, too, took up their land near to the Eby's. Joseph Schneider, Benjamin's brother-in-law, and

This 1855 view of Waterloo clearly illustrates village development north of the Erb Street intersection. Courtesy, Waterloo Historical Society

his wife, Barbara (Eby) Schneider, in 1807 settled on the adjoining lot 17, while Samuel Eby located on lot 3 on the other side of Benjamin Eby. Jacob Erb had already started to clear the southwestern part of lot 17 in the Eby settlement while his brother, Abraham Erb, travelled two miles farther to lot 14, where he could establish a mill site on Beaver Creek. A road was cut almost immediately to link Erb's mill site with the farms surrounding the Eby settlement soon to be known as "Eby's Town" and sometimes simply as "Ben Eby's."

The early road pattern in the German Company Tract also illustrates the unusual nature of the settlement. With no concession lines and with lots drawn up merely to delineate farms of 440 acres, the first roads cut through individual farms at awkward angles, often following the contours of the land or just as often, running through the poorer sections of farmlands. The Great Road from Dundas, which ultimately would become King Street, has the distinction of going in all directions: east and west through Eby's Town (later Kitchener) and north toward Erb's mill (later Waterloo). The explanation for this somewhat unusual development can be found in the requirements of the early Mennonite community. By 1808 a school had been opened in Eby's Town to serve their educational needs, while Erb's sawmill began operation in the same year to provide the lumber for their new

homes. A road to connect the two settlements did not need a surveyor's chain. The permanence of this pattern was merely confirmed in 1816, the year Abraham Erb established his grist mill and the now Bishop Benjamin Eby conveyed the land for the Mennonite meeting house. Together they would serve the physical and spiritual needs of the new community.

Like Abraham Erb's grist mill, the meeting house was of vital importance to the Mennonite colony, for once the community had grown beyond 30 or so families it became impossible to meet in individual homes. Isolated from the "mother colony" in Pennsylvania, the

Mennonites found it especially important for the survival of their beliefs and practices to establish meeting houses as well as schools for their children. Mennonite immigration from Pennsylvania had ensured the steady growth of the German Company lands. There were 355 inhabitants in 1805, 548 in 1807, and 850 in 1815. By 1825 the population was 1,640, of which approximately 1,000 were Mennonites. A decade later in 1835 the population had reached 2,791, of which some 2,000 were Mennonites. By 1834, with 16,858 acres under cultivation, Waterloo Township had one of the highest rates of cleared agricultural land in the province.

Although the number of Mennonite immigrants was not overwhelming, they had established the rural orientation of the township, clearing the lands and creating a distinctive road pattern that would lay the basis for the growth of two separate villages. Berlin would ultimately be established on the lands of Bishop Eby near his meeting house, while Waterloo would come into being around the mills established by Abraham Erb.

The early location of Abraham Erb's mill sites and his close family relationship with so many of the settlers had ensured the success of his mills. But it was more than just chance. Abraham Erb had also seen to it that the roads created to serve the pioneer farmers would also pass by his mills. Not all of the Mennonites shared Erb's desire for roads that would also open the settlement to outsiders. Recent research has indicated that there was significant opposition to some of Erb's plans:

On 5, April, 1819, for example, twenty-eight property-holders petitioned the Judge and the Grand Jury of the District Quarter Sessions to protest the lobby for roads undertaken by "Abraham Erb and some other unfeeling, uncharitable, self-interested" co-religionists.

Their protest, however, was of no avail. Three months later, on July 15, 1819, the plans for "statute roads" in Waterloo Township were approved and "all of them passed through Abraham Erb's Mills."

Those who had opposed Abraham Erb's lobbying for the new statute roads had anticipated that these roads would end the isolation of the Mennonite colony. They would also, of course, make life easier for the farmers who transported their wheat to his mill. The completion in 1820 of the first bridge across the Grand River near Freeport as well as the opening of a new improved Beverly Road to Dundas had begun to draw the Mennonites more fully into the life of the province.

Early mills that had adequate water

power but that were not located near the major roads soon fell by the wayside. Not so for Abraham Erb's grist mill and sawmill. As E. Reginald Good has pointed out, the new statute roads all converged at Erb's Mills:

The first road extended from Abraham Erb's in a northerly direction, through the present day village of Conestogo in Woolwich Township to Pilkington Township. The second road began at Schneider's settlement, in the present day village of Bloomingdale, and ran to the southwest Township Line via Abraham Erb's. The third, and most controversial, road included present day King Street, Kitchener. It was called the Dundas Road because it continued on to Dundas.

This last road, also known as the Great Road, became the main thorough-fare through the township, connecting directly with the grain market at Dundas where flour was transshipped for export to markets in England. It was also the main route for the new immigrants as well as for goods imported from abroad. The government decision in 1836 to macadamize the Great Road would make it one of the major improved roads to the interior. Those mills such as Bridgeport Mills on the Guelph-Waterloo Road, Doon Mills on the West River Road to Galt, and German Mills at the termination of Bleam's Road with the West River Road would fail to develop as Erb's grew.

The possibility of establishing a new Amish colony on the former Crown Reserves for the County of Lincoln (presently Wilmot Township) created the opportunity to extend the boundaries of the German-speaking pacifist areas. That the new road to this area would be called Erb's Road and that it would intersect the Great Road from Dundas at the point where Abraham Erb's mill was located seemed inevitable. The Erb family, led by Jacob Erb, had been responsible for the negotiations with the government regarding this land, including the development of

the prospective Erb's Road, while Abraham Erb and Sam Eby acted as the "Mennonite Trustees" of the survey.

This expansion into Wilmot Township, however, led to a series of allegations of land speculation against the Erb and the Eby families. The Amish contended that their Mennonite brethren had quickly acquired this land only to sell it later at a much higher price, and that they had not intended to establish new farms for themselves or for their children. The report of the deputy-surveyor, Samuel S. Wilmot, as quoted by Good, suggests that there may have been some truth to the charges:

The Erbs and the Ebys, [Wilmot said,] have located a number of lots, the greater part of which are unoccupied, the trifling expense of settlement duty to open roads and pay the survey fees, amounting to about five pounds, enables the monied men of Waterloo to hold lots much to the injury of the poor persons who wish to become actual settlers in Wilmot.

Soon, however, both Mennonite and Amish settlers joined by Roman Catholic and Lutheran pioneers would open new farms in Wilmot Township. For all of them, Abraham Erb's mills at Waterloo would become a focal point.

As these new areas were opened for settlement, Abraham Erb seems to have given little thought to the creation of a village beyond his original grist mill and sawmill. He had sold parts of his land holdings to other Mennonites such as Christian Snider, Christian Bowman, Jacob Snider, Daniel Bowman, and Daniel Eby. The lots that would come to encompass the City of Waterloo, however, were owned by a handful of Mennonites who had simply consolidated their own farmsteads. This, however, was entirely consistent with Abraham Erb's philosophy and with the Mennonite desire to create and sustain their traditional, rural lifestyle. At Cambridge Mills (the present-day City of Cambridge) his brother John Erb had

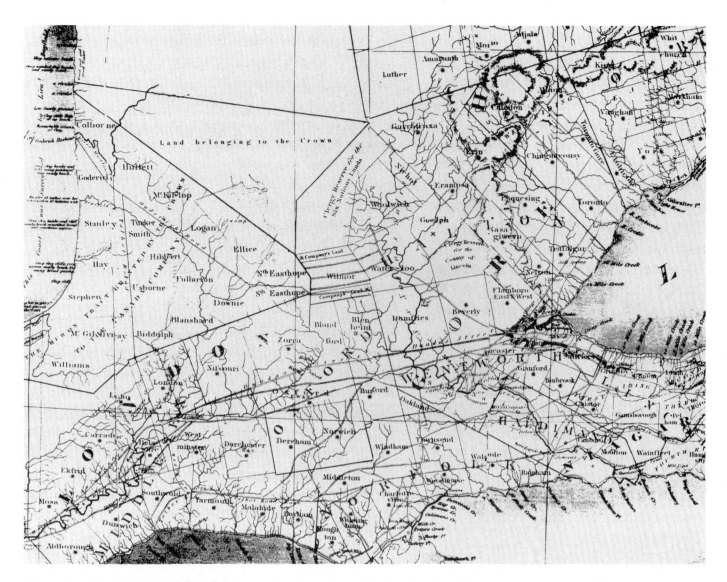

followed a remarkably similar pattern, refusing to survey his land for the development of a village surrounding his mill site.

In 1829, when Abraham Erb sold the 240 acres of land that included his grist mill and sawmill to Jacob Snider, a fellow Mennonite who had arrived from Pennsylvania shortly after the War of 1812, he could look back over many achievements since coming to Upper Canada in 1806. In his own way and faithful to his Mennonite upbringing, Abraham Erb had left his mark on the lands of Waterloo Township. His death the following year in 1830 signified the end of an era in the development of the township. The waves of Mennonite migration that had sustained the unique lifestyle of the community had begun to wane. Some Mennonites from Pennsylvania would continue to come to the "colony" in Waterloo, but after 1829 more of them would be drawn to new lands in Michigan and the American Midwest.

At about this same time, however, the German-speaking settlements in Waterloo Township began to attract an entirely different group of settlers seeking land, religious freedom, and an opportunity to ply their trades and crafts in an area where large urban centres had not been established. These were German-speaking immigrants coming directly from Europe. Although some had come through Pennsylvania, most had not. Arriving at New York from the German ports of Bremen and Hamburg or France's Le Havre, they set out for new lands in the American

This detail from a map of Upper Canada prepared by James Chewitt about 1830 shows the rapid growth of Waterloo and the surrounding townships. Courtesy, Public Archives of Ontario

Midwest. Many travelled on foot; others came on barge ships by canal to Lockport in New York State. At Buffalo they learned of the German-speaking area in Canada where both land and employment were available.

They were also very much impressed by the promise of religious toleration and the freedom from war and strife that had so severely restricted their lives in Europe. Beginning in the late 1820s, this influx of German immigrants would continue well into the 1870s. By the time of Confederation in 1867, a preponderance of Ontario's Germans (nearly 75 percent), numbering 115,189 out of a total of some 158,000, had come to live in the area surrounding Waterloo Township.

The end of the Napoleonic Wars in 1815 at the famous Battle of Waterloo had profound effects not only in Europe, but also in faraway Upper Canada. The creation of the new township encompassing the German Company Tract in 1816, named after the British victory, benefited directly from the mass waves of emigration from war-torn Europe while other parts of the province also gained large numbers of immigrants from the British Isles.

The defeat of Napoleon at Waterloo had led to a series of major changes in the landholding practices in the German states. Many small farmers found themselves forced off their traditional lands, while others saw their standards of living decline; they worried about their childrens' futures. At the same time, skilled craftsmen and artisans found their status threatened and their jobs disappearing. The beginnings of industrialization in some of the German states coincided with the decline of artisanal trades and the weakening of the traditional German "hometown" economic system. Unlike Great Britain, the German states had been slow to industrialize, and the guild and craft orientation of German society had persisted long after it had ended elsewhere in Europe. The proportion of skilled craftsmen in the German states

dramatically outnumbered those in the rest of Europe. Beginning in the 1820s, they began an unprecedented migration to North America which has been described as "the western world's greatest folk movement of modern times."

Immigrants' letters to their families in the German states record the excitement and worry of the arduous crossing of the North Atlantic by sailing ships as well as the attractions of a new life in Canada. Philipp Lautenschlager is perhaps typical of these young immigrants. He left his home in Herchenrode, Germany, on May 13, 1831, and six months later, in November, he sent back a lengthy account of his impressions of life in Waterloo Township:

Here I am with a cooper. I earn nine dollars a month during the winter; in summer I'll earn more. Here a carpenter earns a dollar a day which is two and a half guilders, a blacksmith fifteen to sixteen dollars a month—all craftsmen earn a lot of money . . . also wagonmakers and shoemakers are well paid . . . a hired man earns 110 to 120 dollars a year.

Lautenschlager's description of the opportunities for skilled craftsmen as well as for hired hands and farm labourers would have appealed to many young German immigrants.

Women, too, would have found much that was attractive in his comments on life in Canada:

A female worker earns four to five dollars a month. The women folk do not dress as you do at home; they all dress as the fashionable people of Germany . . . The women have it good; they do not have to go out into the fields. Nor do they have to prepare food for cattle; they cook only for people. In this land the fare is good; three times a day there is meat, butter and apple butter. The bread is as white as your loveliest cakes at home.

Land was plentiful in Waterloo Township, and "not expensive," he wrote, "one may buy an acre for two to three dollars." Lautenschlager urged his father and others to come to Waterloo Township. Not only was the standard of living much higher than in Germany, but, most importantly, there was no fear of war. Instead, he said, "Here . . . Everyone is free. There is money to earn like making hay, if one is willing to work."

Many immigrants followed Lautenschlager's example. The transformation of Waterloo Township resulting from German immigration is evident in the population balance. In 1835, at the beginning of this period, 70 percent of Waterloo Township's population was Mennonite. By 1851 Mennonites represented only 26 percent, while inhabitants of German origin made up 73 percent.

The central location of Abraham Erb's grist mill had placed tremendous pressure on Jacob Snider, Erb's successor, to make lots available for craftsmen and other artisans to locate their shops and homes near one of the most important "cross roads" in the township. At "Ebytown" a blacksmith shop and a roadhouse had been established in the 1820s. In 1830 Bishop Eby had sold a store site to David and William Miller, and in 1832 Jacob Hailer, from Baden, had purchased an acre of land and established a chair and spinning wheel shop. By 1833 there were 25 dwellings, 2 stores, and a few workshops located near the Mennonite meeting house so that Bishop Eby and his brother-in-law, Joseph Schneider, felt it appropriate to name this small hamlet Berlin in recognition of the new German immigrants in their midst.

Jacob Snider, too, had begun to make land available to the German immigrants. As early as 1836 there were 20 Roman Catholic families mainly from Alsace living in the hamlet known as "Waterloo." By this time, too, there were three breweries in Waterloo and, according to the personal experience of the editor of the Berlin newspaper, they provided an excellent quality of beer, with "no unpleasant taste, and is agreeable for drinking and does not cause headaches." In addition, Snider had added steam power to his grist mill. Waterloo also had a sawmill, a general store, a post office, a hatmaker, a shoemaker, a tailor, a blacksmith "and other industries." Henry Bauman opened a hotel in 1839 "in the three story brick building of Daniel Schneider opposite the post office" in Waterloo. Bauman was said to have, "plenty of room in house and stable, healthy food and good drinks. He is a friendly and obliging young man and we wish him many decent patrons and a good business." In 1839, too, another young immigrant, Valentine Boehmer, began a successful cooperage business in Waterloo. By this time there were a sufficient number of German Lutherans residing in the village to begin the building of a permanent church. Jacob Snider provided a site along the Great Road for the sum of five shillings. The Lutheran trustees were Hartman Schnarr, a weaver; John Hilt, a shoemaker; Henry Froelich, a weaver; and George Gutman, a wagon maker. Casper Schneider, a member of the congregation, was engaged as the building contractor.

In 1839 an Evangelical camp meeting was held on David Erb's land between Waterloo and Lexington (presently part of Hillside Park in Waterloo). Leading the prayer meeting were Bishop Seybert and five preachers. The result was the organization of Upper Canada's first Evangelical congregation, which, along with the United Brethren in Christ, had been founded in Pennsylvania by German-speaking settlers in 1800. Although the Evangelical Church would come to be built in Berlin in 1841, many of Waterloo's residents remained active in the congregation, and a Waterloo congregation was soon formed.

By the end of the 1840s Waterloo had become a thriving village. There were a variety of trades and small shops including carpenters, tailors, a lock and gunsmith, a pumpmaker, a limeburner, and four brewers—David Kuntz, Valentine Schwan, Joseph Brandt, and Jacob Kuntz. There was also an engineer, a blacksmith, a stagecoach driver, a tinsmith, as well as

Bildweberey.

Der Unterschriebene Benachrichtiget hiemit seine Freunde und ein geehrtes Publikum, daß er das

Teppichweben,

Angefangen hat, beym Herrn Isaak Schantz, in Waterloo Taunschip, ungefehr eine Meile südlich von der Stadt Berlin; und zwar auf eine ganz neue Art, mit einer Maschiere, auf welcher er die schönsten Muster weben kann. Er hoffet, also, durch gute Arbeit und pünktliche Bedienung, einen Theil der öffentlichen Kundschaft zu erhalten.

Für einfache Teppiche müssen 22 Kott doppeltes Garn seyn, für Zettel—und 18 Kott doppeltes Garn, für Einschlag, und 18 Kott Bindgarn, einfach, und von der neunlichen Farbe wie der Zettel.

Für die doppelten Teppiche, müssen 72 Kott Garn seyn, 36 Kott weiß, und 36 Kott blau, und es müssen 8 Kott auf 1 Pfund gehen, und alles Garn muß doppelt seyn. Für die einfachen Teppiche muß das Garn etwa 9 oder 10 Kott aufs Pfund gehen.

Carl Israel.

August 27, 1835.   1—6v

Nachschrift.

Carl Israel webt einfache Teppiche, mit einen Namen darin, für 2 Thaler und 2 Schillinge das Stück—einen einfachen Teppich zu weben ohne einen Namen, kostet 2 Thaler; und Doppelte

several labourers and clerks.

A stagecoach service owned by Captain Thomas Smith of Winterbourne operated via Waterloo and Berlin to Preston and had sufficient business to offer a regular schedule as early as 1835. When the Dundas road was macadamized in 1837, travel was markedly improved, although it was still not without hazard. One teamster recalled more than a decade later that the stage on a nearby road was upset three times within one day. Ruts in the road, he said, extended "fully half a mile in length . . . Another (stage driver) says he dropped his whip in one of these holes, and his arm was barely long enough to grasp it at the bottom . . . Not a day passes but wagons are injured and horses lamed in different parts." Notwithstanding the difficulties, increasing numbers of immigrants continued to arrive in the settlement.

In 1846 a second stagecoach line was needed to meet the expanded business. George Roos, the proprietor, advertised:

A daily mail coach leaves the hotel of the undersigned (Preston) at 3 o'clock for Berlin and Waterloo. Travellers are taken up and left off at suitable places. At five o'clock in the morning it leaves the hotel of W. Rebscher, Waterloo, calls at the hotels along the route and reaches Preston in time for the south-going mails. The coach is covered and rests on springs for the comfort of the passengers.

A more vivid contemporary description stated that "at cockcrow Waterloo passengers seated themselves in the coach while the whip stored the carpetbags in the boot. With a blare of his horn he was then off . . ." Coach routes crisscrossed the township as German settlements grew in New Hamburg, Crosshill, New Germany, Heidelberg, St Clements, and Elmira. Almost all of these routes passed directly through Waterloo, ensuring the village's economic growth and maintaining close contact with its ever-increasing rural hinterland.

Despite the advantages of Waterloo's location, its development as a village was modest. By 1850 the population numbered fewer than 300. Some authors have suggested that the growth of Waterloo was "considerably delayed by the reluctance of the landowners to sell property for non-agricultural purposes." While this may have been true, the nearby village of Berlin had also developed at a very unhurried pace. It was described in 1851 as "a straggling village" of perhaps 750 inhabitants. As in Waterloo, the original Mennonite landowners had not surveyed their land for village development, but, rather, had made individual lots available in no particular pattern. It was, in fact, the village of Preston, located at the beginning of the German Company lands, rather than either Berlin or Waterloo, that had become the dominant German-speaking village in the township.

The death of John Erb in 1832 had made possible the first major village survey conducted by Squire William Scollick in 1834, creating a linear village pattern along the Great Road from Dundas. The shape of the survey reminded Scollick of his home in Lancashire, and he named the village Preston. The sale of these lands immediately attracted large numbers of tradesmen, artisans, and craftsmen. Despite its English name, "Preston from its early days was the most German centre for Germans," noted a prominent historian, who added, "It is remarkable to find that so many of these German immigrants had a trade and they understood their trade perfectly." By 1851 Preston had become the largest village in the Township of Waterloo. With a population of more than 1,100 inhabitants, Preston had a diversified manufacturing and mercantile base with schools, churches, eight hotels, a large livery business, and several general stores. By the end of the next decade, however, neither Waterloo nor Preston would emerge as the central village in the township. Instead, the intervention of political forces in Toronto

Facing page: Carl Israel, a newly arrived German immigrant, announced on August 27, 1835, that he had commenced a coverlet-weaving business, able to "weave the loveliest patterns." Many of the German immigrants were skilled artisans and craftsmen. Courtesy, Joseph Schneider Haus

creating the new County of Waterloo in 1852 and the selection of Berlin as the county seat changed forever the destinies of the other villages.

Berlin's prestige as the county seat gave it a political and economic influence and made it the centre for German culture and religion. Its newspapers would sup-

plant those in Preston and Waterloo. The German Catholics, too, recognized Berlin's preeminence by deciding to build one large church in Berlin rather than smaller churches in the outerlying villages. Waterloo, for instance, would not get a Roman Catholic church until 1890. As the county seat, Berlin also benefited

Die Alte Kirche (the first Lutheran Church), 1838-1882, gave a sense of permanence to village life and along with Abraham Erb's grist mill was a focal point for early settlers coming to Waterloo. Courtesy, Waterloo Public Libary

from the opening of a branch of the Bank of Upper Canada in 1853. By contrast, Preston would not have its own bank until 1888 although a branch of the Commercial Bank did open in Waterloo in 1861.

The arrival of the Grand Trunk Railway at Berlin in 1856 completely changed the economic orientation of the county away from markets at Dundas and Hamilton and directed to Toronto. It also seemed to signify that the village had come of age, adding a striking new dimension to the economic and social life of Berlin. Its impact was immediately felt in Waterloo. The lure of the railway, the hustle and bustle of new trading opportunities at the Grand Trunk station only two miles away, seemed also to offer a remarkable future to the residents of Waterloo as the age of steam dawned before them. A new village

plan would soon be laid out, leaving behind the "old" commercial area that had developed on the high ground north of the intersection of Erb's Road and the road from Dundas.

It is remarkable that some aspects of the original German influence are still evident along North King Street and Northwest Albert Street, the latter was familiarly called "Die Batchegass" and was once said to "resemble Alt Nurmberg, or some other village in old Germany." The new survey, however, faced Berlin and its railway, with "Waterloo Street" and the newly named "King Street" both announcing their proximity—"One-quarter mile to the Grand Trunk Railway." The past, which had been so much a part of Waterloo's present, would quickly recede as the new age began.

In the nineteenth century crowds from Waterloo and Berlin frequently gathered at the Grand Trunk Station for many festive occasions including excursions throughout Ontario and the American states. Courtesy, Kitchener Public Library

3

Progress and Prosperity

The 1850s was a tumultuous period in the life of Canada West as Ontario was then known. The province's population more than doubled between 1850 and 1860 and continued apace throughout the next decade, culminating in 1867 in the federation of the British provinces and the creation of the new Dominion of Canada. Expansion onto the prairies and the opening of new markets would occur three years later in 1870. The development of these scattered colonies into a nation had been made possible by a growing sense of Canadian independence as well as by the continued immigration of thousands of new settlers from Europe and the British Isles. The advent of new technology, especially the railway, which could move people and their goods over vast distances at speeds that had previously been only a wistful dream, had also played a vital part in making Confederation a reality. In their own way, each of these forces would have a marked influence on the growth of the fledgling settlement at Waterloo.

Speculation about the wealth and prosperity that accompanied railway development spread like a fever throughout Ontario in the 1850s. Cities and towns along proposed routes of the railways eagerly anticipated immense riches, while those that were by-passed feared failure and extinction. Speculators scrambled to secure title for land along the route

This tobacco store, complete with spittoons, stuffed animals, and hardy gents, recreates the ambience of Waterloo life in the 1890s. Courtesy, Waterloo Public Library

through which railways would pass as news of the extension of the new Toronto to Guelph line through Waterloo County to the American border at Sarnia created a great rush of excitement. Two large blocks of land along the proposed railway line in Berlin were bought in 1853 by Sheriff George Grange from Guelph, who had advance knowledge of the route.

The sale of Grange's railway lands generated a great deal of interest as local businessmen watched outside investors drive up the price of land. At the same time, Grange's survey, subdivided into town, park, and industrial lots, was the first major urban plan that any of them had seen. It was described in the press as:

the most desirable opportunity for investment that has yet been submitted to the public connected with railway enterprise, (it is) situated on what is deservedly acknowledged to be the richest agricultural district of Western Canada, backed up by a tract of land extending to the shores of Lake Huron.

On the first day of the sale, Grange was said to have realized "two-thirds of his original purchase price" with lots near the Grand Trunk station selling especially well as this was the area that many believed would soon "become the centre of our business district." Grange's success was carefully noted by John Hoffman, a Berlin merchant and industrialist whose enterprise and ingenuity had already become

legendary. But it was not to Berlin that Hoffman turned his attention. Rather, it was to the neighbouring village of Waterloo.

Born in Pennsylvania in 1808, Hoffman had been trained there as a miller and a mill wright. He first arrived in Waterloo Township in 1825, where he practised his trade. Growing restless, however, he left after five years and moved to Ohio. In 1837 he was back, this time seeking to establish a new career as a cabinetmaker. According to an early account, he tried "in vain" to procure a site for his factory in Waterloo as well as in Bridgeport and Freeport, where water power was available. "Thoroughly discouraged, he and Samuel Bowman, his partner, like others in the same plight, came to Bishop Eby in Berlin who said, 'If that is all, boys, go up the street and build a factory; I'll give you all the land required.' " Whether or not this story is apocryphal, it has been used to illustrate that the reluctance of Waterloo's landowners to subdivide their land encouraged the development of the village of Berlin, a much less favourable site. It might also have been that Jacob Snider, Waterloo's landowner, had found Hoffman to be too brash and too aggressive, for as Hoffman's subsequent career illustrated, he would have more than one conflict with his business partners. One historian, commenting on this trait, described Hoffman as a "young eagle" whose "store nest" soon became too small to hold both him and his partner, Henry Bowman. He also noted that the rivalry with Hoffman continued unabated in several other competing business ventures.

In 1846 Hoffman is credited with a master stroke that transformed local industries. While visiting the United States, he purchased a steam boiler and engine and hired Isaac Shantz to haul the equipment over clay roads "from Buffalo to Berlin with three span of horses." Hoffman's steam-powered furniture factory gave him a major technological advantage over his competitors and revolutionized factory production in Berlin. In 1853 Hoffman was clearly anxious for new and greater opportunities, turning his eyes to the still undeveloped potential of Waterloo, where Jacob Snider had recently handed over much of his land to his son, Elias.

Hoffman immediately approached Elias Snider, offering to purchase more than 300 acres of undeveloped, swampy land away from the existing settlement to the north, facing instead toward Berlin. Like his father before him, Snider at first refused Hoffman, who, along with his son-in-law, Isaac Weaver, then set out for the United States seeking new investment opportunities for the capital they had accrued from the sale of their manufacturing and mercantile interests in Berlin. On reaching New York, however, they received a telegram from John Shuh in Waterloo stating that Snider had changed his mind and that he would accept $37,500 for his land. Hoffman and Weaver acted with alacrity. Returning to Waterloo, they sketched out an ambitious plan for the development of a new village that, when combined with Hoffman's extensive land holdings in Berlin, would come within a quarter mile of the station of the proposed line of the Grand Trunk Railway. Something of the excitement of Hoffman's scheme can be sensed in the editorials of the local Berlin newspaper, which predicted that the area near the railway would soon become the centre of a new business district, away from King Street, and that even rural lands in Waterloo County could be expected to increase in price similar to those near Toronto and Hamilton.

In 1855 M.C. Schofield, a Berlin surveyor, prepared a plan of town and park lots of the Village of Waterloo and part of the Town of Berlin, laid out for John Hoffman, Esquire. The two villages that had begun quite separately were now being drawn inexorably together. Hoffman's ownership of property in both villages had resulted in a single survey plan. In one step he had become the "largest Berlin-Waterloo land owner," acquiring all of the land on "both

sides of the road from the high school (Kitchener Collegiate Institute) to the Zimmerman Hotel" at Erb Street in Waterloo.

Taking their cue from Grange's land sale in Berlin, Hoffman and Weaver adopted a somewhat unusual method of creating interest in the sale of their village lots in Waterloo:

Messrs. Hoffman and Weaver advertised the lots to be sold by auction, and on the day of the sale, a large wagon, drawn by oxen, was loaded with refreshments, liquid and solid. The auctioneer used this wagon as a stand, and moved from lot to lot until all were sold, the people helping themselves to the refreshments they wished, free of course.

So successful were they that the population of Waterloo more than doubled in a single year, rising overnight from 250 to more than 500. At the same time, many of the lands in the Hoffman survey would remain unsold for years to come. His survey, like Grange's in Berlin, was on an excessive scale. Nonetheless, the street pattern with its orientation toward Berlin would foreshadow the subsequent development of the "twin cities" and would make possible the easy sharing of a number of major municipal services in the years to come.

In 1856 the residents of Waterloo sought formal incorporation as a village. A provincial charter was obtained, and on the first of January 1857 Waterloo assumed the dignity of a village consisting of "the northwest quarter of lot number four, the west halves of lots five and six, lots numbers thirteen and fourteen, the north halves of lots numbers fifteen and twenty-two and lots numbers twenty-three and twenty-four on the tract known as the German Company Tract . . ." No one was particularly surprised to discover that among those councillors elected to guide the destiny of the new village was John Hoffman. Indeed, he would continue to serve as a village councillor until 1861 and then from 1863 to 1867 as reeve.

Central School was a Waterloo landmark for generations of students from 1861 until its demolition in 1952, when it was replaced on the same site by MacGregor School. Courtesy, Waterloo Public Library

Hoffman had also been elected president of the newly formed Agricultural Society for the Township of Waterloo, and he was responsible for establishing a cattle market in the village. Along with Waterloo's grain market, the cattle market maintained the village's pre-eminence as an agricultural centre in the face of Berlin's new-found prestige as the county seat for the County of Waterloo. Hoffman and his son-in-law, Isaac Weaver, generated sufficient business at their grain market to take in some 2,000 bushels of wheat daily, selling it to Montreal and Toronto in 10,000-bushel loads.

Hoffman's enterprising initiatives and the rapid growth predicted for Waterloo was clearly reflected in the report of the Grand Trunk Railway *Directory* describing the towns and villages along the route of its rail line. "Only 100 difference in popula-

tion between rival villages," noted the *Directory*, "with Waterloo leading in industries and as (an) important market centre." But it was not to be. By 1861 Waterloo's population had expanded rapidly to 1,274, but Berlin's had grown even more to 1,956. Berlin had become the legal and judicial centre for the county. As increasing numbers of Anglo-Saxon professionals took up residence in the "county town," other businesses soon located there. Among the Germans and Mennonites, however, Waterloo had more than held its own. These differences, which were already evident, would continue to separate the two communities and to shape their future development.

John Hoffman seemed to sense that. By 1870 he was back in Berlin, elected as the second mayor of the Town of Berlin in 1872 (it had been incorporated in 1871). When he died there in 1878, flags were lowered to half-mast on all the private and public buildings and the principal business places were closed. Waterloo's growth would follow its own pace and would continue to draw its strength from the prosperity and stability of the surrounding countryside much as it had done in the days of Abraham Erb.

In part, of course, Waterloo continued to benefit from the rapid growth of the entire province. The older communities on the lake had reached this level of population density much earlier. In 1854 Montreal had nearly 60,000 residents, Kingston,

11,697, Toronto, 30,775, and Hamilton, 14,112. The arrival of the Grand Trunk Railway in 1856, however, had transformed Waterloo County into an inland port, especially for settlers of German origin. In fact, the government immigration agent at Quebec redirected German immigrants there as a matter of course. On June 24, 1857, the Berlin *Chronicle* reported with some sense of consternation that on the previous Friday evening "some 90 German immigrants arrived on the Grand Trunk Railway." The immigration agent had telegraphed their arrival to Berlin and attempts were made to find accommodation for them in the various hotels in Berlin and Waterloo.

These German immigrants had come to Canada intending to go to the Western States. The Canadian agents at Quebec, however, convinced them to come to Waterloo County. Although the local residents energetically strove to find temporary accommodation, they were simply unable to cope with such large numbers. The result was as might have been expected. Half of the immigrants returned to Toronto the next day, hoping to continue on their way to Milwaukee. The *Chronicle* on June 24, 1857, lamented their loss to the community: "They were prepared to work cheap and to live cheap, and would have become producers at once, even upon a small scale—for give to these people half an acre of land, and they will raise as much garden stuff as will keep their families half the year round. But we have lost them and their labour, and the Republic has reaped the benefit of our supineness in this matter."

The Village of Waterloo continued to attract its share of newly arriving immigrants from Germany as well as those from the surrounding German-speaking townships. By 1868 the population had reached 1,788, and eight years later, on February 10, 1876, the former village was officially incorporated as the Town of Waterloo.

To mark its original incorporation as a village, a cannon had been cast at Jacob Bricker's foundry. There was great excitement when the cannon boomed out its message in the early hours on January 1, 1857. Waterloo's ceremonial cannon was used annually to fire a salute of 21 guns in honour of the birthday of Her Majesty, Queen Victoria, each 24th of May. These annual salutes were not without mishap, including one fatality when the cannon "discharged prematurely, and the hardwood ramrod, with the force of a cannon ball, killed a man who was watching the proceedings outside Huether's Hotel two blocks away, severing the head from the body."

The firing of an annual salute was temporarily halted and then resumed from a safer location on the "Show Grounds" near present-day Alexandra School. All the young boys in the village "were always on hand in large numbers to 'assist' in firing the big gun." Even here there was danger as once again the ramrod discharged prematurely, "sailing through the air" to strike the Seagram Distillery on Erb Street, a third of a mile away. After some years, Waterloo's cannon was retired from active service to sit resplendent in a prominent position in Waterloo Park.

A foundry had been located next to the Seagram Distillery on Erb Street for more than a century. In 1982 this building was given a new lease on life by the distinguished architect, Barton Myers, and now serves as an office for Joseph E. Seagram and Sons. Courtesy, Waterloo Public Library

V. R.

Königin Geburtstag
IN BERLIN!
Mittwochs, den 24. Mai 1865.

Der Tag wird als

Allgemeiner Feiertag beobachtet!

und in der folgenden Weise begangen werden:

Spiele und Belustigungen statt:

Nach Beendigung der Spiele wird die große, weltberühmte und unüberwindliche Armee der

KALITHUMPIAN RAIDERS!!

unter den tapferen, ritterlichen und berennten Ober-Schwadron? Seiner Christlichen Gebiet

ALDIBY VONS THEFEL KNECHT UND SCHNITZELBANK.

Top: The Queen's birthday was proudly celebrated by the German-speaking community on May 24, 1865, as Berlin's council declared a public holiday for its citizens. These festivities were often joint celebrations shared equally by Waterloo's residents. Courtesy, Joseph Schneider Haus

Bottom: The Waterloo Musical Society's Band was present at festive occasions throughout the nineteenth century, frequently joining the town's citizens on excursions on the Grand Trunk Railway. Courtesy, Waterloo Public Library

Waterloo's inauguration as a village seems to have prompted its rivals in Berlin to an excessive display of loyalty in 1857 in order to mark the good Queen's birthday. There, the cannon fired several volleys, smashing the windows of shopkeepers who had injudiciously remained open for business. At first it was assumed that the windows had been "unluckily smashed" by the "combustibles." The Waterloo Fire Brigade, with their engine, the artillery company and band, who had travelled to Berlin for the festivities, "appeared to enjoy themselves amazingly." The visitors from Waterloo were undoubtedly bemused at the consternation in the county town as they became aware that the broken windows in Berlin had not been by chance. The "parties in charge of the Cannon" had taken steps "to display their contempt for those who kept open stores that day," commented the editor of the local newspaper. "If we are to have mob-law of this kind," he intoned, "and (if) there is no protection to the peaceably disposed from the quarter it should come from, why the sooner the fact is made known, the sooner will other steps be taken to protect

property and punish the riotous and lawless." Others had celebrated the Queen's birthday in a less dramatic way but one that also marked a major change in the village lifestyle when four car loads of citizens from Waterloo and Berlin had boarded an excursion train to Toronto, the great capital city of Canada West.

These special trains linking Waterloo with major centres had begun the previous year, in July 1856, when the Grand Trunk Railway had provided "accommodation for 1,000 passengers for a trip to Toronto and back for $2.00." Tickets were sold by prominent businessmen in Waterloo, Berlin, and the surrounding area. Excursion trains would remain a dominant feature of Waterloo's social life throughout the century. During August 1879 the local newspaper was announcing that "Excursions are extremely plentiful these times, no one need be without a cheap ride—return trips to Buffalo were as low as $2.50; to New York City for nine dollars, while the Waterloo Brass Band accompanied a special train to Point Edward on Lake Huron near Sarnia." This was described as "the People's Excursion—cheap, comfortable and enjoyable" designed for Waterloo families. The previous week many had joined the more than 400 who went to Toronto along with the band of the local 29th battalion: "The visitors spent the day in the city. In the evening the band paraded King Street (Toronto), playing in fine style. They afterwards serenaded the Rossin House, and were extended the hospitality of the house . . . the party left for home before nine."

Bands and parades were a common part of life in Waterloo. In 1863 the Village Council provided a grant of $100 to assist in the organization of a brass band. The band, present at festive occasions, provided a sense of community spirit that became a hallmark of Waterloo life in these early years. Picnics, too, were a popular pastime. The distillery picnics of the 1870s were particularly well attended:

Headed by the village band, a parade lined up at the distillery and it made a gay scene with flags and banners flying and with all the employees, distillers, coopers, millers, store clerks, bookkeepers and others, and their families, to say nothing of the numerous small boys who swelled the parade and were made to feel welcome.

Many picnics in these early years were held in the "Randall grove," part of the property of George Randall, who owned the distillery and who had purchased Isaac Weaver's house. The house had been set on a prime piece of land in the original Hoffman survey where a pine grove fronted on Park Street near the present Mutual Life grounds. Both Weaver and Randall had made their property available to community groups. Other picnics were held at Quickfall's Bush—a name applied to any wooded grove on the hill east of the town near the Quickfall farm. It was heavily wooded and open to public use.

By the mid-1860s the village had formally acquired a "recreation and showground" of some 10 acres at the present site of Alexandra School. Ultimately, Park Street would connect Victoria Park in Berlin with Waterloo's showgrounds. It became the village's common meeting place, noted an early historian:

sports, tournaments, races, celebrations, saengerfests, and for a time, horse races (were held there). There were many circuses also, and the show ground was always the rendezvous . . . It was the scene of many a close game of baseball, lacrosse or football, and many field days of sport . . .

Fall fairs, too, were held at the showgrounds, supported by a village grant to the North Riding Agricultural Society. By 1869 a permanent "Fair Building" was erected. Waterloo's showgrounds would serve the community well until 1890, when a larger and more attractive park and athletic field would be acquired.

Participation in events such as these resulted in a strong sense of community life and a sense of shared purpose that would distinguish Waterloo from many of Canada's larger cities. The small size of Waterloo's manufacturing establishments encouraged the maintenance of this close relationship. In 1871, for example,

This Sunday School picnic on the banks of the Grand River took place on a late afternoon summer's day about 1890. Courtesy, Breithaupt-Hewetson-Clark Collection, University of Waterloo Library

Top: Employees of Snyder Roos and Company wholesale upholsterers pose in front of their Waterloo store in 1895 during a Labour Day parade. Courtesy, Waterloo Public Library

Bottom: This picnic in Waterloo features ample evidence of the products of the town's major industries— the Seagram's Distillery and the Kuntz Brewery. Courtesy, Waterloo Public Library

Waterloo had only 5 industrial establishments that employed 10 or more workers: J.W. Dodd's woollen mill had 31 workers; M. Wegenast's sawmill and woodworking shop had 22 employees; Jacob Bricker's iron foundry, 20; George Randall's flour and grist mill and distillery, 18; and Absalom Merner's iron foundry, 16. There were another 6 establishments with from 5 to 9 workers. The small size of the village and its diversified economy had resulted in an era of stability and steady growth while avoiding the boom and bust cycles and the widespread unemployment that had become a feature of urban life in many Canadian cities during this period.

Many social problems that seemed remote from village life were, nonetheless, also part of the age. Perhaps most shocking was the case of infanticide discovered by the foreman of a railway work group. He found the dead body of a newly born infant under the platform of the railway station in Berlin. The mother had been a domestic servant from Germany travelling through Berlin to Preston. The child had come "before its time," born in a hotel room near the station. The mother believed the child to have been stillborn, and she had been told by her "betrothed" that he had taken the child and buried it. The "betrothed" had apparently also given the child a sufficient blow to the head to have ensured its death before abandoning it beneath the railway platform. The county coroner issued a warrant for the arrest of the suspected parties.

In some ways, Waterloo residents were spared the "evils" that accompanied the railway in Berlin. The discovery of a case of prostitution in the county town became a "cause cèlébre" in Waterloo when Berlin's police constable was alleged to have assisted the "offending party" and her male consort to depart from Berlin on the next train so that the case would not have to be tried in the court, and the names of her prominent guests would not be made public. The editor of the Berlin *News* was morally outraged, and the Waterloo *Chronicle* observed with great delight: "The Berlin *News* is going for 'Con' Gerbig, the Berlin Town Constable and High Constable Klippert on the charge of favouring the keepers of a house of ill repute in the County Town. It has the promise of a libel suit from the parties who are accused of keeping the said house." In fact, the libel suit was successful while Waterloo's bemused residents looked on with interest.

At the time of its incorporation as a

town in 1876, the new council felt it necessary to provide for the community's safety as well as its public morals. The "Room," known as the "Old Council Chamber," at the Market Building was now officially designated as "the Police Office for the Town of Waterloo." At the same time an omnibus bill of public morals was passed, making it illegal "to bathe or wash the naked person between the hours of six o'clock a.m. and nine o'clock p.m., near any street, highway or dwelling house." Indecent littering or the posting of pictures on walls or fences in the streets of Waterloo, and the use of indecent or insulting language or the uttering of profane oaths was also considered to be a criminal act.

In light of the recent "scandal" in the county town, Waterloo's councillors passed a detailed set of restrictions prohibiting houses of ill repute and making it unlawful,

for any person or persons whomsoever, to keep, maintain and support, or be an inmate or habitual frequenter of, or in any way connected with, or in any way contribute to the support of any disorderly house, or house of ill-fame, or other place for the practice of prostitution, or knowingly own or be interested as proprietor, landlord or otherwise, of any such house with the said Town.

Gambling and other similar activities were also prohibited. Cards, dice, rouge-et-noir, roulette tables, as well as fortune telling, palmistry or "using any subtle craft, means or device to deceive or impose upon any person," were prohibited. Vagrants and mendicants, nightwalkers and prostitutes, and "each and every person wandering about and endeavouring by the exposure of wounds and deformities to obtain and gather alms within the town" would also be in trouble with Waterloo's police.

Unlike frontier towns such as Winnipeg or Vancouver, where a transient popula-

tion and a predominance of males created a social environment in which the liquor trade and prostitution flourished, a strong sense of Victorian morality prevailed in Waterloo. Family orientation had been part of the community from its earliest days. The common ethnic origin of the people and the use of the German language also meant that many of the wandering unemployed who roamed throughout Ontario rarely troubled to stay over in Waterloo. Instead, a strong sense of community with few dramatic social divisions had come to characterize town life in the nineteenth century.

This is not to suggest that life in Victorian Canada was without its personal tragedies. It was not uncommon in this period or in the pioneer era to find public notices such as the following: "I hereby forbid any person or persons harbouring or trusting my wife, Sarah, or giving her any assistance whatever in my name; as I will not be accountable for the same. She has left my bed and board without any provocation whatever. Climson Davis, Waterloo, August 10, 1838." John Youngblut was even more adamant about the sudden departure of his wife, Sarah, for he warned on October 8, 1841, that "whosoever shall lodge, board or employ her in any work or manner, shall feel the whole weight of the law."

Other accounts illustrate the personal anguish of those who emigrated to a new land. Catherine Kreuen arrived in Waterloo from Germany in October 1838 "in a very destitute condition" only to find that her "nearest relative," Conrad Ratz of Grabenon, electorate of Hesse Darmstadt, had left Waterloo. Editors of other newspapers were requested to insert her appeal "for humanity's sake" in the hope that Mr. Ratz might be located.

Illness and disease were also a cause of considerable concern in most parts of the province. Unclean water and poor sanitary conditions (as domestic animals grazed freely throughout the village) were also problems facing the new town council. Blocked drains, rotting vegetables, and unclean privies were common sights in Waterloo as they were elsewhere in Ontario. Beginning in 1857, but especially after 1875, a spate of new municipal regulations were passed into law to regulate these problems. One of the most worrisome concerns was fire, and this can be seen in the priority given to Waterloo's first municipal building in 1857.

Upon the incorporation of Waterloo as a village, Jacob Snider, who still owned a great deal of the land upon which the village would develop, had donated a lot south of the public library as a site for a new municipal building. A simple two-storey brick building was erected, popularly called "Das Spritzhaus" or the firehall. The lower floor served as the firehall, while the upper floor was the council chamber. With the majority of Waterloo's houses in 1857 of wooden construction—either frame, plank or log—and only eight built of brick, the threat of fire was the villager's greatest concern. Wooden buildings, wooden shingles, boardwalks, open fireplaces, and kerosene lamps frequently resulted in major conflagrations that destroyed entire blocks of houses and commercial properties. Once started, such fires were almost impossible to control.

The neighbouring village of Galt, for instance, had suffered a massive fire in 1851 along the south side of Main Street that had destroyed an entire business block. In 1856 fire had struck again, this time on the north side of Main Street. Since the buildings were all constructed of wood, the fire raged through the entire block, destroying everything in its path. Berlin, too, had had its share of tragic fires, one of which in 1853 had destroyed John Hoffman's entire business section. It was partly because of this major disaster that Hoffman had turned his interests to Waterloo. Now as that village's major property owner and elected as a village councillor, John Hoffman was particularly anxious to ensure the safety of his newly adopted village.

As one of its first by-laws in 1857 Waterloo offered a one-dollar premium to the first person to carry two gallons of water to the scene of a fire, 50 cents to the second. "Great was the excitement," described an early historian, "when a score or more of volunteers grasped the long rope attached to the 'engine' and ran along the bumpy streets to a fire, with bells clanging and the 'chief' shouting his orders through a trumpet." Volunteers manned the hand pump, drawing on water supplies that had been located in large underground tanks at strategic intervals throughout the village.

With fairly primitive fire-fighting equipment and in light of the importance of quelling fires as quickly as possible, all able-bodied citizens were expected to be volunteer firemen. On one occasion after a fire near Elias Snider's swamp, the volunteers had all disappeared, and when it was time to pull the engine back to town only six were left. This seemed an excellent opportunity to levy a fine for "neglect of duty" against the community's erstwhile leaders, all of whom were either councillors or future mayors. Christian Kumpf, Harry Nafe, Simon Snyder, Joseph E. Seagram, George Diebel, P.H. Sims, J. Kalbfleisch, and George Moore all paid their fines to the village coffers.

The continuing seriousness of the threat of fire had led the council in 1872 to purchase a hand-pumped fire engine from Rumsey and Company in the United States for $1,700. In 1885 the Town of Waterloo acquired the latest advance in fire-fighting equipment, a steam-powered fire engine that they promptly christened "Bismarck," named after the strong-handed German chancellor, Otto Von Bismarck, who had become famous for uniting the loose federation of German states. The town still did not have its own fire team, however, so when the alarm sounded there was always a race among the local teamsters. The one who first reached the firehall with his team would be awarded a $5 prize. "There were many close and thrilling races," recalled one longtime Waterloo resident, "with the drivers standing on their wagons, and their horses on the full run, it reminded one of the chariot races of ancient times." In 1889 water mains, including fire hydrants, were installed, and the town disposed of "Bismarck" and purchased an "up-to-date horse drawn hose truck." Like all things "up-to-date," the new system undoubtedly provided a more efficient service, but something of the camaraderie and close-ness of village life was lost in the process.

Even without major fires that destroyed entire sections of the town (as in the case of Galt, where inhabitants rebuilt with stone in a self-consciously Scottish style), the look of Waterloo and its urban architecture was fundamentally changed by the town's concern with fire protection. The legacy of wooden houses, which had made up a majority of the homes of Waterloo's residents and of some of its most prominent community leaders, would all but disappear as a result of the town's new by-law. After 1876 homes or commercial buildings constructed of wood were prohibited. As the by-law stated,

Every dwelling house, store, manufactory or other building hereafter erected shall be built of stone, brick, cement, concrete or some other material other than wood, and roofed with slate, metal, tile composition or shingles, laid on some fire-proof material.

The by-law was also directed to existing buildings, forbidding the re-erection of any existing wooden building or even major renovations or repairs to frame or wooden buildings. There was a delightful irony in the fact that Conrad Fenner, a future Waterloo fire chief, took great pride in his attractive clapboard home, compared to the brick houses being put up around him. Nonetheless, the effect of the new by-law would result in a town that was overwhelmingly constructed of brick. Few traces of the earlier architectural styles

would survive, while the presence of locally owned brickyards resulted in the almost predominance of Waterloo's ubiquitous white or yellow brick. The commercial and residential districts were almost all built of brick, often in a uniform and not particularly imaginative style, giving Waterloo its overwhelming Victorian character.

In 1885 the town's total assets were remarkably uncomplicated. The market house and grounds including the Town Hall were valued at $10,000. The town's showgrounds and buildings were worth $6,000. The new 1885 firehall and engine house had cost $2,090, and the cart and hose, plus the old engine house (Spritzhaus—the village's first building erected in 1857) were together estimated to be worth $6,000. Waterloo's combined assets equalled only $27,500.

Most impressive was the Victorian Town Hall, built in 1874 on three acres of land purchased from Elias Snider at the northwest corner of Albert and Erb streets. With its ornate brickwork,

Fire was an ever-present danger in Waterloo and most other nineteenth-century Canadian towns. The horse-drawn "Rescue Hose Company" was a major improvement over the pail brigade. Courtesy, Kitchener Public Library

Flying the new Canadian flag, Waterloo's historic Town Hall remained a landmark throughout Canada's centennial in 1967. Two years later the building was razed. Courtesy, K-W Record Photograph Negative Collection, University of Waterloo Library

stone-trimmed arch, and towers topped by wrought-iron cresting, this building symbolised the optimism and prosperity of Waterloo as it progressed with stately dignity to its new status as an incorporated town. (It would not become a city until 1946, at the end of the Second World War.) An ornate stairway led from the main entrance to the second floor council chamber, while the main floor had municipal offices and the library and market stalls were in the basement.

The size and scale of the Town Hall bespoke much about Waterloo, about its obvious stability, its quiet prosperity, and its relationship to the rich agricultural

hinterland that, from the beginning, had provided its greatest resource. Most of the early hotels and inns had been built to provide food, drink, and lodging for farmers coming to transact business in the village. Names like The Farmer's Hotel and Market Hotel illustrated the village's early orientation, while others such as the Waterloo Hotel and Huether's Hotel also pointed to the Germanic nature of the community.

Waterloo's early industries, too, reveal much about the community's rural orientation. The original Union Mills of Abraham Erb had been substantially rebuilt in 1851, 1855, and again in the 1860s. John Hoffman and Isaac Weaver had also upgraded Erb's original sawmill, converting it to steam power in 1855. One of the earliest manufacturing concerns, a plough shop and foundry established by Abraham Buehler in 1851 on Erb Street, was on the main road coming into the village and in close proximity to the grist mill and sawmill.

The importance of the wheat trade in Waterloo had led in 1857 to the construction of a second grist mill on Erb Street. This was the Granite Mills, which, ultimately in 1883, became the famous Seagram Distillery. By 1861 the Granite Mills, with four run of stones powered by a 30-horsepower steam engine, was producing 12,000 barrels of flour, while its distillery had expanded to nearly 3,000 barrels of whisky per year with the owners having great "difficulty meeting the demands for this whisky." Not surprisingly, there was a large local market for barrels, which were needed for the shipment of both flour and whisky. In the nineteenth century barrels and kegs were the standard containers for most products.

A cooperage business had been in existence in Waterloo since 1839. The arrival in Waterloo of J. Karl (Charles) Mueller, a skilled cooper, from Baden, Germany, in 1853, led to his immediate employment with the Granite Mills. By 1873 Mueller had established his cooperage as an independent business that would continue to flourish as Waterloo's trade prospered.

Whisky and flour were not the only products requiring a cooper's skills. Another prominent Waterloo industry, the brewing of German lager beer, had begun as early as 1835, when there were three small breweries in Waterloo coincident with the arrival of the first German immigrants. The most prominent of them was David Kuntz, a cooper and brewer who had emigrated from Weisbaden, Germany. In 1844 he established a brewery at the site of the present Huether Hotel. When

the Hoffman survey opened up new lands closer to Berlin, he started the famous Spring Brewery at the corner of what is now King and William streets. Located near Waterloo's park and showgrounds, the brewery subsequently became the L. Kuntz Park Brewery in the 1870s when his son, Louis, acquired control of the company.

Like most villages and towns in Ontario, Waterloo had a wide range of stores and mercantile establishments. There were general merchants, tailors, shoemakers, and other similar businesses dating from the 1830s. Tanneries, a carriage factory and a chair factory, a pump maker, a pail factory, a hat maker, a ferrier, a stove maker, a tin smithy, a blacksmith, and a brickmaker provided many of the services necessary to life in the village and the surrounding agrarian community.

The staff at the Kuntz Park Brewery posed in 1894 for this photograph featuring their products in an ornamental display. The brewery was a well-established Waterloo landmark located in the 1870s near the original "showgrounds and park." The brewery has played an important role in the life of Waterloo since 1844, when it began operations at the site of the present Huether Hotel. Courtesy, K-W Record Photograph Negative Collection, University of Waterloo Library

Above: This building on Waterloo's King Street was known for many years as the "Insurance Building" in recognition of the number of local insurance companies, including Dominion Life (now Manufacturer's Life), which once conducted business in its halls. Courtesy, Waterloo Public Library

Right: Waterloo's post office is seen here next to the barber shop and shaving parlor. Courtesy, Waterloo Public Library

cies were directed toward a slower, more organic growth than in many Canadian cities. Waterloo evolved at a measured pace, avoiding both an elaborate "growth ethic" and the bust and boom cycles that occurred elsewhere. In part this was the advantage of proximity to Berlin, where the council had initiated a vigorous policy of financial support for factory expansion in the early 1870s. Waterloo was not in competition, but Waterloo's residents could benefit from the social amenities in their neighbouring county town. Even the arrival in 1877 of a rail connection with the Grand Trunk Railway at Berlin did little to change the pace of life. Instead of creating a new industrial district along the railway line, the railway merely reenforced the existing pattern of development that had been oriented to the rural countryside.

Waterloo differed from other Ontario cities and towns by the presence from 1863 onwards of insurance companies organized on the "mutual" principle, whereby the capital of the company was that of its policyholders rather than that

Those who profited from Waterloo's growth seemed also to be its natural leaders. Merchants and industrialists predominated on village and town councils, often serving consecutive terms over many years. For most of them, municipal office was a serious responsibility and their poli-

Company. It became the Mutual Life Assurance Company of Canada in 1900 and part of the Mutual Group in 1988.

The success of these two companies was followed in 1874 by the organization in Waterloo of the North Waterloo Farmer's Mutual Fire Insurance Company as well as the Mercantile Fire Insurance Company in 1875. In 1889 the Dominion Life Assurance Company, initiated by a group of Waterloo businessmen led by Thomas Hilliard, was chartered by the federal Parliament. The presence of so many insurance companies would come to have a profound effect on the social and economic life of Waterloo. Yet development of the companies in this small Ontario town was entirely consistent with the social stability of the community. Waterloo had clearly begun to establish its own identity as a Canadian town based on a firm belief in progress tempered by the inherent stability of the surrounding countryside—characteristics that would see it through the trying years of the next century.

Left: Moses Springer was active in local and provincial politics, serving first as Reeve of the Village of Waterloo from 1857-1861, 1867-1869, 1873, and 1876, and then as the first mayor of the Town of Waterloo in 1876. Courtesy, Waterloo Public Library

Below: The Honourable Isaac Erb Bowman, scion of two prominent Mennonite families, was a leading politician. Elected to the Parliament of Canada in 1867, 1872, 1874, 1887, and 1891, he was also a business leader serving as president of the Mutual Fire Insurance Company and the Ontario Mutual Life Assurance Company. Courtesy, Waterloo Public Library

of shareholders.

The first of these was the Waterloo County Mutual Fire Insurance Company, established in 1863. Its location in Waterloo seemed a natural evolution of the village's ethos in which co-operation and mutual concern were important values.

The decision five years later to apply the mutual principle to life assurance was the first of its kind in Canada. The obvious success of the fire insurance company had demonstrated its efficacy. At the same time, the desire to retain the profits from the life assurance business in Canada rather than draining the resources of the new country for the benefit of shareholders in Great Britain and the United States persuaded a number of prominent local community leaders including Isaac Erb Bowman, M.P.; Moses Springer, M.L.A.; and Cyrus M. Taylor to support the idea of such a company. The new company was incorporated in 1868, the year after Confederation, and began business in 1870 under the name of the Ontario Mutual Life Assurance

Behind the Berlin Wall

Life in the small village of Waterloo seemed safely removed from the wars and political turbulence of far-distant Europe. Many of the settlers in Waterloo had come there to avoid European wars. Yet it would be these very wars and political conflicts in another land that would leave an indelible mark on both Waterloo and its neighbouring community of Berlin. In 1916, in the midst of one such war, Berlin would lose its name in the face of mounting anti-German prejudice and take instead the name of Lord Kitchener, Britain's famous Secretary of War.

It had all begun innocently enough when the residents of Waterloo and Berlin had decided in 1871 to celebrate their German heritage in a great *Friedensfest* or "Peace Festival" to mark the end of the Franco-Prussian War. The ultimate victory of Prussia over France, however, also signalled the reunification of the German states and the rise of a united and powerful Germany after more than a century of defeat and domination. For many Germans living in the new world this was an occasion for exultant expressions of pride in the traditions of their homeland. Who in Canada would have thought otherwise? With Victoria and her German consort, Prince Albert, on the throne of Great Britain and the Kaiser ruling over a united Germany the future seemed assured for Canada's Germans. Indeed, the consanguinity

Arch near Town H

An engraving of the concert hall
and the festivities surrounding
the great Saengerfest capture the
spirit of these grand nineteenth-
century celebrations. Courtesy,
Kitchener Public Library

Participants in the great Friedensfest celebration of 1871 gathered in front of the Waterloo County Courthouse before proceeding to the festivities in the village of Waterloo. Courtesy, Waterloo Historical Society

of the two royal families seemed to give the Germans in Canada a unique status as well as strong feelings of loyalty to the royal family.

Community leaders sensed the importance of their place in Canada as well as the historic symbolism of the European names of Waterloo and Berlin as they hosted the mammoth *Friedensfest* on May 2, 1871. Attracting an estimated 12,000 celebrants, the *Friedensfest* offered a unique opportunity to express feelings of pride in their homeland. Something of this mood was captured by young Louis Breithaupt, who excitedly recorded the festivities in his diary for May 1 and 2, 1871:

Monday 1 May 1871
I was away to our farm twice to-day getting green trees to decorate our store front for

tomorrow. Everybody is preparing. Wreaths, bows flags &c are up on all the streets in town. The Hamilton Band arrived already in town this evening. The (y) marched through the town, all in uniform. There will be from 7-10 bands & between 300 & 400 singers here tomorrow. It is expected to be a great day if the weather is fair.

Tuesday 2 May 1871
Today was a public holiday as there was a great peace-jubilee in town. This peace jubilee refers to the peace which has been concluded between Germany & France & was arranged by the Germans of Berlin & Waterloo (there was a holiday in Waterloo too). All the stores & businesses of both towns were closed. The programme of the day was as follows: viz - At 6 o'clock in the morning 21 canon-shots, from 7 to 8 o'clock divine worship was held in all the German churches of Berlin & Waterloo, after church the procession went to the R Road Station to meet the visitors who came from a distance, after that the procession moved on to the court-house where an oak tree was planted before the Court House & speeches were held. In the afternoon speeches were held at the market place, from where the procession went to Waterloo where speeches, amusements &c were held. At about 8 o'clock p.m. the Berlin & Waterloo folks met here at the drill shed & formed a torchlight procession, which moved to the Court House where illuminations fireworks &c were going on & the unveiling of "Germania" as the Watch on the Rhein (a transparent) also singing & speaking. The festival closed with the Song of "God Save the Queen." There were from 10,000 to 12,000 visitors in Berlin to-day, the weather was splendid all day. We gave a lunch in the 2nd floor of our old leather store at noon to-day for our customers, friends &c. There were from 50 to 60 guests. The town was fixed up most splendid with green wreaths bows, flags 1/2. Waterloo was not fixed up as nice as Berlin.

The *Friedensfest* was one of great pageantry. A parade with 24 mounted adjutants led an hour-long procession with marching bands and colourful banners. Mass choirs and rousing speeches, punctuated with hearty "hochs," were the order of the day and the German consul from Michigan, Herr Widemann, read a poem specially written for the "fest."

After lunch the procession marched to Waterloo while the bands played "stirring airs." "In the line were thirty-four wagons in which rosy-cheeked girls presented (historical) tableaux." Another program of song and speeches followed, led by Waterloo's reeve, George Randall, and Moses Springer, M.P.P. Then it was back to Berlin where a chorus of 150 voices performed the "Mass des Lobes," followed by a display of fireworks. A grand *Friedensfest Ball* brought the celebrations to a close.

Not all of the residents of Waterloo were of German origin, although 80 percent were as were 73 percent of those who lived in Berlin. The "testimonial" of the English-speaking residents prepared by William Jaffray, George Davidson, and John King presented at the *Friedensfest* provides a rare insight into the relationship between Anglo-Saxons and Germans in the 1870s, pointing to the things that they shared in common "as distinct peoples" and the "many ties to bind us in a single (Canadian) nationality." The ties of marriage between the British and German royal families were emphasized: "the bond of union between your Fatherland and our Motherland is one that has been cemented by relationships the most tender and sacred possible." Other characteristics, too, were shared by both traditions:

in its hatred of oppression and aspirations after true liberty, the genius of our fellow countrymen in both lands is the same; and that in reverence for truth, morality and religion, the observance of law and order, and respect for constituted authority, as well as in the cultivation of all the graces of every day national life, the people of Germany and Britain have long been in mutual accord . . . As Canadians and Colonists, animated by

the same principles and aims and with the same great destiny to labour for and achieve, we are as much with you in everything as it is possible for any two peoples to be.

Applauding the restraint of the German victory and the successful unification of the German states from "the Baltic to the Moselle," the English-speaking delegates expressed their gratitude that "a strong and well-governed (German) Empire, in the very heart of Europe, will, at all times, be a safe guarantee for a prosperous as well as permanent Peace." There also seemed much in common between the German confederation and the creation of the new Dominion of Canada, and "where the German-Canadians were fellow-workers with ourselves in the erection, on this continent, of a great Canadian nationality. A mission so high and noble, (which)

In 1879 these local dignitaries were dressed in formal attire for their presentation to the Governor-General, the Marquis of Lorne, and Her Royal Highness, the Princess Louise. Courtesy, Breithaupt-Hewetson-Clark Collection, University of Waterloo Library

should surely draw us very nearly together . . . We will be laying for our common country a foundation similar to that upon which now stands the powerful and united Empire of Germany."

By the 1870s the predominance of the German tradition in both Waterloo and Berlin was often praised by distinguished visitors to the community. This was especially true in 1879 when the new Governor-General, the Marquis of Lorne, and his wife, Her Royal Highness, the Princess Louise, daughter of Queen Victoria, toured Canada. Local dignitaries planned an elaborate reception to show "admiration for His Excellency and Her Royal Highness and at the same time showing our loyalty and love for Her Majesty 'Our Great Mother' across the sea." Music was provided by Waterloo's newly formed German *Maennerchor*. An address in German was delivered by Hugo Kranz, M.P., and one in English by Berlin's mayor, L.J. Breithaupt. The mayor of Waterloo, Christian Kumpf, the music director from Waterloo, H.A. Zoellner, and Councillor J. Kalbfleisch, were received by the marquis and the princess.

The presence of so many leading politicians bearing such obviously German surnames was a clear recognition of their predominance among the local elite. It was not so much that ethnicity was an electoral issue, although at times it was, but rather that almost all of the major business and commercial leaders in the community were of German descent. So were the schoolteachers and church ministers. Only the professionals—lawyers and medical doctors—were not.

Governor-General Lorne, too, was acutely aware of the cultural values of Waterloo and Berlin. "Here where the virtues of the Anglo-Saxon and German races meet to hasten your prosperity by their friendly rivalry," he said, "we who descend from both English and German parents gratefully accept the tokens of affection given by you here . . . and thank you in the name of our Sovereign." Lorne

then replied to the German delegation speaking entirely in German. The princess and he, he said, were

all the more happy from the fact that we are welcomed in the beloved German language, and the assurance of German faith and friendship given from German lips . . . Though you have received us so heartily and shown your esteem for the Queen, you will still remain good Germans, and you may therefore be proud that you can instruct your children and grandchildren in their forcible mother tongue. The love for the old German Fatherland should never die. It will not interfere in the least with the use of the English language, so much of which comes from the German.

"It affords us the truest pleasure," he said, "to hear from all sides in what high estimation the German settlers are held . . ." The governor-general's concluding remarks offer a glimpse into the political life of a bygone era as he told his audience of the great pleasure it would give him and the princess "to inform the Imperial family of Germany how happy and prosperous you reside here in Canada, being regarded as those who bring good fortune to the country." The princess, Louis Breithaupt noted later in his diary, "spoke an excellent German."

Lord Lorne would not be the last vice-regal representative to speak so highly of the bonds of unity between England and Germany. As late as 1911 another "royal" governor was sent to Canada. This was His Royal Highness, the Duke of Connaught, third son of Queen Victoria. The Duke of Connaught brought with him his dutchess, the former Princess Louise Marguerite of Prussia, and when they travelled across Canada it was not uncommon for citizens to fly the Union Jack and the German flag side by side, giving the impression of a strong Anglo-German accord. As the clouds of war formed over Europe in 1914, the end was near for this quite remarkable tradition. In 1879, however, nothing would have seemed more remote.

The German community in Waterloo was certainly sensitive to the uniqueness of its place in Canadian society. There had even been some concern that the special "German" address to the governor-general might cause uneasiness. On September 10, 1879, the Berlin *Daily News* had urged that "We hope this matter will unitedly and heartily be entered into by all our citizens—even in the matter of the German address—for there are comparatively few people in this county who have not more or less Teutonic blood in their veins." The editor of the Waterloo *Chronicle*, for one, did not agree, complaining that all those presented to the vice-regal party represented only the Germans. "The 'Dutchmen' (Mennonites) and the English were not worth representing," he lamented, "being like a certain class down South, known among the darkies as 'no' count, white trash."

While some indeed may have begun to resent the changes in the community that had resulted from the increasing numbers of German immigrants as evidenced by

German plays and *Turnvereins* (gymnastic festivals), German choirs and German *Saengerfests* or singing festivals, the predominance of German folk songs, German styles of dress, and German imported goods, a majority clearly did not. In the last quarter of the nineteenth century the citizens of Waterloo witnessed a remarkable flowering of German cultural traditions. The most obvious of these was the series of nine grand *Saengerfests* staged between 1874 and 1912, bringing together German choral societies from across Ontario and the American states. These *Saengerfests* attracted tens of thousands to Waterloo and Berlin for the purpose of singing German songs and listening to performances of instrumental works composed by the great German composers. The programs also included German folk songs—"songs of the old homeland"—as well as cantatas, oratorios, overtures, and operatic excerpts designed to instill a sense of pride in German culture.

Beginning with the 1871 *Friedensfest*, these festivals also aroused a high degree of patriotism in the German citizens, allowing them to express their strong feel-

In preparation for visitors arriving for one of the many Saengerfests in the 1880s, Waterloo is decked out with boughs and garlands. Courtesy, Waterloo Public Library

A crowd gathers in Waterloo at the corner of King and Erb streets to celebrate a traditional German singing festival or Saengerfest. These melodious affairs drew thousands of visitors to Waterloo and Berlin. Courtesy, Waterloo Public Library

the nineteenth century." Bismarck's success had overcome the traditional weakness of the German states, providing instead a strong, united leadership in Europe. The singing festivals in Waterloo had evolved in part from this philosophy, and the elaborate rituals that they followed were "deeply planted in Germany's past." As one author has suggested, "These Saengerfests represented a German tradition rooted in the perception of a powerful and united Germany and are clearly an expression of the nationalistic and historical themes dominant in nineteenth century German culture." While political philosophy may have been less evident in Canada, the songs and the philosophy of the *Saengerfests* drew heavily for their inspiration on nationalistic German traditions, and German patriotic songs were the choirs' mainstay.

A recent study of *Saengerfests* in Waterloo and Berlin has illustrated their strict adherence to these traditions:

Meticulous care and preparation was given by the citizens of Berlin-Waterloo . . . in an attempt to recreate visually the pageantry and atmosphere of an ideal outdoor medieval festival. Buildings in the towns were embroidered with flags, banners, greenery, and floral arrangements to recreate the appearance of historical castles. The additional lining of the streets with triumphal arches transformed the industrial centre into a medieval community . . . The military practice of firing cannons each morning of the Saengerfests announced the transformation of Berlin-Waterloo and . . . symbolized a warning of protection against any intruders who threatened the security of the German state.

ings toward the homeland both "overtly" and with great "enthusiasm." Waterloo's Mannerchor and Berlin's Concordia Mannerchor, both founded in the 1870s, were choirs of exceptional quality and their leadership was recognized throughout Ontario. In 1873 Waterloo's H.A. Zoellner drafted the constitution for a German-Canadian *Sangerbund*, whose purpose was to unite all of the German singing societies in Canada, hoping thereby "to unify the present German settlements . . . and to promote and maintain the German language, customs and traditions." The first meeting of the *Canadian National Sangerbund* was held in Waterloo from August 31 to September 3, 1874. The sense of pride expressed in the great *Friedensfest* of 1871 was not to be forgotten by Waterloo's German-Canadians.

The *Sangerbund* seems to have originated "from the German desire to unite the many states of their homeland during

The details of the various social events at the *Saengerfests* followed a formula drawn from German history. This included uniforms, flags, and banners.

The 1886 *Saengerfest* was led by Louis Zimmer "wearing an emperor's cloak and helmet, and assisted by an aide." According to the local newspaper, "both looked very impressive in their military garb and swords." At a time when Canadians in neighbouring Anglo-Saxon communities were revelling in Rudyard Kipling's tales of military adventure and glory in far-off India and Africa, the German community's pride in the traditions of its past seemed harmless and even somewhat archaic. As the two great imperial powers began their headlong rush into one of the most devastating clashes that the world had ever seen, however, the position of Canada's Germans became decidedly uneasy.

Many of Waterloo's residents had long ago begun to think of themselves as German-Canadians rather than as Germans in Canada. By 1911, 90 percent of Waterloo's residents had been born in Canada. Few had ever seen Germany even if the census listed 76 percent as being of German ethnic origin. German immigration had slowed to a trickle in the later decades of the nineteenth century, and Waterloo had attracted few of those German intellectuals or professionals who represented the rising wave of German nationalism elsewhere.

German immigrants coming to Waterloo had been mainly craftsmen, labourers, and artisans. As a result, one author has suggested that, "although a semblance of spiritual contact with Germany was maintained by newspapers (singing festivals and German choirs), a predominantly Canadian character also manifested itself early in their development." Nonetheless, when war against Germany was declared in August 1914, communities like Waterloo were seen, from the outside at least, as being altogether too German.

In addition to the *Saengerfests,* the German character of Waterloo had been main-

Left: The building of "Die Neue Kirche" (St. John's Lutheran Church) in 1882 attests to the predominance of the Lutheran congregation in Waterloo and to its enduring German traditions. Courtesy, Waterloo Public Library

Below: St. Louis Roman Catholic Church, constructed in 1891, symbolizes the growing prosperity and stability of life in Waterloo at the time as well as the central importance of religion in the community. Courtesy, Waterloo Public Library

tained by the predominance of German-speaking religious traditions that gave a distinct sense of identity to the local community. At the beginning of the twentieth century more than half of Waterloo's residents were members of a German-speaking congregation, St. John's Evangelical Lutheran Church. St. John's, which had originally been organized as Waterloo's first parish in 1837, had built a new church in 1882 to accommodate 1,200 people. By contrast the Anglicans in Waterloo were not even listed on the 1891 census, and, in 1887, at the time of the expansion of the Lutheran congregation, were meeting for the first time on the second floor of the Devitt block on Erb Street. The Presbyte-

On October 30, 1911, a crowd of some 1,500 Waterloo "notables" gathered on the lawn of the Waterloo Lutheran Seminary to celebrate its official opening. Courtesy, Waterloo Public Library

rians had erected St. Paul's Church on George Street in 1888, although the 1881 census had listed only 96 members. Even the Roman Catholics, who were predominantly German-speaking and among the earliest residents in Waterloo, had only 330 members in 1891. By 1911 they had rapidly increased to more than 900.

Members of congregations such as the Methodists and Evangelicals had not been without opportunities for worship in the German language. And of course the Mennonites had built a new church on Erb Street in 1903. Others, too, had made the trip to Berlin, where a greater variety

of denominational services had been available from mid-century. In Waterloo, however, the Lutheran tradition was predominant. The Lutheran presence was also felt in the town's social and political life. Many of the mayors and members of council had come from St. John's congregation. The families of the workmen and those of the factory owners frequently worshipped at the same church (and in the German language), which heightened the bonds of unity and community life in Waterloo.

There is remarkably little evidence of sectarian strife in nineteenth-century Waterloo. The organization and funding of St. Louis Roman Catholic Church in 1890 provides an interesting illustration of early ecumenism. Support was initially sought from within the Catholic community, but from the beginning the entire town was also involved. As Theobald Spetz later recounted:

It is worth while to state that the non-Catholics of Waterloo had been for years urging their Catholic fellow citizens to build a church, and promised them their assistance, because they thought it a good plan to increase the population of the town. When the trial was made the committee found them ready to redeem their promise quite nobly.

The canvas resulted in $2,584 in subscriptions from Waterloo Catholics and $1,469 from the other "non-Catholic" residents of Waterloo. Roman Catholics in Berlin contributed an additional $742, while donations from other Berlin residents added $272. One young man visiting a local bar room contributed to the fund, saying, "So you are going to build a Catholic church in Waterloo, I will give $10 for it, if it is going to hurt Berlin."

Congregations that offered a more fundamental challenge to the social order, however, were not particularly welcome. A local diary entry recounts the short shrift given to the Salvation Army: "August 4, 1892 The Salvation Army went to Waterloo to convert the heathens, but Waterloo did not like their music. Three young men were before Justice of the Peace Mackie for disturbing them."

The original organization of St. John's Lutheran Church in the 1830s had not been without its own difficulties, and the history of this parish reveals much about Waterloo and about community life in this nineteenth-century Ontario town. Unlike Anglicans and Presbyterians and to an extent the Roman Catholics and Mennonites, the early Lutheran settlers had no established Church body to aid them in their new life in Canada. Nor were there Canadian mission boards or theological seminaries to supply them with pastors or churches. The first Lutheran minister to visit Waterloo in 1835 was the Reverend John Bernheim who had been "commissioned" by the Lutheran Ministerium of Pennsylvania "to visit, as a travelling missionary, such sections of Canada as have need of the Gospel and the Holy Sacraments." "The inhabitants of Waterloo Township are chiefly German," he noted. "The larger and wealthier part is Mennonite, the smaller and poorer part has lately emigrated from Hessen, Alsace and Wurtemberg."

Pastor Bernheim's task was far from easy. He was deeply concerned about the unfortunate religious conditions that he had uncovered. "Where the good seed of the divine Word should bring forth fruit hundredfold, the greater part falls by the wayside and is trampled underfoot, on the other hand the seed of the enemy and of infidelity grows luxuriantly." The problem was that many of the German immigrants had left Europe during an era when "rationalism" had come to question the spiritual authority of the church, finding its exponent in Waterloo in the person of the Reverend Frederick W. Bindemann. A former Prussian cavalryman, Bindemann had arrived in Waterloo Township two years earlier in 1833 and had founded his version of Lutheran congregations in Waterloo, Berlin, and Preston. Pastor

Bernheim found Bindemann firmly entrenched in Waterloo. "Already these eight months a certain Bindemann sows the seeds of Universalism in this place . . . The fatal poison spreads through this corner of the earth like a cancer and consumes all piety," he wrote. ". . . If the Word of God were not my support, I should leave at once and return (to Pennsylvania)."

Blocked in his attempts to preach in Preston, Reverend Bernheim attempted to address the Lutheran congregation in Berlin, but this experience, too, was to be most unfortunate:

About 20 Germans had collected at the taverns during divine worship; they became drunk and made much noise till mid-night. It appears that Satan goes against me with violence, but I have a protector, who is infinitely more powerful than he . . . through which I have so often been delivered, I will still trust. I hope the Lord will fulfill Psalm 91, V. 8, also in this instance, and that the issue will be glorious.

Although Reverend Bernheim returned to Pennsylvania with little outward success, the continuing immigration of German Lutherans resulted in the establishment of a congregation in Waterloo in 1837, and in 1838 the cornerstone was laid for a Lutheran church. The Reverend Frederick Bindemann, however, began to serve as the first pastor, but not according to proper Lutheran doctrine.

The official history of St. John's records the following description of these turbulent times:

Pastor Bindemann was proving himself a very unfaithful shepherd, for instead of preaching Jesus Christ and Him Crucified, he proclaimed to them an empty rationalistic message which left their souls empty and dissatisfied.

Asked to resign in 1841, Bindemann did not depart without causing further trauma and division. Although the church doors were closed to him, "several times . . . he forced his way into the church and held services with his followers." In the words of the Reverend Immanuel Wurster, who subsequently came to the Waterloo parish, "This hireling (Bindemann) hurt the congregation inestimably." This was not the only controversy in Bindemann's lengthy career. With some concessions to Lutheran teaching and character, he continued to serve St. Paul's Lutheran Church in Berlin until his retirement in 1864, when he was given a flattering testimonial. Yet, when he died on November 29, 1865, at the age of 75, it was the pastor of the New Jerusalem Swedenborgian Church who officiated at his funeral, and he was buried in the Mennonite cemetery with the early Mennonite pioneers rather than with his own congregation.

The Bernheim-Bindemann controversy points to the somewhat unique position of the Lutheran Church within a Canadian context. Far removed from Germany, with services and a liturgy originating in a German context, a prayer life entirely in the German language, they were dependant on pastors trained abroad or in German-speaking communities in the United States, remote from Waterloo and often from a social context quite unlike that which had come to exist in Canada. Developing a successful Lutheran parish life in Waterloo was not an easy matter. The most explicit statement of this dilemma occurred in the 1850s. With no synodical organization in the Lutheran Church in Canada to rule on a candidate's fitness, a fair number of imposters found their way into the ministry:

Many had never been regularly ordained . . . who with flattering words and smooth manners succeeded in deceiving the early settlers, . . . Some even were men with criminal records, who, fleeing from their homeland in Europe came to Canada and the United States, and took up the ministry as their calling . . . Thus it happened that the good work done by Rev. Wurster was undermined and practically destroyed by his successor, Rev. Th. Huschmann, who served less than a year, and who was compelled to resign on account of his immoral life.

Other pastors, however, led exemplary lives and the faith of the pioneers was more than rewarded. The Lutheran congregation flourished and on February 26, 1882, decided to build a "more commodious house of worship." No sooner had the new church been opened than new problems surfaced on the horizon. Pastor J. L. Braun announced that he was no longer able to remain in the Lutheran Canada Synod, and the congregation was again divided. Difficulties would remain until 1911, when St. John's was once more united to the Canada Synod. For reasons that were not altogether dissimilar to those that had plagued the congregation in Waterloo, it was decided that the time had finally come to establish a Lutheran Seminary in Canada. The decision to locate the seminary in Waterloo, in the centre of one of Canada's largest Lutheran areas and where the German language and culture was predominant, seemed particularly appropriate. Not surprisingly, the establishment of a Lutheran seminary was strongly encouraged by Waterloo's Lutheran business elite, and its role in the final determination of the site may well have been the deciding factor.

Led by J. Charles Mueller, a prominent industrialist and a member of Waterloo's town council in 1904 and 1906, as well as the former chairman of its board of works and now president of the town's Board of Trade, Waterloo had actively intervened to convince the Evangelical Lutheran Synod to locate its Theological Seminary there rather than in Toronto. Negotiations had been well underway to establish the Lutheran Seminary as a part of the University of Toronto, where several other denominations had already located their seminaries. The articles of agreement with the University of Toronto had already been drafted when the Waterloo Board of Trade and its staunchly Lutheran president, J. Charles Mueller, offered to donate five acres of land, free-of-charge, convincing the committee to reconsider. It was not only the offer of free land, although that was a considerable inducement. The president of the General Council was also concerned that the "unionistic forms of a common Christianity" found at major universities would weaken the "Lutheran principles" of its students. By contrast, a Lutheran seminary, set in the midst of a predominantly Lutheran and German-speaking community such as Waterloo would tend to strengthen their secular identity.

For their part, the members of the Board of Trade voted unanimously for a $1,750 subscription to buy a five-acre site for the seminary. The mayor, the president of the Board of Trade, and three prominent community leaders conducted a campaign to collect the subscriptions. Subsequently, three members of the council of the Board of Trade became trustees of the property. (Title deeds were handed over to the seminary on July 10, 1924.)

It was a proud day in June 1911 when 1,500 people gathered in St. John's Evangelical Lutheran Church in Waterloo to celebrate the decision to locate Canada's first Lutheran seminary in their town. A procession led by the seminary board of directors marched the few short blocks from King Street to the new location on Albert Street, where it was met by the town's Lutheran mayor, W.G. Weichel, and a very happy president of the Board of Trade, J. Charles Mueller. For his part, Weichel would soon be elected to represent Waterloo North in the Parliament of Canada, where he would suddenly find himself preoccupied with defending Waterloo and its German heritage. Within three years, when war was declared against Germany, that same German character that had so appealed to the leaders of the Lutheran Church would provoke a profound crisis both for the Lutheran

Church and the Town of Waterloo.

The declaration of war against Germany in August 1914 seemed to condemn not just Germany, but also many aspects of the German tradition in Canada. German flags and banners, which had been so much a part of the *Saengerfests* tradition, now became suspect. Use of the German language in stores and churches, in homes, and on the streets quickly became a sign of apparent disloyalty to Canada.

Waterloo's citizens immediately rallied to support the war effort. Their individual contributions to the Patriotic Fund led the nation. Early the following year Waterloo's Member of Parliament, W.G. Weichel, rose in the House of Commons to try to explain that it was possible for German-speaking Canadians to have been proud of their heritage without being disloyal to Canada. Pride in the race from which they had sprung and in Germany's

The honourable William G. Weichel was one of Waterloo's most popular political leaders, serving as mayor in 1911, 1922, and 1923; as M.L.A. for Waterloo North in 1923 and 1926; and as the Member of Parliament in Ottawa from 1911 to 1917. He was also a hardware merchant and a director of the Waterloo Mutual Fire Insurance Company. Courtesy, National Archives of Canada

progress in science, art, music, literature, and philosophy were shared by many, he said, "But, Sir, they are not proud of the violations of the neutrality of Belgium . . . (Furthermore) German art, German music, German science is one thing; but Prussian militarism is another, and the reason why so many people of German origin have left their old fatherland was to escape military domination." Weichel was undoubtedly right, and anyone who thought about it would have agreed. But war stirs up strong emotions and second thoughts in these matters are often too little and too late.

Within weeks of war being declared, the bust of Kaiser Wilheim I, erected in

Berlin's Victoria Park to recall the great "Friedensfest" of 1871, was toppled from its pedestal and unceremoniously dumped into the lake. The kaiser was rescued and retired to a backroom in Berlin's Concordia Club. On February 15, 1916, a group of soldiers from the local 118th Battalion broke into the Concordia Club, removed the bust, and paraded it down King Street. The obvious sign of "treachery" represented by the bust aroused other soldiers and civilians, who then ransacked the Club, seizing German memorabilia from the storage rooms and destroying much of the clubhouse. Local police looked on helplessly.

Nor was Waterloo to be spared as simi-

Dedicated in 1897, the bronze bust of Kaiser Wilhelm I in Berlin's Victoria Park was regarded as a lasting symbol of the bond between Germany and England. By 1914, however, in a portent of things to come, an empty pedestal was all that remained. Anti-German vandals had thrown the Kaiser into the park lake. Courtesy, Waterloo Historical Society

lar wartime tension and anti-German feelings spilled over from Berlin. On May 5, 1916, after a large recruiting rally was held in Waterloo's market square just before midnight, when emotions had built up all day, 30 soldiers in uniform entered Waterloo's German social club known as the Acadian Club. They went on a rampage, smashing tables, chairs, lamps, pictures, chandeliers, and anything that could be moved. According to a later report of the minister of justice, "some ten or more soldiers of the 118th Overseas Battalion Canadian Expeditionary Force, stationed in the City of Waterloo," entered the Acadian Club "for the purpose of obtaining and taking away a bronze bust of the

Emperor of Germany." Reinforced by 30 or 40 more soldiers and "organized in the character of a mob, (they) returned to the Acadian Club and practically demolished all of the furnishings contained in the said rooms."

Despite the acknowledged guilt of the battalion and the inability of either the military or the local police to intervene, the Canadian government chose not to reimburse the Waterloo club for the damages. As the minister of justice explained, "in view of the racial ill-feeling which appeared to exist in that locality, . . . they were not disposed to recommend that the battalion be assessed for the amount of these damages because they feared that further ill-

The dumping of the Kaiser's bust into the lake in 1914 was merely a prelude to greater unrest as anti-German feeling intensified. These men "rescued" the bust from a watery grave in Victoria Park. Courtesy, Kitchener Public Library

feeling might be engendered."

Such feelings had become part of community life as members of the 118th battalion harassed young men on the streets for failing to sign up for overseas service. In March 1916 the parsonage of the Reverend C.R. Tappert, a Lutheran minister in Berlin and a part-time instructor at Waterloo's Lutheran Seminary, was broken into by a group of 60 soldiers led by the re-doubtable Sergeant Major Blood. "Within minutes, Tappert was being dragged behind horses through the streets, his face bloodied, his body twisting as he fell into unconsciousness while the pavement scraped off his flesh." He

left Berlin and Waterloo shortly after. The soldiers were given a suspended sentence and the minister of militia blamed the victim, as he had warned the House of Commons some two weeks before the attack on the Reverend Tappert:

For some time the feeling of loyal and law-abiding citizens of both British and German extraction in Berlin and Waterloo and adjoining localities, have been more or less exasperated by the language and actions of a Lutheran clergyman—an American citizen—and by a German-born Canadian subject named Asmussen, who whether with good or bad intent, have been semi-apolo-

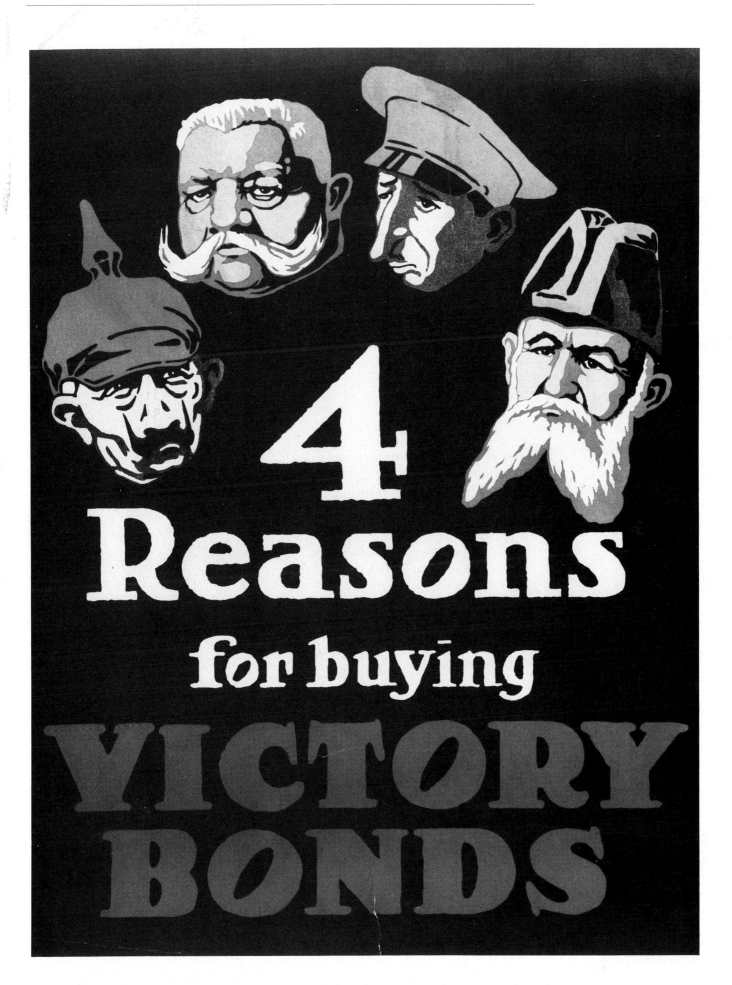

gists for German atrocities and Kaiserism. It is asserted that one of these men recently stated that "the conduct of the British, in the war has been about as bad as the Germans" . . . These utterances, coupled with the general tension of mind throughout the country over the war, gradually wrought up a number of people to a high pitch of feeling.

The townspeople breathed a sigh of relief on May 22 when more than 10,000 citizens lined the streets of Berlin and Waterloo to say farewell to the 707 men of the 118th Battalion, who set out for further training in London. Life in the community calmed down—if only temporarily.

The turbulent events of that May in 1916 were not quite over. The previous week the residents of Berlin had begrudgingly agreed by a majority of 81 of the 3,057 votes cast to change the name of their city. Many now believed that "Waterloo" should be the proper name for the "twin cities." But this, too, was not to be. Instead, the name of the recently deceased British secretary of war, Lord Horatio Herbert Kitchener was chosen, and Berlin, Canada's German capital, no longer existed.

When the dust had settled, the raid on Waterloo's "German" Acadian Club revealed a great deal about this Canadian city. The club had a membership of some 60 men, nearly half of whom had already enlisted for the armed forces, and soldiers had always been welcomed into the club. From the beginning of the war its members had readily supported local patriotic events including the Red Cross and the Patriotic Fund, while the "ring leader" of the raid was a disgruntled former member "who had not paid his dues for a considerable period." His actions, one suspects, had more to do with personal spite than with promoting Canada's war effort.

Despite their German ethnic origin, Waterloo's citizens would have offered a measure of Canadian identity that many more typical Canadian towns could not have equalled. At the beginning of the

war only eight residents had registered as enemy aliens (as being born in Germany and not yet nationalized Canadians). J.C. Mueller, who had led the campaign for the Lutheran seminary, also found time to organize the Waterloo Patriotic Fund, raising more than $50,000 by 1917. So successful was he that Waterloo was said to have the highest per-capita contributions to the fund in all of the Dominion. Like most other Canadian communities, the churches and women's volunteer organizations were active in support of the war as was the St. Quentin Chapter of the Imperial Order of the Daughters of the Empire, organized in 1917 and led by Regent Mrs. H.M. Snyder. Mrs. George Wegenast headed up the major fund drives

more personal insight was revealed when a businessman in Los Angeles had asked Louis Breithaupt in 1918 "why we do not help our German brethren in Germany," and Breithaupt had replied quite bluntly that "he was *too British* to discuss that with him."

As wartime tensions at last began to recede, Waterloo, as was most of Canada, was caught in a crippling influenza. The Spanish influenza, which had played havoc with Europe, reached the town in October 1918, closing schools, factories, and the local hospital. More than 2,000 citizens were reported "down with the malady" as the pages of the Waterloo *Chronicle* seemed to be little more than one large obituary column while the board of health issued urgent calls for help. By November "twice as many had died from the influenza as had been killed in action in four years of war." In fact, the war ended for Canadians on November 11, 1918, exactly 10 days after Emma Breithaupt had written so despairingly about the influenza. Now

Left: Citizens of Waterloo gathered before their historic Town Hall to celebrate Armistice Day on November 11, 1918. The end of the Great War brought jubilation and tremendous relief. Courtesy, Waterloo Public Library

Below: In 1914 Caspar Braun, a general contractor, built a large, new plant in Berlin for the Dominion Rubber Company. (Braun is standing at the top right of the structure.) By 1916 the plant employed 604. While companies like Dominion Rubber were a natural outgrowth of Berlin's manufacturing tradition, Waterloo would establish a tradition of its own as home to many large insurance companies and would earn the sobriquet "Hartford of Canada." Courtesy, Waterloo Historical Society

for the Red Cross. Perhaps the sentiment that best describes Waterloo's role in the war was that expressed by W.H. Breithaupt of the Waterloo Historical Society, who noted that although thousands of miles away, the war "most vitally affects us here in Waterloo County as an integral part of the vast, far flung, world encircling British Empire. Notwithstanding the descent of many of us from a country and people now hostile," he said, "we refuse to stand second in loyalty and sacrifice to any part of the British Dominions." A

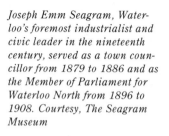

Joseph Emm Seagram, Waterloo's foremost industrialist and civic leader in the nineteenth century, served as a town councillor from 1879 to 1886 and as the Member of Parliament for Waterloo North from 1896 to 1908. Courtesy, The Seagram Museum

the community would turn to welcoming its soldiers from the front and beginning life anew.

For the town of Waterloo, much like the Canadian nation, the Great War had been a time of testing. Waterloo had found its place within the nation as Canada had achieved its sense of identity as an independent nation within the British empire. No longer was Waterloo merely an adjunct to Berlin. In its recruitment for the war effort, in its fund raising, and with honour for its fallen soldiers, Waterloo had stood on its own.

In the years immediately preceding the war, Waterloo and Berlin had seemed to be growing even closer. The need for shared services was exemplified in the Berlin and Waterloo Street Railway, which had joined them in a physical way and made the movement of people and goods all the more intimate. A common waterworks system was introduced in 1888, and the erection of the Berlin-Waterloo Hospital in 1894 at the border of the two towns on land donated by Joseph Seagram of Waterloo seemed to draw them closer still. They also shared the nearby high school and the cemetery, which was located midway between the two towns. Urban expansion in the 1890s also seemed to pull the two communities together. The location of the massive new tire factory of Dominion Rubber as well as several smaller factories in the hinterland between Berlin and Waterloo created new demands for housing and municipal services. By 1900 the label "twin cities" had become both commonplace and credible as the suggestions that they unite became more frequent.

The war put an end to that. Berlin's overpowering sense of pride in its German identity and in the virtues of the Made-in-Berlin label of its manufactured goods was replaced by a new-found reticence. It would take time before the name of Kitchener would replace the memories of Berlin. It was also a community badly divided from within. By contrast, Waterloo's identity had emerged from the war years stronger than ever. Pride in community and in Waterloo's achievements was expressed without reservation and without comparisons to the former city of Berlin.

The Great War had heightened the differences between Waterloo and Berlin and had reaffirmed Waterloo's distinctive identity. While Berlin had been proudly proclaiming its Germanic virtues in the years preceding 1914, Waterloo had become renowned in quite a different way. The prominence of the Seagram Distillery, and, even more, the dominance of the famous Seagram Stables in Canadian racing circles had been sources of great pride for Waterloo and its citizens. Seagram's stables had won the Queen's Plate in eight consecutive races between 1891 and 1898, while Joseph Seagram had been elected as

Waterloo's Member of Parliament in three general elections.

Waterloo's residents had shared in the victories of the Seagram Stables in the sport of kings, "looking for the flag on the distillery flagpole to see if a Seagram horse had won the Plate." The influence of the Seagram family in Canada's Anglo-Saxon social elite also did much to ameliorate the sense of Waterloo as a German community. Joseph Seagram was a close personal friend of the former Governor General, His Excellency Lord Grey, and a member of Canada's most prestigious social clubs: the Rideau in Ottawa; the National, the Albany, and the York Clubs in Toronto, as well as the local Waterloo Club. His contacts in politics and finance had given Waterloo a singular identity from that of Berlin.

During the war years, too, Waterloo was led by Mayor Dr. W.L. Hilliard, an ardent Methodist lay leader whose commitment to the British war effort was beyond reproach as the Methodist Church rivalled all other denominations in Canada in its support for the war. Two of Waterloo's other prominent companies, Dominion Life and Mutual Life, were outstanding in their financial support for Canada's war effort, and Mutual Life listed on its board of directors the former prime minister of Canada, the Rt. Hon. Sir Wilfrid Laurier. If anything, their financial commitment to Victory Bonds and the Patriotic Fund ensured the jealousy of neighbouring communities, who envied Waterloo's overpowering record. By the end of the war, Waterloo had clearly distinguished itself as a community both separate and different from Berlin-Kitchener. The reality of the "twin cities" also meant that they were separate "cities," each with its own character and identity. Waterloo now faced the future in its own way and at its own pace, confident of its place in Canada's society.

5

Coming
of Age

At about 1:55 p.m. on a hot
Saturday, July 19, 1924 a CPR
train pulled up at the Erb Street
crossing in the Town of Waterloo. A second train arrived at 2:45 p.m.
that same afternoon. Getting off the train
were the first of about 1,500 Russian
Mennonites who would come to Waterloo
County in 1924.

Loaded with all their worldly possessions,
these Mennonites, driven out by the hor-
rors of the Russian Revolution, had
arrived in Waterloo nearly 120 years after
their co-religionists had begun to clear
this land in the backwoods of Upper Canada. As they made their way "under the
curious gaze of the local residents" who
lined historic Erb Street from the railway
tracks to the Erb Street Mennonite
Church, many must have reflected on
their own past life in Russia as well as on
the opportunities and challenges that lie
before them in Canada. Feelings of
uncertainty and sadness for those whom
they had left behind mingled with a sense
of thanksgiving and relief as terror and
repression were replaced by a life in
Waterloo that offered safety and freedom.
    One of these young Russian Menno-
nite emigres, Woldemar Neufeld, has provided a most remarkable and vivid recol-
lection of his impressions of Waterloo.
In his paintings, Neufeld depicts town
life in Waterloo from 1928 to the 1980s.

The 1945 Victory Loan Parade once again demonstrated the generosity of Waterloo's citizens to support Canada's war effort. Courtesy, K-W Record Photograph Negative Collection, University of Waterloo Library

"We had heard in Russia," he later recalled, "that in America there would be no time for play, or for art, that people just worked hard to buy cars and have electric lights. And here (in Waterloo) the city fathers had put up a modern amusement . . . We had so much fun on that slide and right beside a schoolhouse!"

The "city fathers" and especially those businessmen who in 1890 had formed Waterloo's Board of Trade would have been delighted by his appreciation of the importance of Waterloo Park in the life of the town. It had been the Board of Trade that had first recognized the need for better recreational facilities and had led the campaign to purchase the 75-acre farm of Jacob Eby that nestled along the border of

Above: The first group of Russian Mennonites wend their way along Erb Street under the gaze of curious spectators in 1924. Courtesy, Waterloo Public Library

Right: Wading in the Grand River posed a threat to the modesty of these proper Victorian young ladies from Waterloo and Berlin. Courtesy, Breithaupt-Hewetson-Clark Collection, University of Waterloo Library

A precise documentarist, he has captured the ambience of Waterloo life by combining the reality of buildings and streetscapes with feelings of wonder and appreciation for the town. One can sense, for example, the feelings of home town pride in the Town Hall and civic square as well as the pleasure of young children following an ice wagon along dusty streets, hoping for free chunks of ice to while away a hot summer's day. Neufeld was fond of the picturesque grist mill, a Waterloo landmark since the days of Abraham Erb, which still dominated the town's main intersection. The mill pond, too, on Silver Lake, was especially important. From a vantage point in Waterloo Park his paintings often portray "the serenity of this lake in the midst of the town." It was, he said, "such a soothing place for people seeking a little peace." It was also a place to go swimming on a sultry summer day, while along the edge of the lake a "romantic path" wound its way through large overgrown willows.

His charming painting of a toboggan slide in Waterloo Park on a hillside adjacent to the 1820 log schoolhouse, which had been moved to the park in 1893, offers a rare insight into Canadian life.

the mill pond. The board had considered the possibility of trying to extend the town's existing showgrounds as a park or, as an alternative, to develop a park near the border with Berlin next to the cemetery. The Board's members, however, strongly preferred the Eby site.

Leaving little to chance, J.H. Roos, secretary of the Board of Trade, had prepared a petition signed by 250 electors of the town. He presented it to council, petitioning for the adoption of the Public Parks Act, the new provincial legislation enacted to provide for such purposes. On September 1, 1890, the by-law (to provide for the adoption of the Public Parks Act) passed with a 217-vote majority. When the first board of park management was

established, its membership consisted of Christian Kumpf, Isaac Erb Bowman, Dr. J.H. Webb, Walter Wells, and Jacob Conrad—all prominent members of the Board of Trade.

A Toronto engineer was contracted to aid in the design of the new park, and Andrew McIntyre was appointed as the park's first superintendent. Thousands of cubic yards of earth were moved to create the terraced central park area:

Ten men and two teams of horses worked for 3 1/2 months to level slopes and fill in hollows. Fences, derelict buildings, and old tree stumps were removed, and over 2,000 trees were planted to create shaded picnic areas, walkways and drives.

The athletic grounds, with the hillside rising above them, soon attracted hundreds of spectators.

Taking advantage of a popular sport of the day, the Waterloo Bicycle Club built a bicycle track around the athletic field and in 1895 hosted the Annual Meet of the Canadian Wheelman's Association. More than 10,000 visitors came to watch the championship races. The lake, too, was in frequent use in the summer, providing not

Two young ladies enjoy a restful moment in front of the newly constructed 1902 Erb Street Mennonite Church. Courtesy, Waterloo Public Library

These "Wheelmen" from neighbouring Berlin pose outside Rich's Ice Cream Parlour before setting off on a jaunt to the country. Courtesy, Waterloo Public Library

Waterloo Musical Society recruited the prominent New York concert master, Professor C.F. Thiele, to lead their band. Not only would Thiele add a striking new dimension to the musical life of Waterloo, but he also persuaded the Seagram family to erect an elaborate, open-style band shell in memory of Joseph E. Seagram, who had died that year. The combination of Thiele's leadership, the community's love of music, and the splendid new facility in Waterloo Park began an era during which both the band and the town would receive international acclaim.

For young Woldemar Neufeld, the Waterloo Band Shell held many other happy memories. "Here, beside the lake," he reminisced, "girls and boys learned to observe each other. It was a central meeting place . . . I began to appreciate Canadian girls at these concerts. Sometimes I'd even ignore the girls and just listen to the band, because I was used to good music at home . . . Our whole family would get all dressed up and stroll over on a Sunday afternoon or evening; it was the one thing we were allowed to do on Sundays."

Not all visitors to Waterloo in these years were as enthusiastic as the young Woldemar Neufeld. One who was not was Frank Darling, a partner in the prominent Toronto architectural firm of Darling and Pearson, who had come to town to advise George Wegenast, the manager of the Mutual Life Assurance Company, about possible sites on which to erect a new head office. Darling's assessment of

only good swimming, but also good fishing. A pavillion and a boathouse were erected to accommodate the town's rapidly growing leisure activities. The park also hosted the local softball leagues out of which developed a renewed rivalry between Waterloo and Berlin.

After 1901 the entrance to the park was through an attractive Memorial Gateway. It was erected in honour of the late "beloved Queen Victoria," and constructed of brick and Indiana limestone, with "beautifully designed wrought iron work" forming the sides. An overhead arch surmounted by Thomas Edison's new invention—electric lights—completed the gateway. As the twentieth century began, Waterloo's park had clearly become a focal point for town life. The size of the town emphasized its centrality, for no one lived beyond a half-mile distance from the park.

Waterloo's flourishing musical life, too, found its natural focus in the park. This was especially so after 1919 when the

Waterloo's most prestigious "town site" facing on Albert Street opposite the Town Hall and slightly to the north of the office of Mutual Life was quite blunt. "(It) should be unhesitatingly condemned, the outlook is most unsatisfactory, facing as it does upon a firehall, a cattle market, and the Town Hall, none of them objects either of beauty or of interest."

The possible acquisition of the Devitt Block on King Street south of Erb, set back "some little distance" from the line of King Street, he reported, would "unquestionably (be) the best site . . . ," but it had one major flaw. Its proximity to the Snider grist mill posed the possibility of serious damage in the event of a fire to that ancient wooden structure. Despite its location in the very heart of the town, it would be very inexpensive to purchase. Expansion would also be possible, Darling noted, for "The properties at the back, all the way to the mill-race are not now, and probably never will be, of any great value."

In addition to the "town sites," the Toronto architect had also evaluated a number of possible "country sites" slightly beyond the main business centre. One of these "at the bend of King St. facing upon a small park and looking up the street towards the town of Waterloo" was rejected because of its proximity to the Kuntz brewery as well as the cotton-felt factory of Aloyes Bauer. Others further south on King Street seemed singularly inappropriate except for the Randall prop-

A visit to the park did not necessitate casual attire at the turn of the century. It could also be an opportunity for dressing in high style. Courtesy, Waterloo Public Library

erty at the border with Berlin, which had served as the town's picnic grounds before Waterloo Park had been created in the 1890s. Darling's description of this site and of the vistas that it offered of the surrounding countryside reveal a town that still retained a predominantly rural ethos:

Nothing could be better—it lies high, . . . any building located on it would be conspicuous from whatever direction it might be approached, nobody passing up or down the main road could help noticing it. The views from it across the country in every direction must in summer be charming, and could not be interfered with by all the building up of the locality in a generation . . .

Mutual Life accepted Darling's recommendation and for $18,000 purchased 6.79 acres at the corner of what would become King and Union streets in Waterloo. Dar-

Taking a break from the summer's heat, these youngsters cavorted in the fountain in the park near the Kuntz (now Labatt's) Brewery. Courtesy, Waterloo Public Library

ling's firm was retained, and a new head office in the "modern renaissance style" was completed in 1912 at a cost of $275,000. As he entered the new Mutual Life building and looked at the few desks in the main hall, George Wegenast, the general manager, is remembered as saying: "Gentlemen, we will never fill it."

Subsequent additions were soon to come and many in number. By 1921 Mutual Life's head office was overflowing. The 39 employees who worked there in 1913 had been augmented by some 100 others, and a major addition was necessary. Six years later there were 255 employees and the building was again enlarged. A decade later in 1939 there were 369 employees and more space was needed. Additions to the building would continue to be necessary in 1953, 1967, 1976, and 1980, culminating in 1987 when a large, 13-storey tower was erected. The site of the 1912 headquarters of Mutual Life quickly became a dominant Waterloo landmark. Its classic proportions and dignified elegance marked the entrance to the town and was a visible sign that one

had entered Waterloo, leaving behind the more heavily industrialized vista of Berlin-Kitchener's smokestacks.

By the early years of the twentieth century many of the prominent buildings that today give Waterloo its historical character were already in place. The Commercial Block that still stands on the southeast corner of King and Erb streets had been built in 1858, one year after Waterloo had been incorporated as a village. A number of prominent businessmen such as John Hoffman, Isaac Weaver, and William Hespeler, who would be responsible for the original grist mill that later developed into the Seagram Distillery, had conducted business there. It was here, too, in 1888 that a group of Waterloo businessmen, including the former Member of Parliament Isaac Erb Bowman, John Shuh, P.H. Sims, Thomas Hilliard, and Simon Snyder, decided to start the Dominion Life Assurance Company. By the time that Mutual Life moved into its new head office, Dominion Life had grown to the point where it took over Mutual's previous 1880 building at 15 Erb Street across the

Above: The much-acclaimed Waterloo Musical Society Band and its pre-eminent conductor, Professor C.F. Thiele, gathered in front of the Mutual Life Building during the 1930s. Courtesy, Waterloo Public Library

Left: Hoffman Wegenast and Company linked together two prominent Waterloo families and founded a thriving furniture manufacturing business at the corner of King and Allen streets. Later the establishment was absorbed by the Canada Furniture Company. Courtesy, Waterloo Public Library

square from the Town Hall. Dominion Life would remain at this central location until 1954, when a new head office was built in the countryside on a park-like setting on Westmount Road. In 1988, under a new corporate title known now as Manufacturers Life, the company would move to a splendid site overlooking Blue Springs and the Westmount building would be acquired by the Economical Mutual Insurance Company.

Next to the original 1858 Commercial Block on King Street was the large and imposing Central Block, which had been erected in 1881. With its heavy-bracketed eaves and arched windows, this building gave Waterloo a predominantly Victorian look that contrasted with the much simpler appearance of the adjoining 1850s architecture. This new-found sense of sophistication was most obvious in the elaborate renovations to Waterloo's two major hotels. The Huether Hotel, by virtue of its proximity to the Town Hall and market, had long occupied a prominent place in the life of Waterloo. In the 1880s it had been expanded with a new

mansard roof and iron cresting consonant with the style of Waterloo's new Town Hall. Within a decade, the Huether Hotel had undergone even more extensive renovations, adding an elaborate facade on King Street with stone-capped arched windows, an Etruscan tower, and a series of balconies overlooking King and Princess streets. Within its new "High Victorian" splendour, the Huether Hotel boasted 40 well-lighted rooms and 7 parlours. In 1886 rooms in the hotel rented for one dollar per day, and the hotel's menu contained "all the delicacies of the season, as well as the substantials," while its Lion brand lager beer had "a widespread reputation throughout Perth and Waterloo counties."

The town's major business intersection at King and Erb streets had been the site of an hotel since 1840. Known first as the "Farmer's Hotel," a two-storey building with a row of dormer windows stretching along King Street, it had played an important role in the life of the early village. Destroyed by fire in 1850, it was immediately rebuilt to its original design. By 1880 a two-storey addition was built on the rear. Known as the Bowman House in the 1860s, it remained in the Bowman family until 1882, when Henry Zimmerman acquired possession. Another fire in 1889 destroyed a major portion of the original 1850 structure facing on King Street.

With a sizable mortgage of $15,000 from the Ontario Mutual Life Assurance Company, Henry Zimmerman rebuilt the hotel, adding a third storey and renaming it the Zimmermann House. With an elaborate cornice and prominent 1890 datestone in its peak, the Zimmermann House looks today much as it did in 1890 when it was described as perhaps the finest hotel in Waterloo and "a rival to any in nearby towns." Renamed the Hotel Lewis in 1904 after a change of ownership, it was said to be "Newly furnished throughout, electric lighted and steam-heated. Commodities and accommodation for commercial travellers. Electric trains from Galt and Berlin leave every twenty-minutes." Rates in 1906

The Bowman House had been present at the corner of King and Erb streets since 1840. By the time this photograph was taken in the early 1880s a two-storey addition had been added at the rear of the building. Courtesy, Waterloo Public Library

were two dollars per day. The interior, "remodelled from basement to attic," was finished in quarter cut oak, and "furnished with a view to comfort and ease." With 30 bedrooms, "the parlours are furnished with an eye to preserving that home-like atmosphere so that the overall appearance is of a large elegantly decorated house."

In some ways this last phrase captured the mood of life in Waterloo. The town was undoubtedly prosperous. Population had grown from 1,594 in 1871 to 4,956 in 1915. These increases were steady and measured, but not overwhelming. Employment in Waterloo's factories had also kept pace. There had been 218 industrial workers in 1871 and 1,050 in 1915, increasing as a percent of the population from 13.7 percent to 21.2 percent. This latter figure would remain fairly constant throughout the period of town life, settling at 18.5 percent in 1931. The value of goods purchased in its factories had also increased substantially, from $661,000 in 1871 to $3,561,000 in 1915. Compared to other similar-sized towns in Ontario, Waterloo could be proud of its record. It was also a matter of some pride that the businesses that had grown and expanded were primarily local companies owned by Waterloo's citizens rather than by outside investors.

Waterloo's industrial growth had occurred especially during the years 1901 to 1914 and had been encouraged and stimulated by the establishment of the Board of Trade in 1890. The town had also developed a "progressive factory policy" during these years. A recent study by Elizabeth Bloomfield has concluded that "Waterloo undertook a formidable burden of debt for industry's sake" with loans to individuals and their companies totalling $131,100 as well as numerous exemptions from municipal taxes or fixed industrial tax assessments usually significantly below the actual property value. Although these "inducements" benefited the manufacturers, most of whom were Waterloo businessmen, they also had the over-

whelming support of the town's ratepayers since all cash bonuses had to be approved by the voters.

Waterloo's Board of Trade worked assiduously to ensure support for these new industries as well as to attest to their likely success. One of the first of the "new" companies to receive a financial incentive to locate in Waterloo was W.A. Greene's shirt and collar factory on William Street. On the Board of Trade's advice, the town provided a $7,500 loan, a site valued at $500, a 10-year tax exemption, and free water. The establishment of a furniture factory by Emil Schierholz was aided by the offer of a free site, a $5,000 loan, and a 10-year tax exemption. When put to the citizens of Waterloo, 416 voted

Top: The Berlin and Waterloo Street Railway ushered in the era of public transportation in 1889, when horse-drawn streetcars began operating on a daily schedule. The line was electrified in 1895, and electric trolleys became a symbol of the close association between Berlin and Waterloo. Now known as Kitchener Transit, the utility encompasses 15 routes and covers 18,200 kilometres daily. Courtesy, Kitchener Public Library

Bottom: The Zimmermann House stands at the height of its nineteenth-century elegance shortly after being rebuilt following a disastrous fire in 1889. Courtesy, Waterloo Public Library

By the mid-1800s more than 800 young women were employed by the garment, button, and confectionery industries in Waterloo and the neighbouring town of Berlin. These Weigands Shirt Factory workers paused momentarily from their labour to be photographed. Courtesy, Doon Heritage Crossroads

in favour and only 55 against. Similar offers were made to a boot and shoe manufacturing company. After a disastrous fire at the Schaefer-Killer furniture factory, which threatened the loss of 125 jobs, the town granted a $15,000 loan and a 10-year exemption from taxes.

One of the most interesting cases to come before council was that of the Mueller cooperage. It was rumoured that

Mueller, prominent citizen of Waterloo though he was, was considering "an informal inducement" to relocate in Berlin. The Waterloo Board of Trade urged council to provide a three-acre site costing $1,800 and to exempt the new cooperage from taxes for 10 years. A large majority of Waterloo's ratepayers were in favour, although 111 were opposed. Questions were raised about the propriety of aiding an already prosperous business and about the possible conflict of interest since J. Charles Mueller served on Waterloo's town council at the time that these terms were negotiated. In the end, fear of Berlin's rivalry removed any other doubts. The problem of a perceived conflict of interest between the business leaders who guided the town's growth and those who sought municipal favours was not an easy one. Yet a careful examination reveals no direct conflict of interest. Rather it indicates the limitations faced by a town the

size of Waterloo with the need for expansion and the growth of municipal services while attempting to balance business expertise and a willingness to serve one's town. Waterloo's ratepayers seemed to agree, for they voted in favour of financial assistance to companies that would provide employment for themselves and for their children.

Many prominent Waterloo companies and institutions were aided during these years. The Mutual Life Assurance Company was granted a fixed assessment for its

These young women were employed in Roschman's button factory about 1890. The stern-faced man in the second row from the top may be Roschman himself. Courtesy, Waterloo Public Library

"Champion Threshing" machines and "Waterloo" steam engines are lined up for a parade on King Street. Courtesy, Waterloo Public Library

new head office "to ensure that it would remain in Waterloo." When the Lutheran Seminary was proposed, community leaders on the Board of Trade "subscribed towards the cost of land" and then stood bond for the seminary. Reitzel's planing mill was originally rejected, but subsequently granted a reduced assessment for 10 years. The Quality Mattress Company, now Waterloo Bedding, was granted a $10,000 loan and a 10-year exemption by a majority of 302 votes to 73. The Globe Furniture Company was granted a $50,000 loan, a $1,000 site, and a 10-year exemption to expand its plant with the requirement that it spend $125,000 and increase employment from 150 to 200.

There were very few cases of industrial support during the years of the Great War and its aftermath. In 1929, however, when plans were unveiled by the H.V. McKay Company of Australia to construct a new factory in Waterloo to produce "one man, self-propelled combine harvesters" the whole town seemed to become involved. The new factory was estimated to cost

$275,000 and promised to employ 1,500. The town offered to fix the factory's assessment at $25,000 for 10 years and to install roadways, sewers, sidewalks, and storm drains. Land was acquired for a 30-acre factory site from Canada Barrels and Kegs at less than market value, while Canbar was compensated by the town with a reduced assessment on its remaining property.

When put to the vote these measures received overwhelming support from the citizens of Waterloo with 1,126 in favour and only 8 opposed. The report in the Waterloo *Chronicle* vividly describes the town's mood:

Citizens of Waterloo celebrated the splendid victory at the polls on Monday following the almost unanimous vote given by bylaw to grant the Sunshine Waterloo Co. Ltd. a fixed assessment. Immediately after the result was known a parade was formed, headed by the Waterloo band, members of the town council, officials of the company and other citizens in motor cars, followed by several of the famous Sunshine threshers, and proceeded to the Memorial Park.

The Board of Trade had previously feted the visitors from Australia in a dinner attended by more than 100 members. The industrial policy recommended by the Board and initiated by Waterloo's council had done much to establish a diversified industrial base. It also prevented Waterloo from the fate of so many small towns in Ontario that had begun an inexorable decline in the face of competition from Toronto and other large urban centres.

Waterloo had also begun to change in

other ways. In 1911 the land at the town's main intersection of King and Erb streets, which had been set aside by Abraham Erb as "a town square of liberal dimensions," now came under scrutiny. Waterloo's council planned to pave King Street, which had been "in a very rough condition for a number of years." Ownership of the "town square" resided not with the town, but with William Snider, who had retained title as part of the 1829 purchase of the original mill site. Not wishing to pay taxes on the frontage of the square on both King and Erb streets, Snider offered to deed the square to the town. Council refused, demanding that Snider pay the full tax on the property.

The town square, which had been a central part of Waterloo's identity for more than a century, was lost forever as Snider promptly sold the land to the Molson's Bank. In 1914 the Bank erected a classic "Beaux Arts" style bank. Of cut grey stone with Ionic columns, curved pediments, and keystones above the windows, the Molson's Bank gave Waterloo its only monumental bank building, capturing that sense of Canada's pre-eminent banking tradition. Standing at the corner of Waterloo's central business intersection, that bank now recalls its own traditions in contrast to those of Abraham Erb in the previous century.

Waterloo's other "official" building, the 1911 post office, designed under the influence of the famous Ottawa architect, Thomas Fuller, quickly became a landmark in the town. It, too, owes a great deal to politics. Although Waterloo had had a post office since 1835, there had never been a major government building in the town. Nor would its population normally have merited one. The Board of Trade, however, had aggressively sought the assistance of William Lyon Mackenzie King, the new Member of Parliament for Waterloo North.

The post office building was a direct result of his patronage. A native of Berlin, Mackenzie King was paranoid about the possible influence in the riding of Joseph E. Seagram, the distiller and former Conservative Member of Parliament. King had once told the Liberal leader, Sir Wilfrid Laurier, that he would like to show him that "there is something more than money and whiskey in North Waterloo, something that neither of these can reach." In the 1908 election Seagram had not been a candidate nor had he taken an active part in the election, and King won by a small majority.

Instead of "whiskey," Mackenzie King thought to use political patronage to hold the riding. As Minister of Labour and a member of Laurier's cabinet, he actively garnered political favours for Waterloo North. Not only did Waterloo receive a magnificent new post office and federal building "worth $35,000," but the town also became an official customs port. Free mail delivery was extended and improved. When Waterloo's popular mayor, W.G. Weichel, won the next election in 1911, Mackenzie King was hard pressed to explain his defeat. Instead of the reciprocity bill that had led to major losses by the Liberal party in most urban areas, he blamed his old rival, Joseph Seagram: "The distiller, and his allies had

Top: Prime Minister Sir Wilfrid Laurier campaigned for William Lyon Mackenzie King in North Waterloo in 1908. A smiling King is seated on the left side of the platform. Three years later, rejected in his home constituency, King blamed his bitter defeat not on Laurier's reciprocity policy, but rather on the mischief of former Conservative Member of Parliament Joseph E. Seagram. Courtesy, National Archives of Canada

Bottom: William Lyon Mackenzie King, shown campaigning in 1908, represented North Waterloo in the House of Commons from 1908 to 1911. A native of Berlin, he succeeded Sir Wilfrid Laurier as Liberal Leader in 1919 and became Prime Minister of Canada in 1921. As the local Member of Parliament and, after 1909, as Minister of Labour, King's patronage became an important factor in the advancement of Waterloo. Courtesy, National Archives of Canada

corrupted the people and joined all forces opposing reciprocity. Had there been no bribery, had bribery been even less than wholesale," King claimed, "I would have won out." The truth of King's allegations remains unsubstantiated. The town of Waterloo had clearly benefited from his fear that he would lose the riding, and although Mackenzie King would go on to become Canada's longest-serving Prime Minister, he would never again run in North Waterloo.

Mackenzie King's concern about the prominence of the Seagram family had come not merely from the physical size of their distillery or the popularity of its products. Nor was it just the town's pride in the Seagram Stables, race track, and farm on Waterloo's eastern border, which would later be developed as the site of the Tower's plaza. Many of the residents of Waterloo and Berlin had also recalled with some affection that it was Joseph Seagram's donation of "Greenbush," the 13 acres of land on which he had planned to build his home, that made possible the

establishment of the Berlin-Waterloo Hospital. The hospital was as much of a landmark as the post office would ever be.

Although Waterloo's somewhat isolated location had spared it from many of the illnesses that had infected towns and cities along the lakefront, where unsanitary conditions and migrant travellers constituted a serious social problem, the new scientific theory that disease was spread by germs had resulted in demands for the development of hospitals in many Ontario towns and also for the proper treatment of sewage and industrial wastes as well as for supplies of clean water. Waterloo would add each of these services in the next two decades. The water system had been first in 1888, and sewers had followed shortly after. Waterloo's residents had benefited from the fact that Berlin, with its larger population and greater difficulties arising from its manufacturing industries, had been forced to deal with these problems before they had become a serious concern in the smaller

Before women were widely accepted in the work force, girls from Waterloo and Berlin were expected to attend household science classes at the Berlin High School. Two world wars in the space of a generation, however, dramatically changed the role of women in society. Courtesy, Kitchener Public Library

town. In this respect, it was only natural that a hospital would be a joint facility to serve the needs of both towns.

Moses Springer, Waterloo's long term reeve and Member of the Legislative Assembly, was one of the first to recommend that the hospital be common to both Waterloo and Berlin. A public meeting was held at the high school, midway between the two towns, on June 10, 1893, followed by a subsequent meeting on July 18 to consider possible sites. Joseph Seagram's offer to donate his 13-acre property was eagerly accepted. Seagram had intended to build his home on this site, but on learning that it lie entirely within Berlin, he promptly refused to consider it.

The gift was not only from Joseph Seagram, but also from his wife, Stephanie, a significant inclusion given the important role that the Women's Auxiliary would have in the operation of the hospital. Seagram also specified that the hospital would be non-sectarian, "that no person shall be refused admission . . . by reason of his or her Nationality, Race, Color, Religious belief or want of Religious belief." In many ways this last clause illustrated the openness and lack of sectarian strife in Waterloo where the Germans, although a majority in the community, were clearly in a minority in Canada. In Waterloo there had always seemed to be a greater sensitivity to the rights of other minorities than in many other Canadian towns and cities.

The hospital was a joint project of both towns. The residents of Waterloo donated $5,000 toward the new project, while Berlin with its much larger population contributed $10,000. The new building was of red brick, "its outline and style quite modern and pleasing, while its beautiful site favourably heightens its architectural effect." The cornerstone was laid on September 19, 1894, and "a thousand children's voices led by Professor H.A. Zoellner of Waterloo joined in singing the stirring national song, 'Red,

White and Blue,' at the same time waving hundreds of flags in unison, while a salute of 16 guns was fired by the Artillery brigade, all of which was very impressive."

The hospital was governed by a board of trustees, eight from Berlin and four from Waterloo. The first chairman was George Randall, Waterloo's former mayor and town councillor. Others from Waterloo were Christian Kumpf, another former mayor; John Shuh, a businessman and former town councillor; as well as James Lockie; and, of course, Joseph E. Seagram, who was rewarded with a life membership on the board in recognition of his substantial donation. Twelve doctors comprised the hospital staff: eight from Berlin and four from Waterloo.

Despite the initial enthusiasm for the hospital, its early years were marred by an unusual problem—a lack of patients. The provincial hospital inspector reported that when he had visited in 1899 there were only 13 patients. "Situated between two prosperous towns whose united population was between 11,000 and 12,000, and being the only hospital in the part of the county, a much larger attendance might be expected," he noted. Compared to other parts of Ontario, he continued:

The Berlin-Waterloo Hospital was built in 1894 on land donated for the purpose by Joseph E. Seagram. Seagram abandoned a plan to construct a residence on the site when he realized the property lay entirely in Berlin, not in his beloved Waterloo. Refurbished upon completion of a nine-storey addition in 1951, the original building was renamed the Kathleen Scott Pavilion, in honour of the former hospital superintendent. Courtesy, Kitchener Public Library

The Waterloo Garage once stood prominently in the centre of Waterloo near the site of the present "Old English Parlour," which is also a former garage and tire depot, illustrating the adaptive reuse of historical buildings. Courtesy, Waterloo Public Library

Waterloo does not appreciate the establishment of a hospital in its midst, or else the inhabitants are particularly exempt from sickness and accident . . . The Hospital idea is quite a new feature among the Germans who are naturally very conservative, and considerable hostility will have to be lived down before they take kindly to treatment in such an institution.

There was something of truth in both parts of his explanation. Waterloo's relative isolation from many of the larger cities and the problems of congested urban communities had led to a healthier lifestyle. Similarly, the social cohesion of the community meant that concern for the sick was a family responsibility. A sick relative was treated in one's home, not in a public hospital ward. These were values that would remain an integral part of life in Waterloo. They were also features that made life there attractive.

The inherent stability and social conservatism of the community is also evident in the lack of industrial unrest. While strikes and walkouts became more frequent in the early years of the twentieth century, the workers of Waterloo felt little compunction to join. The first major

industrial strike would not occur until 1941. Similarly, the high degree of home ownership (estimated at more than 80 percent by the twentieth century), did much to instill pride in the community. Factory owners understood this, too. Workers who owned their own homes were less likely to strike and risk losing their property. The location of Waterloo's factories near the central business district and along King, Erb, and Regina streets, provided an important focus for community life. At the same time, the dispersion of residential areas around the central part of the town meant that Waterloo had never developed an overwhelming working-class district as was so common in most industrial communities. Of course, the stability of employment offered by insurance companies, a distillery, and a brewery meant that

unemployment (the bane of all workers) was rarely a problem. The steady growth of Waterloo during these years also saved the town from the boom and bust cycles that created social unrest and serious discontent in other cities.

The styles of housing on so many of Waterloo's older streets illustrate the prosperity and stability of community life where the homes of merchants and manufacturers are commonly interspersed with those of workers and shopkeepers.

Prestigious Victorian styles like those of Thomas Hilliard's on William Street or David Bean's grand Italianate residence on George Street provide ample evidence of the town's prosperity. Waterloo's elite built their homes in the styles that had become fashionable throughout the province. In the look of the town there was little that would identify its

The Waterloo Cricket Club, active in the 1920s and 1930s, was led by its captain, T.W. Seagram. Courtesy, Kitchener Public Library

Germanic past, although on King and Albert streets there were a few remnants of the earlier "Mennonite Georgian" style. The newer residential buildings were usually one and one-half storeys in height, with gable ends facing the street, often with a porch or stoop at the front entrance. Perhaps in keeping with styles that may have been common in Germany, where land was scarce and urban homes frequently two- or three-storeys high, the dimensions of these homes seemed to emphasize their height. But if this was a cultural statement, it was difficult to distinguish these homes from others in Ontario, except perhaps that they were larger, built on lots with 66-foot frontages, and with well-cultivated vegetable gardens in the rear. Row housing, which had become a common feature of many Ontario towns, was conspicuously absent in Waterloo.

There was a surplus of residential land until after World War II. As a result, homes were often built by individuals rather than by developers. Older residential streets such as Albert and Menno have a remarkable range of housing

Left: As early as 1894 a Berlin-Waterloo Baseball League had been formed, and a strong rivalry existed between the two communities. Reorganized in 1931 by E.F. Seagram, the Waterloo "Tigers" adopted the Seagram colours of black and gold. Courtesy, Waterloo Public Library

Below: Lawn bowling was a popular Waterloo pastime organized in 1900. Waterloo's team, shown here, won the Ontario Championship in 1906. Bowling greens were located next to the Waterloo Club on Erb Street as well as at Mutual Life's head office. Courtesy, Waterloo Public Library

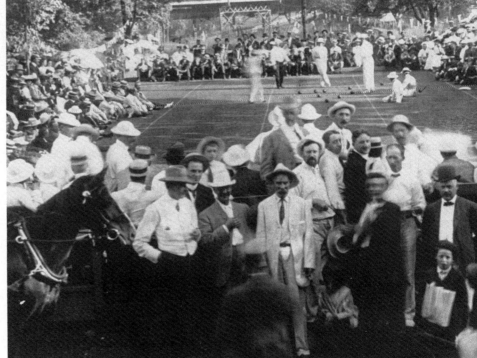

ST. PAULS

The active role of the churches in organizing sports teams was a response to industrialization as church attendance dropped and new roles were defined. St. Paul's team won the "Church League" championship in basketball in 1922. Courtesy, Waterloo Public Library

styles from the 1850s and 1860s to the midpoint of the next century. High Victorian Gothic peaks sit next to small bungalows, offering not only an interesting visual effect, but also clear evidence of the social cohesiveness that seemed to characterize town life in Waterloo.

The presence of so many insurance companies in Waterloo has left a dominant impression on Waterloo's streetscape as well as on its social and economic life. The Waterloo Mutual Fire Insurance Company had been the first in 1863, followed by the North Waterloo

Farmers' Mutual in 1874, and the Mercantile Fire Insurance Company in 1875. Mutual Life had commenced operations in 1870 and Dominion Life in 1889, while the Ontario Equitable Life and Accident Insurance Company was organized in 1920, the Merchants Casualty Company in 1924, and the Pilot Automobile and Accident Insurance Company began in 1927. A related company, the Waterloo Trust and Savings Company, which would later be absorbed by Canada Trust, had also developed in Waterloo in 1912.

Waterloo's stability and steady prosper-

ity had provided the environment in which the idea of insurance and "life assurance" could grow and flourish in the 1870s and 1880s. By the 1930s these companies would themselves contribute to the maintenance of Waterloo's lifestyle. In 1940 the *Financial Post* placed Waterloo on its municipal "honour roll," noting that:

It is an important financial centre, with four banks and the head offices of three life insurance and four fire and casualty insurance companies—an exceptionally large

number for a town of less than 9,000 people. There probably is no more stable source of income than is distributed throughout a community by such companies.

Even during the Great Depression of the 1930s Waterloo's employment remained remarkably steady, and the town's political leaders could proudly report in 1939 that "relief had never cost the town anything." This is not to suggest that poverty and suffering had not existed as they had throughout Canada, but rather that there

Waterloo and Kitchener were caught up in the war effort as this photograph representing a 1943 drive to "stamp out U Boats" clearly illustrates. Courtesy, K-W Record Photograph Negative Collection, University of Waterloo Library

Facing page: The Waterloo Memorial Arena, dedicated to the memory of Waterloo's citizens who had died in two world wars, became home to the Waterloo Siskins. Courtesy, K-W Record Photograph Negative Collection, University of Waterloo Library

Below: Rationing and shortages had affected Waterloo's citizens throughout the duration of six years of war, and, when peace finally arrived in 1945, few were prepared to continue these sacrifices in the face of new demands for consumer goods. Courtesy, K-W Record Photograph Negative Collection, University of Waterloo Library

was considerably less in Waterloo and that in the later years of the depression expenditures on social welfare were paid from funds collected by private subscription rather than by the municipal dole.

As Waterloo's residents faced the problems of industrial development, the uncertainties of the economic depression of the 1930s, and the fearful lead up to World War II, they looked with pride on their community's stability and its strong religious ideals. A wide range of leisure activities, many of them centred on Waterloo Park and sponsored by local industries, churches, and community groups had also done much to strengthen town life. Organized sporting events, drawing citizens together both as participants and as spectators, were prominent in Waterloo. As people came to live in towns and cities, the pressures of urban and factory life in addition to the absence of open, natural recreational spaces had resulted in the increasing importance accorded to organized

sports. In this respect Waterloo and its residents were well-served, especially by the presence of companies such as Mutual Life and Dominion Life, both of which emphasized the importance of sports for the physical and social well-being of their employees.

Mutual Life, in particular, provided facilities where management and workers could mingle on the bowling greens and the tennis courts. Dominion Life donated the funding for the establishment of tennis courts in Waterloo Park for the use of its employees and the town's citizens. Other industries, too, assisted in the organization of team sports for their workers. In 1920, for example, the Kuntz Brewery, Seagram's Mutual Life, A. Bauer, Dominion Life, Equitable Life, John Forsyth, and McPhail's, as well as three private clubs, competed against each other in Waterloo's lawn bowling league. One estimate suggests that as many as 500 bowlers played in the various leagues and tournaments.

If lawn bowling seemed to attract the professionals from the middle-strata of Waterloo's companies, these same companies also supported teams in hockey, softball, rugger, and baseball leagues. With their wider mass appeal, hockey and baseball flourished throughout the industrialized centres of Canada. The relationship between sports teams and the industrial leaders in the town was recognized in 1931 when the Waterloo "Tigers" were reorganized, with E.F. Seagram as president and gold and black, the colours of the Seagram Stables, now adorned Waterloo's pre-eminent baseball team. These teams also provided a strong sense of community identity as teams from Waterloo competed against others from rival municipalities. In a town like Waterloo, with the overwhelming presence of nearby Kitchener, the success of these municipal teams took on a new importance and continued to assure Waterloo's separate identity.

During the 1920s and 1930s Waterloo had an exceptional range and diversity of sporting teams. Schools, industry, commerce, and social agencies provided sporting opportunities for both men and women. Not insignificantly, the churches were often in the forefront of this movement, led by Anglicans, Lutherans, and Roman Catholics and by the Kitchener-Waterloo Young Men's Christian Association. Church leagues in basketball, hockey, baseball, and soccer had large numbers of players. At the very time when concern was being expressed about the decline in traditional church attendance, participation in sporting events was reaching an all-time high. These teams brought young and old together, encouraged the development of athletic skills, and, when teams or individuals from Waterloo were successful in competitions elsewhere, the town shared in the pride.

Municipal teams had also become well established. In 1938 the Waterloo Siskins hockey team won the Ontario Juvenile Championships and in 1940 captured the Ontario Junior B Championship. The

Waterloo Tigers won the Inter-County Baseball Championship in 1934 and 1935. In 1936 they won the championship of the Ontario Intermediate A league. In 1939 and 1940 they advanced to the Senior B league, winning both the Inter-County and the Ontario Baseball Association championships, giving the town and its residents a strong sense of local pride.

With the advent of World War II in 1939, the nation and the town seemed to turn their attention to national issues. Many remembered all too well the tragic loss of life and the strain on their town's unity in the previous war. Waterloo and its citizens would be once again called upon to participate fully in this great crisis. When the peace treaty was declared in 1945 and Canada and its allies travelled to Paris in the summer of 1946 to fashion a new world order out of the devastation of war-torn Europe, the residents of Waterloo felt that the time was also right for their town to play a greater part in the new Canada.

Council petitioned the Ontario Legislature to elevate the Town of Waterloo to a City. The "City of Waterloo Act" was passed on April 3, 1947. One month earlier, in February, the new Memorial Arena had been opened, dedicated to the memory of Waterloo's citizens who had died in the two world wars. The symbolic timing of the two events, looking to the past as well as to the future, seemed especially appropriate. On January 1, 1948, the City of Waterloo was born.

CHAPTER 6

Looking to the Future

When Ontario's Premier, the Honourable George Drew, officially declared Waterloo's status as a city on January 8, 1948, at a formal dinner in the auditorium of the Mutual Life Assurance Company, no one could have anticipated the changes that were to come. The boundaries of the new city were exactly those outlined in the original act that had incorporated the first limits of the village in 1857. Nor had the city's population growth been so great as to necessitate any radical departure from the traditional lifestyle. With barely more than 10,000 residents, it was thought that Waterloo would not likely reach 15,000, the minimum population for a city, for at least another quarter century. Certainly neither Premier Drew nor Waterloo's mayor, W. L. Hilliard, would have believed it possible that in less than two decades Waterloo would be internationally renowned as a "university town" or that the local newspaper would be referring to something called a "University of Waterloo," describing it as a "city within a city" that had attracted more than 7,000 students, 500 professors, and a total staff of more than 2,500. Nor could they have guessed that the tiny Lutheran Seminary Arts College, with an enrolment of fewer than 200 in 1948, would have 2,000 students by 1968. There were nearly as many University students in Waterloo in 1968 as the total population when

The 170-acre Quickfall farm on Lincoln Road, which had been a Waterloo landmark since 1846, was developed into a 149-home subdivision in 1960. This ended a tradition of six generations of the Quickfall family. Courtesy, K-W Record Photograph Negative Collection, University of Waterloo Library

The contrast between the two eras is strikingly captured by the city's own review of its activities after its first full year of cityhood: the major event of the year had been the picnic in June when the schoolchildren were given a holiday to celebrate Waterloo's new municipal status. The chief of police reported that there had been no major crime in Waterloo during the year, "although safecrackers got away with a small sum of money in June when they blew up a safe at Litter's store." The break-in occurred, the chief offered by way of explanation, "on the night of the Waterloo Music Festival." He also noted that:

Juvenile crime continued at a low ebb with only one juvenile delinquency case heard in Waterloo during the entire year. No traffic deaths occurred in the city although there were nine persons injured in accidents. A 3 1/2 year old boy drowned in a cistern on April 18. It was the only violent death. A night officer was added to the Waterloo police department to bring the total strength to ten while a two-way radio receiving set installation was shelved for another year.

Above: Ontario Premier George Drew proudly shows Waterloo's cityhood proclamation at the formal dinner to inaugurate city status. Courtesy, K-W Record Photograph Negative Collection, University of Waterloo Library

Below: Waterloo's citizens celebrate cityhood at a dance in the historic market building. Courtesy, Waterloo Historical Society

cityhood was proclaimed.

J.F. Scully, the city's auditor, had reported in 1948 that Waterloo's population in the previous decade had increased only marginally and that during the entire 10 years of the 1930s only 357 "new residents" were added. In 1982, when the still "new" University of Waterloo with 22,999 students officially became the second-largest university in the province, no one had any doubt that the city of Waterloo had undergone a major transformation.

The city's population had increased to 10,736 from 10,640 the previous year. Whether residents were aware of it or not, Waterloo was about to enter the most remarkable period of its history.

Although the pace of life in Waterloo may have seemed unchanged from previous years, this was more of an illusion than it was a reality. For one thing, many of Waterloo's leading companies were no longer "Waterloo" companies. The era of small town, family-run firms that had characterized much of Waterloo's lifestyle was ended. In 1928 the Seagram Distillery was acquired by the newly created Distillers Corporation of Montreal, headed by Samuel Bronfman. In the following year the Kuntz Brewery, which had been in the Kuntz family since 1844, was sold to E.P. Taylor and Canadian Breweries Limited, becoming part of the O'Keefe Brewery.

Teen Town was organized in 1949 as a common meeting place for young Waterloo boys. Courtesy, Waterloo Historical Society

Even the Waterloo Manufacturing Company, once described as the largest industry in the county and which had carried the Waterloo name across Canada emblazoned on a series of agricultural implements, was reorganized in 1930 into a new company with H.V. McKay Ltd. of Sunshine, Australia, called Sunshine-Waterloo Limited. These changes, of course, were not restricted to Waterloo and were part of a much larger trend toward amalgamation and worldwide consolidation of industries. But the effects were noticed and not always applauded.

With international companies came international unions, and in 1941 organized labour began to "flex its muscles" when the Canadian Labour Congress called for a strike against the Waterloo Manufacturing Company, charging that wages were being kept unfairly low while the company was making excessive profits from the war effort. The Canadian government intervened due to the exigencies of wartime production, and the matter was quickly settled, but no one doubted that in the postwar era there would be a fundamental change in the attitudes between management and labour.

The years of the Second World War (1939-1945) were in many different ways a watershed in Canadian life, and the

prosperity that followed the war created much of the unparalleled economic growth that marked both Waterloo and its neighbouring city of Kitchener. Its legacy has been described in the words "affluence" and "population boom." Much of the evidence for this can be found in a 1944 survey conducted by the Canadian Chamber of Commerce in Waterloo, Kitchener, and the surrounding villages to aid the Canadian government in postwar planning. Covering all city businesses and more than 10 percent of all households, it was even by modern standards an extremely thorough analysis of the local community. What the survey found, in its own words, was "an industrial revolution."

The war also created a social revolution as women were called upon "to do men's

work" and it was soon discovered that not only were women capable of doing all but the heaviest of jobs, they also did them well and often better than the men who had preceded them. Daycare centres, income tax revisions in favour of working women, and steps toward social and educational equality were direct, if not always immediate, benefits of the war. The employment figures for Kitchener-Waterloo also tell part of this story. In 1939 the two cities had a work force of 9,239 men and 4,288 women. Over the next four years, 3,198 men and 131 women joined the armed forces. Yet by 1943 the two cities employed 11,411 men and 6,824 women—a net growth in the work force of 8,037 employees. Not only was there a massive increase in the work force, but

this astonishing growth had also "bestowed widespread benefits on all classes" as the average wage rose substantially. The result of this new prosperity was a meaningful redistribution of income. Waterloo took on that "middle-class" aspect that has marked it ever since new streets were opened and dotted with rows of neat bungalows and the inevitable ranch-style houses. The conclusion to the 1944 survey was both accurate and prophetic as it observed that "there can be no doubt that in material comforts the population of Kitchener-Waterloo lives, on average, considerably better than it did in 1939—in spite of heavier taxation and even after purchasing War Bonds and War Savings Certificates to the tune of $17,500,000." With a 91 percent increase in bank deposits between 1939 and 1943, the residents of Kitchener-Waterloo were poised to take advantage of the remarkable range of products available to them in what would soon be labelled (not always without criticism) as the "consumer society."

The immediate postwar years led to a dramatic population explosion and a generation popularized as the "baby-boomers." Added to the hoards of newcomers fleeing the devastation of Europe and the confident expectations of many veterans that the deprivations of the war years were not in vain, the 1950s saw rapid expansion not just in industrial growth but also in the need for educational facilities. When Waterloo became a city in 1948, its four elementary schools—Central, built in 1861; St. Louis, a Roman Catholic Separate School built in 1905; Alexandra, opened in 1905; and Elizabeth Ziegler, established in 1931—had seemed more than adequate. Rising enrolments led to the construction of Our Lady of Lourdes in 1948 to serve the "west side" of the city, while Empire, the first of what would seem an unending list of "new subdivision" schools, was opened in 1954. Two years later St. Agnes was established for the rapidly growing Lincoln Heights subdivision on the east side of Waterloo. Before the decade of the fifties had ended, another public elementary school named after longtime school trustee, Harold Wagner, was opened in Lincoln Heights. There were now more than 3,000 children in the elementary system, and there were no signs of the pressure abating. Clearly Waterloo would also need its own secondary school. In 1958 a 20-acre site was acquired in the north end of Waterloo not far from the site of the first postwar housing boom of some 83 wartime houses, described in 1949 as "Waterloo's biggest individual construction project." It would be here, on September 6, 1960, that Waterloo Collegiate would open.

If elementary and secondary schools had faced tremendous pressure to expand, Ontario's universities were also struggling to keep pace, but with very limited access to public funding. Due to federal offers of support for those veterans who wished to pursue higher education, soldiers returning from the Second World War had caused a sharp rise in enrolment. In 1945-1946 more than 20,000 of them attended universities, expanding the number of full-time students from 38,516 to more than 60,000 by 1946. The graduation of

Facing page and below: This prank played on the freshmen students at Waterloo College in 1947 has come to symbolize the high spirits and "clean" fun associated with university life. Courtesy, Waterloo Historical Society

University leaders J.G. Hagey, Father C.L. Siegfried, and an unidentified man meet to plan the curriculum for the new University of Waterloo. Courtesy, K-W Record Photograph Negative Collection, University of Waterloo Library

time, plans were outlined for future science and engineering faculties.

In Waterloo the Lutheran Seminary had also begun to address the needs of the postwar era. Affiliated with the University of Western Ontario since 1925, the first class of six graduates from Western's "Waterloo College" had completed their program in 1927. Weathering a series of financial crises in the 1920s and 1930s, the college had nonetheless received substantial community support and had maintained a steady enrolment of some 50 students. Like so many institutions in the postwar era, the college's enrolment jumped from 70 to 169 students, and in 1947 an expansion program was announced to try to raise $100,000 for a new teaching and administrative building. Tenders were received, and in 1953 a ceremony for the ground breaking was performed by the college's new president, the man who more than any one single individual would transform the look of the city of Waterloo—Joseph Gerald Hagey.

As Waterloo College's new president, Hagey was in some ways an unlikely choice. For one thing, he was a layman in an institution that had traditionally been headed by Lutheran clergymen. Although a graduate of the college, he was a businessman, not an academic. He had been the national public relations and advertising manager for B.F. Goodrich, but he was also active in his church and in his alma mater, serving on its board of governors and, in 1951, as the board's vice-president. At a time when the college was struggling with an ever-increasing demand for service to its students, yet governed by a traditional clerical structure, Hagey offered an alternative as a prominent Lutheran layman with proven administrative experience. On April 29, 1953, he accepted the board's offer to become executive administrator and president of Waterloo College. What followed over the next decade was a truly remarkable saga ending with not one, but three new universities in Waterloo—Waterloo Lutheran University, the

these veterans did not result in a decrease of student numbers. Instead, more students than ever before sought to attend university. Now it was not thought of as a privilege. It was a fundamental right in Ontario's postwar society. This, too, was the beginning of a profound revolution in attitudes toward university education and in the accessibility of Ontario's universities.

The first local institution to respond to the challenge of the new demands for university education was the Roman Catholic St. Jerome's College. Established in 1865 in St. Agatha and a prominent landmark in Berlin and Kitchener since 1866, St. Jerome's entered into an affiliation with the University of Ottawa in 1947 and quickly announced plans for expansion, including the admission of women to its classes. A major new university site, called Kingsdale, was acquired on the eastern boundaries of Kitchener and in 1953 the Ontario premier who would preside over much of the university growth, the Honourable Leslie Frost, opened the college's arts building and library. At the same

new University of Waterloo, and the somewhat new (although in many ways much older) institution, the University of St. Jerome's College, leaving its seminary campus at Kingsdale and moving its arts programs to Waterloo in a federation agreement with the University of Waterloo.

As president of Waterloo College, Gerry Hagey was acutely aware of the increasing demand for post-secondary education. In his report to the board of governors of the Evangelical Lutheran Seminary of Canada in 1955, he pointed to the need for Waterloo College to plan to meet these new challenges. He also alluded to the possibility of increased government funding that would allow the college to be placed on a more secure financial basis as well as to better serve the community and its students. Hagey faced a myriad of problems. Waterloo College had neither the land nor the finances to expand. University education, whether at Waterloo, Western, or Toronto also involved other faculties than arts. The choices seemed to be either to limit the size of the faculty or to find new funds to acquire land, extend the faculty's areas of expertise, and provide an enlarged and enriched university community. The problem was that denominational colleges like Waterloo College and St. Jerome's College were church-supported and therefore ineligible for provincial funding. There had to be a way around this obstacle.

The Roman Catholic Assumption University at Windsor had found one solution. "By establishing a non-denominational institution, which then entered into affiliation with the parent college, indirect government funding could be obtained." Hagey was worried that if he did not act promptly, St. Jerome's would. To put it bluntly, he later recalled, "some of the Protestant people" were complaining that "it was a shame Waterloo (College) had let St. Jerome's get ahead of them."

The board of governors at Waterloo College was reticent about expansion,

fearing that the Lutheran character of their college would be diluted. Nonetheless, Hagey persevered:

It was with the threat I had of St. Jerome's adopting a program such as I had suggested—meaning that the faculty of science would be separately incorporated—that I was able to get the Board of Governors to approve . . . I strongly recommend that we do it or we might find ourselves as an affiliated college with St. Jerome's. That, of course, seemed very—you might say— offensive to Waterloo College.

The result was the establishment in 1955 of a separate board of governors of a new organization to be called the Associate Faculties of Waterloo College.

The new board of governors was composed of prominent businessmen from Kitchener, Waterloo, and the surrounding area. Business interests, not religious affiliation, determined the membership. Ira G. Needles was appointed chairman and Carl Dare, secretary, while prominent Roman Catholics such as industrialist

The Engineers' sign on the Hotel Waterloo in 1958 clearly established their presence in Waterloo. Future high jinks would include painting the word BEER on the top of Waterloo's water tower. Courtesy, K-W Record Photograph Negative Collection, University of Waterloo Library

Henry C. Krug and the publisher of the Kitchener-Waterloo *Record*, John E. Motz, also played an active part. In 1956 the Canada Synod of the Lutheran Church agreed in principle to the affiliation agreement and the following day the rector of St. Jerome's College, the Reverend C.L. Siegfried, announced that "when the time comes . . . we shall hope to become a part of the new university and to lend our full support and co-operation to its foundation."

Four years and countless hours of negotiations later, the heads of the three institutions announced that on July 1, 1960, "an agreement had been reached by which Waterloo College and St. Jerome's College will become federated with the University of Waterloo . . . arts students enroling at the colleges will receive their degrees from the new University . . ." But it was not to be. At the last minute a special meeting of the Lutheran Synod was called recommending that their church college "pursue a course of independence." The Synod was in a position to overrule its board of governors, and so it did, but not without new divisions in the Synod itself and among the faculty. Gerry Hagey was the one most affected. His dream had been "to transform the Lutheran College into a University and it had been his moral suasion that had encouraged negotiations through the worst of the crises." The final break with the Synod marked the beginning of independence for the new University of Waterloo. Hagey would spend the next decade transforming what he once described as the "matchbook on a farm and a farmhouse" into one of Ontario's foremost universities.

At the same time as St. Jerome's College entered into federation, the leaders of several other churches negotiated for three new colleges to become affiliated with the university. The Anglican college, Renison, was first; followed shortly afterward by St. Paul's, a college of the United Church of Canada; and the Mennonite's Conrad Grebel College. In their own way, each of these church-related colleges

would add significantly to the attractiveness of the new non-sectarian university while the original concept of the associate faculties, which had also included a work-study or, as it would be popularly known, a co-operative education plan, would quickly lead Waterloo to the forefront of Canada's university system.

The timing of the co-op programs could not have been better. On the night of October 4, 1957, an announcement was made that had startled mankind. The Soviet Union had launched Sputnik I. The excitement started all over again. National and industrial priorities were about to be drastically altered. New relationships would have to be formed between universities and business with a new emphasis on science, engineering, and computers. In a way, the old universities and the old ways had let us down. New, brash, and vital upstart universities like Waterloo would be given a unique chance to prove themselves.

On July 1, 1960, another new institution, Waterloo Lutheran University, had also begun its first year of operation as a degree-granting institution created by the same act of the provincial legislature that had established the University of Waterloo and, under a new nomenclature, the University of St. Jerome's College. In the beginning there was an inevitable spirit of competition and some acrimony. Relations between the universities, however, quickly developed into a healthy rivalry and a shared commitment to academic excellence. The rapid growth of Waterloo's universities strained the community resources to the point in 1973 when the Eastern Canada Synod of the Lutheran Church in America voted 212 to 56 that W.L.U. become an autonomous and fully-funded, provincially supported university. Out of this decision W.L.U. now became W.L.U. once more, but this time the initials stood for Wilfrid Laurier University (named after Sir Wilfrid Laurier, one of Canada's pre-eminent Prime Ministers).

The 1960s were exciting times both for

Chicopee Ski Club, in its early years, offered a pleasant respite from the Canadian winter. Courtesy, K-W Record Photograph Negative Collection, University of Waterloo Library

the city of Waterloo and its two universities. There is probably no more striking contrast between the old Waterloo and the new city than that revealed in Waterloo's centennial celebrations in 1957.

The Waterloo that was depicted was a Waterloo of the past. It was a Waterloo in which men like Daniel Snyder, John Hoffman, Moses Springer, or George Randall, Waterloo's prominent politicians in the 1850s, would have felt quite comfortable. The Waterloo they had helped to create was still evident. Companies like Seagrams, Mutual Life, and Dominion Life had grown and expanded, but the dynamics of the city had not changed. Members of council had many surnames that would have been familiar to them— Bauer, Bauman, Ratz, and Snider. Even the physical size of the city had not altered significantly from the original Hoffman survey

in the 1850s. The first of the new subdivisions extending beyond Waterloo's boundaries was yet to come, although in 1957 it was in the planning stages. Even these changes maintained a tie with the past. When the former 100-acre Seagram Stables and, since 1936, the J.M. Schneider stockyards at Bridgeport Road and Weber Street, were being developed into Waterloo's first shopping plaza, the local newspaper proudly announced that "one stable used by J.E. Frowde Seagram for wintering his race horses would not be torn down . . . In effect, this means a 'reprieve' for the famous Seagram Stable, established in 1888." No such reprieve would be likely in the spectacular growth of the next decade.

With Mayor James Bauer at the controls on June 15, 1960, a huge excavating machine dug the first shovel of ground at

Waterloo Square to officially signal the start of construction of Waterloo's $5-million downtown shopping development on King Street. "In one stroke," Bauer confidently proclaimed, "the (shopping) centre will advance the heart of the city by 50 years." Alex Rubin, president of Toronto Industrial Leaseholds, the developers who planned to participate with the city in the new project, was presented a symbolic "key to the city" by Mayor Bauer. Rubin's comments contrasted the old Waterloo with his vision of the new:

The battle of Waterloo (he said) seems to be over. All around is destruction. The heart of your city is levelled to the ground. We can survey around us the flattened corpses of ancient buildings. Historically, then, there is nothing to do except to celebrate and then to withdraw.

It is at this point that we change history . . . Out of this flat ground will shortly rise a fine series of beautifully architectured buildings. The heart of the city will beat with renewed vigour.

No one could have better expressed the optimism of the 1960s and the faith in a brave new world that could be rendered out of concrete and plastic. Nor could anyone have expressed more clearly the disdain for the past and a shocking disregard for tradition. In its own way, this would be a major part of the legacy of the 1960s.

Waterloo's business district had been in serious trouble. A market survey in 1960 revealed that Waterloo shoppers did only 25 percent of their business in their hometown. Fifty percent was done in Kitchener and the remainder elsewhere. With the revised plans for Waterloo's business

In the 1960s Waterloo claimed to have more horse-drawn traffic than any other Ontario city. These privately owned stalls were located in the centre of the business district. Courtesy, K-W Record Photograph Negative Collection, University of Waterloo Library

Top: A July 1961 photograph of Waterloo Square under construction shows both the destruction of existing buildings and the erection of the steel girders for the new mall. Courtesy, K-W Record Photograph Negative Collection, University of Waterloo Library

Bottom: A view of the central business district of Waterloo in the 1950s, before the development of Waterloo Square, illustrates the close proximity of factories, commercial enterprises, civic government, and church steeples. Courtesy, Waterloo Public Library

district adding 40 new stores, it was anticipated that "most of the buying could be done at home." In one sense it was the proximity to Kitchener's larger retail district that had forced Waterloo's council to initiate the Waterloo Square project. For James Bauer and his council this was the first time in Canada that a municipality and a developer had shared in a cooperative venture. The city acquired and demolished the buildings of two prominent Waterloo companies, the Waterloo Manufacturing Company and Snyder's Furniture factory. With incentives from the city, both firms had agreed to relocate in Waterloo and to build new plants away from their Main Street locations. In addition the city also purchased "an old garage, a tenement house and two homes on Caroline Street." The total cost for the city was estimated at more than $1.3 million with a debenture debt of $909,000.

From the beginning this dramatic leap into the future was plagued with problems. The original development was at first delayed and then renegotiated. Then it was criticized as a "white elephant," and complaints abounded that the developer was lacking in commitment. Only in 1964, with expansion of both the University of Waterloo and municipal services at the city and county level, was the vacant office space filled. Ownership of the square changed again and again, sometimes by outside investors and other times by local interests, but never without controversy. For many, Waterloo Square had come to symbolize the problems of 1960s redevelopment. It had not enough parking, not enough green space; it was not connected to the rest of the downtown; it was a suburban mall trying to masquerade as a city centre, and the list goes on. Over the next two decades planning study after planning study worried over Waterloo Square and the surrounding businesses with ever-changing guidelines to reassert the central importance of the city's core area. Waterloo was not alone in this regard. The prob-

lems were common to many North American cities, but in Waterloo the problem seemed more urgent if the city was ever to retain a sense of its identity.

An even greater threat to Waterloo's identity had come in 1970, when Dr. Stewart Fyfe, who had headed a review of local government, recommended the amalgamation of Waterloo with Kitchener to create one new city. Worrisome, too, was the comment of Darcy McKeough, the minister of municipal affairs, whose department was reviewing the Fyfe Report, when he warned that "it is imperative that the people of these two cities seriously contemplate whether it is realistic for them to remain apart." When 83 percent of Waterloo's voters cast their ballots against amalgamation in a public opinion poll in September 1970, Fyfe was astonished at the overwhelming anti-amalgamation vote. The people of Waterloo, he opined, really do have a strong sense of identity. Nonetheless, he added, "It is (only) a question of time before an

"K-W merger study needed," agreed these panelists in a 1959 debate led by Magistrate J.R.H. Kirkpatrick; Sandy Baird, then a Record *columnist; and Anna Hughes, a Waterloo alderman. Courtesy, K-W Record Photograph Negative Collection, University of Waterloo Library*

Facing page: Catching an afternoon in the sun, both the occu-
pant and the building will soon
be gone in the wake of Waterloo's
continuing industrial expansion.
Photo by James Stevenson, Photo
X, Waterloo

amalgamation takes place."

A question of time, it may have been,
but it was also a question that had been
debated time after time. The answer was
always the same, a resounding no. Even
in 1857, when Waterloo first sought incorporation as a village, the act as passed in
the legislative assembly had provided for
its amalgamation with Berlin "whenever
the councils of the town and village petitioned the lieutenant-governor of the
province." Interestingly, this clause was
not present in the acts incorporating the
Town of Waterloo in 1876 or the City of
Waterloo in 1948. This does not mean that
the idea had died.

Official proposals, usually emanating
from Berlin and later Kitchener, seemed
to occur at least every 10 years. Sometimes they were attended with a certain
civility as was recorded by the Berlin
business and civic leader, Louis Breithaupt, in his diary of February 29, 1888:

*We met the mayor and council of Waterloo
at our council chambers this evg. & had a
friendly discussion of matters pertaining to
the mutual welfare of the 2 towns, such as
street ry, [sic] removal of cemeteries, amalgamation, etc. Afterwards the Waterloo gen-
tlemen were entertained at an oyster supper
at Mattell's Grand Central Hotel & a very
pleasant time was spent.*

Other meetings were strikingly unpleasant. One of these in 1904, under the aus-
pices of the Berlin Board of Trade, urging
that the two towns act jointly in the purchase of the street railway and in supplying
light and power, quickly degenerated into
acrimony and rancour. Problems quickly
arose about the probable name of the new
town as well as the location of a town hall
and the sharing of the municipal debt. Carl
Kranz, mayor of Berlin, said that he would
never consent to seeing Berlin's name
dropped while those from Waterloo replied
that "Waterloo had been on the map since
1816. To take it off would disfigure the
map of Ontario." Others suggested that

"Berlin's conduct as a town had not
inspired confidence in amalgamation, alleg-
ing that 'Berlin had acted shabbily and
even dishonestly on the matter of Waterloo's share of street railway profits'. . ."
In the ensuing uproar several aldermen
rose to leave, when, over the noise, Berlin's
future mayor, W.H. Schmalz, could be
heard proclaiming, "When the time does
come for Berlin to engulf Waterloo, I know
it will be a pleasant morsel."

A rather different scenario had occurred
in 1916 in the midst of the war when
Berlin's citizens faced the prospect of a
name change. The name Waterloo was
proposed along with a union of the two
municipalities. This time Waterloo council
seemed more amenable, but Berlin's was
not. Berlin in fact "would not even give its
Waterloo counterpart a hearing." The
debate reached the pages of *Saturday
Night,* Canada's national magazine,
describing the "packed meetings" and
"padded petitions" utilized in promoting
the choice of the name of Kitchener, while
"the sound suggestion of the change to
Waterloo was not even allowed to intrude
itself, there being a feeling among the tub
thumping 'changers' that Kitchener would
be a better 'business getter.'" And so the
debate continued.

It arose again immediately after the end
of the Second World War. In 1954 the idea
of a merger of the two municipalities
was described as a "hot potato" and the
"kiss of death" to whichever council would
make the first move. In 1959 Waterloo's
council voted overwhelmingly "not to participate with Kitchener in a study of amalgamation." Waterloo preferred the quality
of government and the personal relationships between council and its citizens that
could be maintained. This philosophy,
which worked so well in the 1950s, would
come under serious strain in the 1980s,
but long before that the continuing crises
of amalgamation would have to be faced.
In the meantime the local newspaper
delighted in regular spoofs and opinion
(Continued on page 137)

Above: Although not giving in to that temptation of the modern age, the automobile, this young Mennonite has seen fit to attach a ten-speed bicycle to the rear of his horse-drawn buggy. Photo by James Stevenson, Photo X, Waterloo

Right: A toboggan hill in the winter is a popular location for these Waterloo children. Photo by James Stevenson, Photo X, Waterloo

Facing page: This tree-lined road captures the timeless serenity of autumn near Waterloo. Photo by James Stevenson, Photo X, Waterloo

Facing page: Waterloo's skyline is beginning to change as the 13-storey tower of Mutual Life joins the company of the Marsland Tower at King and Erb streets. High-rise residences also begin to reshape the look of the city. Courtesy, Mutual Life

Left: The campus at Wilfrid Laurier University has added an attractive element to city life in Waterloo. Courtesy, Wilfrid Laurier University

Far left: Sunrise over the Grand River is as impressive in the 1990s as it must have been to the Indians who travelled along its shores long before the white settlement. Photo by James Stevenson, Photo X, Waterloo

Left: The Martin Meeting House offers a sense of serenity and timelessness as the commercial malls and factory buildings draw ever near. Photo by James Stevenson, Photo X, Waterloo

*Above and right: Charles Bronf-
man's decision to create an
international museum at the site
of the Seagram Distillery has
created a prominent heritage
landmark and reasserted the
importance of understanding
our past in order to build a better future. Photo by James
Stevenson, Photo X, Waterloo*

Above: Progress seems to have stood still as these two boys ponder their fate in the afternoon sun. Photo by James Stevenson, Photo X, Waterloo

Left: Baseball is as much a common pastime among these children in the countryside as it is in organized T-Ball leagues throughout the city. Photo by James Stevenson, Photo X, Waterloo

Facing page, top and bottom: While many Waterloo residents were employed in the giant tire factories of Uniroyal Goodrich, this blacksmith was still plying his trade for visitors to Waterloo coming by horse and buggy. Photo by James Stevenson, Photo X, Waterloo

Facing page: The "Star" quilt is an excellent example of this colourful form of folk art that flourishes in Waterloo County. Photo by Susan Burke, The Joseph Schneider Haus

Left: Apple orchards proliferated with the arrival of the Pennsylvania Mennonites. Scenes like this are common in the gardens of many older Waterloo homes and on the "high tech" campus of the University of Waterloo. Photo by James Stevenson, Photo X, Waterloo

This detail is from an 1823 bookplate for the Bible of Bishop Benjamin Eby, the spiritual leader of the early Mennonite community. It is one of the finest examples of the Fractur tradition, which illuminated many early documents. Photo by M. Bird, courtesy, Canadian Harvest Collection, The Joseph Schneider Haus

The harvest brings an end to the warm days of summer as this farmer prepares for the inevitability of winter. Photo by James Stevenson, Photo X, Waterloo

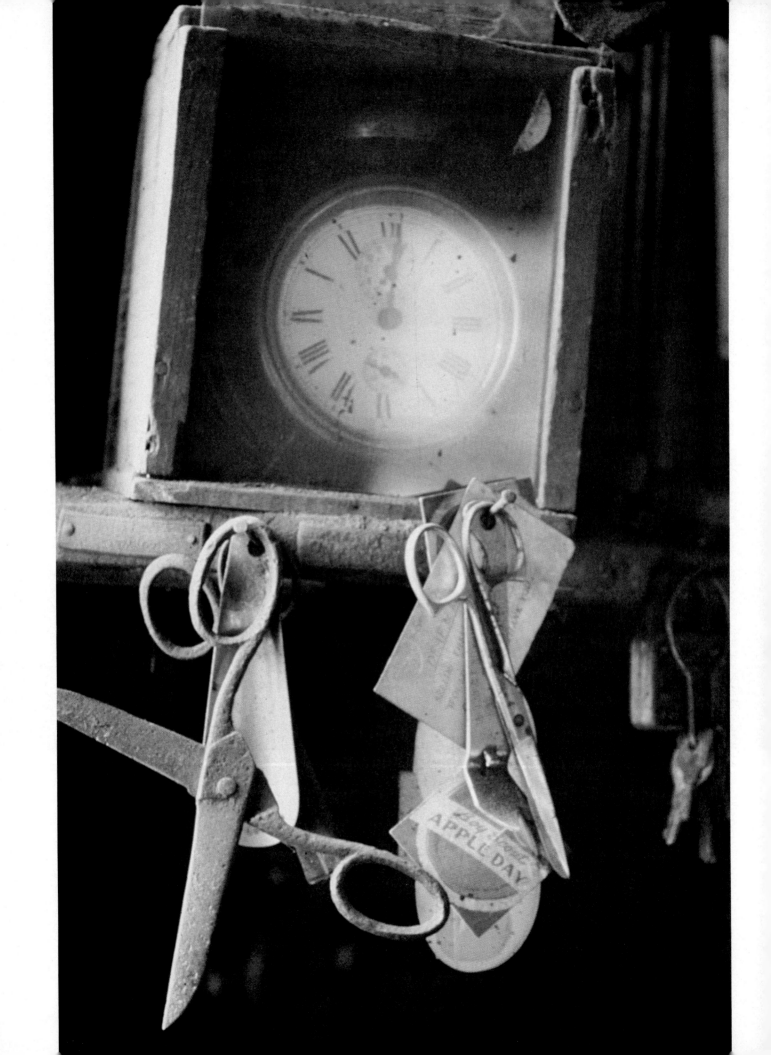

Above: This artist's rendering depicts a playful moment on the toboggan slide in Waterloo Park next to Waterloo's first schoolhouse, which had been relocated to the park in 1893. Courtesy, Woldemar Neufeld and Sand Hills Books

Left: The Barn Raising by Peter Goetz depicts the strong sense of community spirit still evident among Waterloo County's Mennonite and Amish communities. Courtesy, Sand Hills Books

Facing page: The hands of time seem suspended in this repair shop. Photo by James Stevenson, Photo X, Waterloo

Pages 130-131: This view of Waterloo's business district looking north along King Street depicts the area as it looked in the early twentieth century. Courtesy, Woldemar Neufeld and Sand Hills Books

DEORSAM'S BOOK STORE

Woldemar Neufeld

Above: Once known as the Mill Pond or Waterloo Dam, Silver Lake adds an attractive dimension to Waterloo life. Courtesy, Woldemar Neufeld and Sand Hills Books

Right: Waterloo's civic centre, where so many major events in the life of the town had been celebrated, appears in this Woldemar Neufeld painting. Courtesy, Woldemar Neufeld and Sand Hills Books

Woldemar Neufeld

Above: A Waterloo streetscape by Peter Goetz illustrates the growth of the City of Waterloo around the focal point created by St. Louis Church. Courtesy, City of Waterloo

Left: Peter Goetz's painting of the Erb-Kumpf house captures the timeless serenity of Waterloo's oldest home, portions of which were built by Abraham Erb, circa 1812. Courtesy, City of Waterloo

Facing page: The Carnegie Library's classical revival style has graced the intersection of Albert and Dorset streets since 1905, serving as a public library, a police station, and as the proposed gallery for Waterloo's collection of Woldemar Neufeld paintings. Courtesy, Sand Hills Books

*In Waterloo's early years the fire-
hall and town market were central to community life. Both
were demolished in the 1960s
when so many historic buildings
gave way to the march of
progress. Courtesy, Woldemar
Neufeld and Sand Hills Books*

surveys of such possible new names as Kitchenwater, Waterkit, Kitwater, or Kiterloo.

By 1970, however, the mood had changed. Rapid municipal growth and the demands for new services had caused the province to review overlapping municipal structures across Ontario. Many of these powers had been unchanged since the original Municipal Act of 1849. The Fyfe Report was the first step in this review of the governing structures in Waterloo County which led ultimately to the creation of the Regional Municipality of Waterloo in 1973. When Fyfe had originally urged amalgamation of the two cities, many had concurred with its inevitability. Some might even have secretly agreed with Jack Weber, a Waterloo resident who also chaired Kitchener's planning board, when he suggested that in many of their services Waterloo's taxpayers were benefiting from their proximity to Kitchener. In

his inimitable style, Weber declared, "We just feel that Waterloo should join us and pay their share of the load instead of always having their hands in our pockets."

The gauntlet was thrown down. Waterloo responded with an anti-amalgamation drive led by former city planner and the present mayor, Brian Turnbull, and Dr. George Priddle, a geography professor at the University of Waterloo. The committee of business leaders, industrialists, professors, and housewives launched a campaign titled *Think Twice* including a barrage of statistics to explain why Waterloo should oppose amalgamation. The success of their poll showing 83 percent opposed to amalgamation reaffirmed both the separate identity of Waterloo and the strength of their feelings.

Despite outward similarities, Waterloo had always been different from Kitchener. Although close geographically, there had long been a dramatic difference in the

As these Waterloo women gathered to celebrate the city's 125th anniversary, they felt confident that the threats of amalgamation were laid to rest. Courtesy, K-W Record Photograph Negative Collection, University of Waterloo Library

Above: University construction was a hallmark of Waterloo life throughout the 1960s. Courtesy, University of Waterloo Archives

Right: The Dana Porter Library, which rose to become a focal point on the university campus, contains more than two million volumes. Courtesy, University of Waterloo Archives

temperament and operation of the two cities. In the years after 1945 these differences had increased. The presence of two major universities in Waterloo in addition to the ever-growing insurance industries had merely enhanced the city's distinctiveness.

In 1958 the sale of 180 acres by Major Holdings to the fledgling associate faculties of what would become the University of Waterloo had inexorably changed the destiny of the tiny city of Waterloo. Before long the university would expand its campus to nearly 1,000 acres, absorbing the eight existing Mennonite farms into the largest integrated university campus in Ontario. As early as 1965 the two universities had become Waterloo's second-largest industry, surpassed only by the insurance companies. Henry Koch, the Kitchener-Waterloo *Record's* business editor, predicted that by 1970 the two universities "would have mushroomed into a $60,000,000 industry" that would "pour more than $20,000,000 into the local economy in a 12-month period." The continuous building programs on the two campuses were accountable for the

The University of Waterloo's 1965 graduates faced the future with assurance. Courtesy, K-W Record Photograph Negative Collection, University of Waterloo Library

All roads lead to Waterloo as seen in this "Founder's Day" celebration in 1982 with Waterloo aldermen Mewhinney, Voelker, and Thomas in historical attire. Courtesy, K-W Record Photograph Negative Collection, University of Waterloo Library

extremely low unemployment rate in Kitchener and Waterloo, while realtors and those in the service industries had difficulty keeping pace with the rapid growth. The 1965 survey also tried to measure the cultural impact of the universities as more than 2,000 people from the "twin cities" attended night courses at the two institutions in addition to numerous plays, musicals, visiting lecturers, and political speakers. On the

other hand the city struggled to provide new streets, traffic lights, sewer extensions, and sidewalks as well as additional police and fire protection. When all was said, however, Waterloo had changed dramatically.

By way of measure, the decade between 1961 and 1971 was one of exceptional growth. Waterloo's population had grown by 424 percent since the end of the war. The social disparity between the blue

collar working class of Kitchener and the more white collar higher economic social status of Waterloo became evident, not only in the dramatic differences in types of houses in the two cities, but also in average family incomes. Waterloo's in 1981 was $31,224, while Kitchener's lagged far behind at $26,278.

Waterloo had also expanded its manufacturing employment much faster than Kitchener and with a noticeable concentration on technology-oriented firms, many of them related directly or indirectly to the universities. In 1950 Waterloo had 55 industrial plants employing 2,572 workers. By 1970 there were 79 plants and 5,483 workers—a 96.9 percent increase. In 1980 this had increased again to 132 plants and 7,314 workers or a growth rate of an additional 33 percent. A 1982 study has suggested that in the 14-year period between 1967 and 1981 the University of Waterloo's faculty, grad-

uate students, and former graduates had established more than 60 companies. Even if this figure tends to exaggerate the university's efficacy by counting companies that were merely consulting firms set up by faculty members, there were still another one-third that were actually "operating at arm's length from the University and were developing or manufacturing a product."

The City of Waterloo reluctantly began to come to terms with its new status. In 1964 Waterloo no longer referred to itself as "the Hartford of Canada," which had emphasized its role as a centre of the insurance industry, and in 1967 it was claiming second place only to Toronto as a "university city."

The establishment of the universities also changed the physical look of Waterloo. The size and scale of their park-like campuses created a tremendous pull toward the north-northwest counter-

The Waterloo Siskins meet the Kitchener Rangers in a 1984 hockey match that had as much to do with the rivalry of the two cities as it did with the game of hockey. Courtesy, K-W Record Photograph Negative Collection, University of Waterloo Library

balanced only by the Conestoga Parkway. The area along Weber Street, which had once been the centre for industrial growth, was quickly ended. The Beechwood subdivisions developed by Major Holdings from the original farm lands from which the university had also been carved quickly became an extension of the traditions of Westmount ending forever the hopes of Kitchener's Forest Hill to acquire that mantel while Waterloo's new booster publications described the city as "a dynamic leading edge community . . . with vision."

All this growth has not been without cost. In the early 1980s the local newspaper began to note that it was "hard to recognize the old town," and walking tours of the historic central residential district were oversubscribed as people tried to reestablish contact with their community. Under the terms of the Ontario Heritage Act, Waterloo began cautiously designating buildings of historical or architectural interest while the historical depictions of

life in an earlier era by prominent artists such as Peter Goetz, Woldemar Neufeld, and Peter Etril Snyder gained in popularity as did the delightful works of fiction by Edna Staebler. Then came the momentous decision by Charles Bronfman to develop by 1984 an internationally renowned museum on the site of the original Seagram Distillery. Waterloo's past had taken on new meaning.

Politicians, too, began to reconsider the frenetic pace of the previous decades. Headlines such as "Waterloo Growth Surpasses Toyota," "Economic Excitement Continues at Waterloo," or "Lakeshore plan to add 3,000" began to be replaced by others stating, "Quality of Life at Stake as Waterloo Plots Growth" and "Aesthetics Important." People began to complain about "traffic jams, water shortages, loss of farmland and the deteriorating quality of the city's creeks and lakes."

Some experts examining the development of modern cities have noticed that the form of the city systems has changed

Facing page, top: Construction of the Conestoga Parkway had a great impact on the urban development of Waterloo. While the growth of two universities brought a focus to one section of the city, the Parkway and its access to Highway 401 stimulated the expansion of subdivisions in another. Courtesy, K-W Record Photograph Negative Collection, University of Waterloo Library

Facing page, bottom: The presence of Waterloo's two universities changed the face of the city and redirected development toward the two contiguous campuses. Courtesy, University of Waterloo Archives

Below: The effects of rapid growth were not always beneficial. As Waterloo grew, the need for more housing drastically changed the urban landscape. Gone were the days when aesthetics, not utility, were a major consideration of architects and planners. Courtesy, K-W Record Photograph Negative Collection, University of Waterloo Library

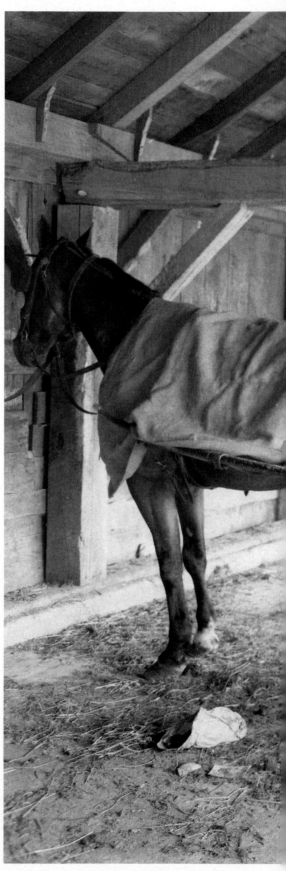

Above: Oktoberfest brings hundreds of thousands of visitors to celebrate Canada's great "Bavarian Festival." In 1983 Prime Minister Brian Mulroney and his wife, Mila, attended Oktoberfest. They were watched over carefully by Waterloo's Member of Parliament, Walter McLean. Courtesy, K-W Record Photograph Negative Collection, University of Waterloo Library

Right: When Waterloo's new City Centre was opened in 1988, a horse stall was built in an adjacent parking lot to replace this privately owned structure that had been removed during the construction. Courtesy, K-W Record Photograph Negative Collection, University of Waterloo Library

markedly since the end of World War II. Like Waterloo these new "post-industrial cities" have attempted to retain a traditional city centre, and they are generally surrounded by suburbs, some intervening farms, open space areas, and neighbouring villages. In many ways Waterloo conforms to this image. Every day people come in from the rural areas for shopping and recreational activities. Their presence is dramatically symbolized by the horse shed adjacent to Waterloo's new City Centre. Many others also travel to the surrounding countryside for a less hectic lifestyle or for dinner at one of the small pubs and hotels scattered across the rural area proclaiming their country ambience. Were he to return to the site of his Union Mills, Abraham Erb (one suspects) would have a great deal of sympathy for the plight of Waterloo's civic leaders. The tension between growth and stability was as troubling for his generation as it is for this, and the forces that had led Erb and his family to leave their homes and friends in Pennsylvania and set out for Waterloo township were not so different. He might well have been amused by the idea of a "rural renaissance" in Waterloo, espousing the values that he knew too well, for despite Waterloo's reputation as a centre for high technology, the enduring presence of the rural countryside seems entirely in harmony with its past and offers the assurance of a promising future.

7

Partners in Progress

Waterloo, eight years into its second century and unofficially decades older, is upscale, uptown, and upbeat. Similarly, the businesses, industries, and institutions depicted on the following pages are representative of family enterprises founded in the early nineteenth century alongside high-technology ventures less than 10 years off the drawing board.

A strong element of stability driven by vision, hard work, and ambition will be noted in this Partners in Progress section. In the case of some retail, commercial, and manufacturing entities, which claim several generations of pioneering merchant or factory background in the area, steady progress is a way of life. For others, who have chosen Waterloo as an ideal setting for innovative consumer and industrial operations, the environment is a decided asset.

A brief overview of the economic base points to a key factor in this measured growth—diversification. Not only is Waterloo the head-office site of six Canadian insurance companies (a story in itself, dating to the 1860s), it also accommodates two major universities: Wilfred Laurier and the University of Waterloo. Uptown Waterloo, as the central business section is known, offers a

superb small-city mall surrounded by specialty shops, restaurants, hotels, and heritage attractions developed from disparate backgrounds of Mennonite settlement to beer-making expertise.

The rise of a high-technology sector in the north-end industrial parks simply adds another dimension to traditional manufacturing and service components. Many of the new corporations have

During the Second World War, 131 women from Waterloo and Kitchener joined the armed forces. At the same time, 2,536 women from the twin cities entered the work force, placing them in the vanguard of a movement that caused a social revolution in Canada. Courtesy, National Archives of Canada

access to and support the educational community. In recognition of benefits to the local economy, Waterloo has joined forces Kitchener, Guelph, and Cambridge to form a marketing front under the banner of Canada's Technology Triangle.

An abundance of recreational facilities completes the quality of life scenario enjoyed by these Partners in Progress organizations, which have chosen to participate in this literary work. Spacious parks, well-kept athletic fields, ski and hiking trails, and programs for all seasons contribute to the rise of contemporary Waterloo.

From this background emerges an urban profile of surpassing excellence, from a vibrant downtown core to an ever-changing skyline.

THE WATERLOO CHAMBER OF COMMERCE

To fittingly commemorate its centennial, the Waterloo Chamber of Commerce is preserving an impressive record of achievement while advancing on new frontiers as a positive voice for the business community.

The 770-member organization has tracked a diverse route in the advocacy of economic, educational, and civic amenities since incorporation as the Waterloo Board of Trade on April 22, 1890. Cornerstones of free enterprise, voluntary teamwork, and partnership with the city flourish today in keeping with solid foundations laid in the early years.

The Waterloo Board of Trade was organized mainly through the efforts of Julius H. Roos, a leading citizen of the day, with the support of Mayor George Moore. A public meeting in the town hall on March 11, 1890, led to formal organization and election of the following officers on May 2, 1890: Christian Kumpf, president; William Snider, vice-president; Julius Roos, secretary/treasurer; and directors R.Y. Fish, Mayor Moore, P.M. Sims, Simeon Snyder, W.H. Riddell, H.J. Grassett, George Wagnast, John Shuh, T.E. Bowman, A.G. Babbick, Richard Roschman, and J.M. Scully.

To the credit of that early alliance

Christian Kumpf, the first chairman of the Waterloo Chamber of Commerce, which, at the time, was known as the Waterloo Board of Trade. Photo circa 1890

of public-spirited citizens, such valued assets as the beautifully appointed Waterloo Park stand, a full century later, in testimony to their vision. The ensuing years have seen the board of trade later renamed the Waterloo Chamber of Commerce.

It played an integral role in the 1902 campaign for hydro-electric

power, promoted new industry, improved post office accommodation, and bettered transportation facilities.

Not the least of the board's contributions was its influence in securing a Lutheran theological seminary for the town in 1911. The board, with Charles J. Mueller as president, arranged for the town to donate five acres of land and for the purchase of the former Merner residence on Albert Street to house the five-member faculty and four students. This was the beginning of Waterloo College (subsequently Wilfrid Laurier University) and the start of a long-running chamber of commerce interest in widening the local educational establishment.

The chamber also provided an initiative for city status with a resolution in June 1946, but the final decision was a resounding 2,673 to 163 "yes" vote by the citizens on December 6, 1946. As a result, the Ontario Legislature enacted the City of Waterloo Act conferring separate identity and detachment from the County of Waterloo, effective in 1948.

For many years until the early 1980s, the chamber performed as an industrial commission for the city. Then, with the advent of a permanent municipal development committee, chamber focus shifted to meeting the needs of existing firms. Throughout its history, the chamber has been an active proponent of improvement to the downtown core. Tourist promotion has been a major concern, especially over the past few

Waterloo's first schoolhouse was built in 1820. After 1842 it was moved to King Street and became known as K-W Collegiate. It was then converted to a residence and later moved to Waterloo Park.

The cedar arches of the Saengerfest Celebrations held along King Street North are seen here circa 1880. Today the festival is called Sounds of Summer.

decades, as attractions have proliferated in the city and surrounding area. From its office at Bridgeport and King, the chamber provides information and hospitality to visitors to Waterloo on behalf of the city.

Recently the chamber has begun to develop a higher promotional profile for the area by promoting Canada's Technology Triangle in collaboration with surrounding chambers of commerce. As well, the Waterloo Chamber of Commerce has introduced a new logo, backed by the slogan "For Your Business Future," as an image-enhancing measure. All of this activity, plus the mainstream of chamber programs, is communicated to the membership by a monthly newsletter.

An active contingent of 150 volunteers lends ongoing support to Waterloo Chamber of Commerce projects. An active board of directors contribute to policy making, direction setting, and in-depth discussion on issues that face the business community.

Supporting volunteer activities, ensuring member needs are met on a day-to-day basis, and providing

continuity of programs and services, the staff work alongside of the volunteers to make a strong chamber.

The Waterloo Chamber of Com-

merce has published this illustrated history of the city in celebration of its 100 years of progress. This is one of the many projects planned in 1990 to commemorate past achievements and mark the beginning of a new era. Celebrating progress since 1890, the centennial theme is reflected throughout the accomplishments of the past, and the future promises continued strength in the organization's growth.

This busker entertained shoppers in Uptown Waterloo in September 1989, giving them a sneak preview of the Waterloo Buskers Festival to be held in August 1990.

LATEM GROUP

A family-founded and -operated metal-finishing specialist is servicing a large roster of consumer-based industries from its headquarters facility in Waterloo.

The Latem Group, at 475 Conestogo Road, with complementary divisions in London, Ontario, represents several plateaus of dramatic growth from a single trophy shop founded by James Nother, Sr., more than two decades ago.

Presently, the niche pursued by Nother from a basic knowledge of metal surfacing and treatment flourishes under the direction of his children who supervise 100 personnel in an increasingly high-tech environment. At Waterloo, son Liam, president of Latem Industries Waterloo, handles overall responsibilities as well as supervising a local staff of 30 highly skilled, dedicated people who are typical of a company-wide attitude.

The Latem Group industrial complex traces to a 1955 decision by the founder and his wife, Mary, to emigrate from Dublin, Ireland, to London. Employment with the CNR, and later Kellogg's, was followed by the opening in 1968 of a small downtown trophy store in the Forest City. James Nother, Sr., moved the business into a 10,000-square-foot building on Horton Street in 1972, then doubled the area in 1978 to include manufacturing. Son James Jr. is currently president of the trophy enterprise at the same location.

In the meantime, the cornerstones of the metal-finishing business were laid at plants on Kitchener Avenue in London in 1977 and on Webster Road in Kitchener the following year. The latter facility was transferred to Bridgeport Road for the year 1980 and subsequently to the present site, where it has quadrupled in size to 24,000 square feet.

The London holdings have expanded impressively, too, with the development of Latem London Inc. and Latem Custom Coating from limited bases in the mid-1980s to joint occupancy of a 50,000-square-foot structure on Sovereign Road. General managers are daughter Michelle, of Latem London Inc., and son Paul, general manager of Latem Custom Coating, who work in con-

The Latem Group, a metal-finishing specialist, services a large roster of consumer-based industries from its headquarters facility in Waterloo.

junction with their father in the London division.

Expertise in deburring, polishing, powder painting, die-chromating —essentially laundering metal components—is the principal strength of the company. Metal stampers and die-casters in the automotive, appliance, and sporting goods sectors comprise the mainstream of custom orders, but the firm also fine tunes parts for steel, computer, and some plastics applications. In addition, the Latem Group makes polishing compounds, washes, rustproofing materials, and stripping agents at Waterloo, supplying these products.

The crowning touch to its know-how, state-of-the-art equipment, and depth of experience is Latem's versatility and fast turnaround in keeping with principles instilled from inception by James Nother, Sr.

James Nother, Sr. (seated), founder, with Liam Nother, president of Latem Industries.

BERESFORD BOX COMPANY LIMITED

A quarter-century of creative folding-carton making continues to advance on new frontiers of technology and skill in the modern manufacturing facility of a leading Waterloo industry.

Beresford Box Company Limited represents the vision of its founder, the late Jack F. Beresford, a former banker turned businessman, who built the firm from a handful of employees and a single offset press. From its inception on September 30, 1964, to his untimely death in 1985, he spearheaded expansions in plant, equipment, and market. Beresford would have applauded the major relocation in 1986 to 607 Kumpf Drive and the equipment acquisitions that have accompanied it.

The niche for a new player in the folding carton field was originally pursued by Jack Beresford in a failed attempt to buy a division of Toronto-based Campell Containers. With two associates, who have long since left the business, he then launched the present company in the basement of an industrial building at 12 Laurel Street (now Bridgeport Road). From

The modern plant of Beresford Box Company Limited on Kumpf Drive houses total design, printing, die-cutting, and finishing operations for quality folding cartons.

less than 10,000 square feet that was plagued by recurrent flooding, Beresford Box moved to a former shirt factory at 210 Regina Street North. There it expanded to 40,000 square feet by 1979, with its capability greatly enhanced by multicolor lithographic presses and ancillary die-making and pre-press installations.

Today some 150 skilled personnel are engaged in the various functions of administration, preparation, production, and shipping amid the hum of four-, five-, and seven-color printing presses, as well as cutting, creasing, gluing, and window-patching machinery on 83,000 square feet of closely co-ordinated assembly in north-end Waterloo. A $1.75-million Planeta press, acquired upon the opening of the new plant, was topped in 1988 by the allocation of $3 million for a 6.5-color Heidleberg Speedmaster C.D., designed specifically for boxboard; a Bobst SP 102 CE Diecutter; and a computer-assisted system for carton design.

Such infusions of capital are consistent with the firm's broader product line, which sees Beresford Box serving more types of industries with a wider range of colors and coatings. Refinements to the mainstream carton output, augmented by innovations such as blister cards, contribute to current annual sales

Founder Jack F. Beresford built a leading Waterloo industry over two decades of aggressive management.

exceeding $14 million. In the long run the founding principles of quality product, excellent service, and competitive prices have cultivated a large, diverse clientele, including local food processors such as Schneider and Dare.

Ownership is vested in the second generation of the Beresford family: Greg, of Elmira; Jill, Toronto; Sandra, Guelph; and Chris, Elora. All have been involved in the business. Key management positions are held by Dennis Boehmer, general manager; Jeff Fisher, plant manager; and Wayne Goldie, sales manager.

LA-Z-BOY CANADA LIMITED

A leading Waterloo area industry of 60 years' standing is flourishing and expanding again on the crest of rising demand for high-quality home furnishings. La-Z-Boy Canada Limited has survived the trauma of depression, a world war, and recession to regain momentum as the largest motion chair manufacturer in this country.

Today the company is in full flight, employing more than 500 city residents at its sprawling, and only, Canadian facility at 55 Columbia Street East near Weber. More than 600 units, principally the world-renowned La-Z-Boy reclining chairs, are shipped daily to retail clients from coast to coast.

The original Canadian connection was forged in 1929, shortly after the founding of the La-Z-Boy Chair Company in Monroe, Michigan. Develop-

This is the original 1929 agreement for Deluxe Upholstering Company Limited to manufacture La-Z-Boy chairs in Canada.

ers of the unique chair were cousins Edward Knabusch and Edwin Shoemaker, whose enterprise has proliferated to a current complement of 19 manufacturing plants in the United States, plus a headquarters building in Monroe and licensees worldwide. The Waterloo operation stands alone as the parent's only subsidiary outside of the United States.

Their quest for a Canadian manufacturer led Knabusch and Shoemaker to an agreement with Deluxe Upholstering Company Limited in Kitchener. Deluxe was a small firm that had just been launched by Schreiter's Furniture, and it was located on the corner of Charles and Gaukel streets until moving to King Street a few years later.

Like many businesses of that era, Deluxe verged on bankruptcy in the early 1930s, leading to a takeover by employees Helen Wagner, Ralph Connor, and Bill Sterne. Wagner later joined in buying out Sterne; she then assumed full ownership upon Connor's death. For most of her proprietorship, the company was managed by "Soapy" Soanes as president, with Ed Manser as plant manager and Ralph Stauffer as superintendent. An acquisition in 1938 was Canada Furniture Manufacturers Limited.

The outbreak of World War II saw an exodus of Deluxe employees into the armed forces, while the balance engaged in making a transition to war production. Then as now their craftsmanship and versatility

The old King Street site of Deluxe Upholstering Company Limited.

came into play as they turned out camera cases, escape hatches, and sections for the famed Mosquito bomber. One of the most effective Allied airplanes, the prolific Mosquito outperformed most enemy aircraft.

As the Waterloo industry returned to peacetime output, the mainstay La-Z-Boy product was soon supplemented by boat seats, beauty salon chairs, and Niagara Massage chairs en route to the growth that by 1961 resulted in the firm surpassing its American counterpart in per capita sales. The latter continued to prosper, despite having to continually protect valued patents from pretenders. In 1961 the U.S. division opened up a huge market with a

Oct. 16th, 1929.

The Floral City Furniture Co. Inc.,
Monroe, Mich.

Dear Sirs,

Arrangements have today been made between Mr. E.M. Knabusch, representing your company, and Mr. Armand Schreiter, representing The DeLuxe Upholstering Co. Ltd., that a contract will be drawn up forthwith between the above mentioned companies covering the exclusive sale and manufacture of the La-Z-Boy chair, in Canada.

The following items to be incorporated in said contract.

Royalty of $2.00 per chair for first ten thousand sold.
Royalty of $1.50 per chair on all sales over ten thousand.
Complete hardware mechanical units purchaseable at $1.25 per unit.
Additional hardware purchaseable at cost as required.
Royalties payable quarterly.
In case of suit by the Floral City Furniture Co., against any infringement on patent, compensation is payable to the DeLuxe Upholstering Co. Ltd., in proportion to damages collected.
Floral City Furniture Co. to prosecute all infringements in Canada at their own cost.

The Floral City Furniture Co., to supply the following at once.

Photographs of the La-Z-Boy chairs, #480 and #99 in colors.
One frame #480 KD new hardware.
One chair #480 new hardware, in muslin.
One frame #99 KD new hardware.
Spring construction for seat and backs for chair #99.
Copy of patent.
The Floral City Furniture Co. to notify the Kroehler Mfg. Co. Ltd., Stratford, Ont. to forward to the DeLuxe Upholstering Co. Ltd., Kitchener, Ont. the model and setup frame now in their possession.

It is agreed that the above contract and other details will be attended to by Mr. E.M. Knabusch immediately upon his return to Monroe, Mich.

THE FLORAL CITY FURNITURE CO. INC.   THE DELUXE UPHOLSTERING CO. LTD.
per   per
Edward M. Knabusch   A. Schreiter.

and receiving increased the total facility to 300,000 square feet.

Over the years the fortunes of La-Z-Boy Canada Limited have improved, not only from skill and dedication on the shop floor, but also from executive leadership. Longtime president Soanes was succeeded in 1976 by Dave Eby, with Ab Geng as plant manager. Don Playford took over in 1983 upon Eby's retirement. Playford retired in April 1986, when he was replaced by Crandell Murray, who is vice-president and general manager. Iain Douglas, former owner of Baetz Furniture in Kitchener, is vice-president/sales and marketing, and Don Schott, formerly with Leigh Instruments, is plant superintendent. Exemplifying the community awareness of company personnel, Murray serves as vice-chairman of the board of governors of Lutherwood, a non-profit agency helping children and families in distress.

new mechanism—the footrest attached to the chair.

In 1968 Deluxe was purchased by the prominent Canadian brewer Molson Companies Limited as a running mate for the Molson-owned Vilas Furniture of Cowansville, Quebec. Coincidentally, Globe Furniture on Canbar Street in Waterloo went bankrupt that year, whereupon the La-Z-Boy operation was moved in, renovations made, and manufacturing commenced under plant manager Ted Douglass. Subsequently a vacant Molson plant in Elmira was utilized to assemble wood parts cut in Quebec and supply the finished units to Waterloo. An addition to the

A showcase of today's popular styles of chairs, sofas, and accessories.

Waterloo plant in 1978 resulted in relocation of the woodroom and frame assembly to the city, where all of the La-Z-Boy facilities in Canada were then consolidated.

The La-Z-Boy Chair Company purchased Deluxe Upholstering Canada Limited from Molson Companies in 1979 in a period of rising national sales. The firm rode out the recession of 1981-1982 to emerge in an improved economy with plans afoot for a new building. On January 2, 1985, La-Z-Boy Canada moved to its present site, occupying the former home of Leigh Instruments and Marsland Engineering. At that time the building was completely renovated, the office was moved from the Weber to the Columbia Street side, and departments were added for metal fabricating, wood finishing, and foam cutting. An up-to-date heating and energy conserving system allowed the company to heat by burning its own scrap wood.

The move to Columbia Street, which was followed by the firm attaining $40 million in annual sales while adding sofas and sleepers to the product line, entailed a second extension in 1989. A 50,000-square-foot addition for storage, shipping,

Crandell Murray cuts the ribbon to officially open the latest addition to the Waterloo plant, still the only La-Z-Boy Chair Company subsidiary outside the United States. Helping to celebrate the occasion are (from left) Ben Clayfield, assistant superintendent; Iain Douglas, vice-president/sales and marketing; Crandell Murray, vice-president/general manager; John Spier, personnel manager; Terry Weber, shipping supervisor; and Don Schott, plant superintendent.

J.L. CORTES ARCHITECT CORPORATION

Jorge and Maria Cortes

A career and family relocation undertaken in the aftermath of the Cuban Revolution comprises a fascinating foreword to the annals of an established Waterloo architectural practice.

Jorge and Maria Cortes were students aligned with the movement that overthrew the Batista dictatorship prior to their graduations as architects from the University of Havana in 1965. Jorge became the first architect in charge of rebuilding Levisa, a city in Oriente Province flattened by bombing. He was also assigned to the design and construction of several major industries in Oriente, which was the birthplace of the revolution.

Their professional and political backgrounds created formidable obstacles to their growing desire to leave Cuba. However, in 1970 the couple and three small children were able to take up residence in Spain. Fluent in English, Jorge found immediate employment with American development companies on such projects as the Bacardi plant in Malaga, Kemsearch Corporation in Madrid, La Manga International Golf Club on the Mediterranean, and housing for low-income families in Barcelona.

Uneasiness over political and social stability in Spain, and a chance meeting with a Canadian booster of the Kitchener-Waterloo region, precipitated a second major move by the Cortes family. They arrived in Canada in September 1971; within 48 hours of the plane's touching down,

Jorge was working as a masonry estimator. Six years in drafting, design-build, and a variety of contracting culminated in a gratifying dual achievement when, in 1977, Jorge and his family became Canadian citizens and Jorge earned a master's degree in Architecture from the University of Toronto.

During a one-year stint as area chief architect for the Canada Mortgage and Housing Corporation, he opened an office at 421 King Street North in Waterloo in October 1978. Seven years ago the firm acquired its present facilities at 222/224 King Street South in Waterloo to accommodate additional clientele and staff. The firm's personnel includes Maria Cortes, who also heads a separate consulting business; son Jorge, who manages construction, site reviews, contracts administration, and computer programming; plus an administrative and technical staff.

The J.L. Cortes Architect Corporation specializes in a full range of residential, commercial, and institutional buildings. Although based in Waterloo, the firm is currently involved in the design and construction of projects in Toronto, Hamilton, London, Peterborough, Owen Sound, and Waterloo County. It is presently completing a $21-million, 200-unit family complex on the former Massey Ferguson properties in downtown Toronto.

The company's office in downtown Waterloo.

CLEMMER INDUSTRIES LIMITED

An historic presence in Waterloo and a distinguished record of achievement enhance the reputation of one of the foremost steel tank manufacturers in North America.

Clemmer Industries Limited, a growing high-tech company with 130 employees, has evolved from a makeshift machine shop in the early part of the century to computer-assisted design and production. Innovative from the beginning, the firm has earned credits for technological advancement in the agricul-

Some of Clemmer Industries early products included mortar boxes, hog feeders, stone boats, snowploughs, feed carts, and cattle back-scratchers (shown here).

tural, industrial, and consumer goods sectors.

The enterprise bears the signature of founder Jonas Clemmer, who opened a service station and mechanical repair service at 12 Herbert Street in 1923. He installed the first electric arc welder, but it remained for younger brother Nathan, who bought the business in 1935, to widen horizons. With the arrival in 1939 of Arnold Meyers (the lone employee then), the firm embarked on machining and metal forming for local industry and agriculture. It made mortar boxes and hog feeders, cattle back-scratchers, stone boats, snowploughs, and feed

carts. Soon their venture's expertise advanced into pressure vessels, silos, iron railings, and mortar mixers.

Meyers, who stayed on to attain partnership in 1950 and ownership in 1958 upon Nathan Clemmer's retirement, recalls dismantling the stables of the old City Hotel livery on King Street, where the Clemmer operation relocated in 1941. As demand for such items as basement oil tanks, boilers, and custom equipment increased, a move to the present site at 446 Albert Street, on 10 acres of the old Clemmer family farm, was carried out in 1959-1960. There, the company flourished with added lines of liquid storage and material vessels, corrugated culvert, highway signs, and a variety of metal fabrications. The original 60-by-80-foot plant was expanded many times over, while the site was extended by the acquisition of 11 acres in 1978. In 1988 a new 96-by-240-foot finishing building was added to the facility.

Upon the arrival of Arnold G. Meyers in 1939, Clemmer Industries Limited began machining and metal forming for local industry and agriculture. Meyers was owner of the company from 1958 to 1988 when it was sold to Meridian Technologies, Inc.

These large metal silos for bulk storage of chemicals, granules, and liquids are part of Clemmer Industries' current line of products.

Under Meyers' direction, the firm pursued a creative course of experimentation, development, automation of manufacturing equipment, and marketing. It invented a nylon die-electric bushing to isolate underground tanks and make them corrosion resistant and recently perfected an emergency vent-and-fill fitting for farm and construction site utility tanks. Earlier Meyers, who is self-taught in engineering, electronics, die making, and a host of trades, assembled one of the early versions of rotary lawn mowers in the Clemmer plant and marketed some 6,000 units under the Lawn King label. His firm was driven out of the mower business by multinational competition, but he takes pride in the current operation of some of those mid-1950s Lawn Kings.

Over the years Clemmer Industries Limited people turned out boilers for high-rise, industrial, and commercial use; assembled a hook-strip system for plush fabric reels; and registered a number of world patents. Corporate objectives centered on quality products and employee incentive and security are being perpetuated by Meridian Technologies Inc., which purchased the company from Meyers in 1988.

ABROYD COMMUNICATIONS LIMITED

The resources of a highly specialized multidisciplined Waterloo engineering/contracting company play an integral role in the ongoing expansion of broadcasting and telecommunications systems in Canada and abroad. ABROYD Communications Limited is one of four major companies in Canada that specializes in the design, supply, and installation of towers and related services and products for an industry that spends up to $40 million per year in Canada and more than $500 million per year internationally.

Since June 1984 ABROYD has worked on more than 200 projects ranging in size from small rooftop mounts to towers in excess of 1,000 feet including many modifications to existing structures. ABROYD's highest profile product continues to be its line of aesthetically pleasing, multitapered self-supporting towers developed for Ontario Hydro's Telecommunications Network; more than 50 of these towers, in heights of up to 450 feet, have been built since 1974.

ABROYD also holds Canadian manufacturing and distribution rights for two specialty products relating to lightning prevention and special "ultra-low resistance to ground" grounding systems—namely, the LEC Lightning Dissipation Array® and Chem-Rod® systems.

ABROYD's present 20-member staff, led by president Ab Nightingale and vice-president John Verlis, both professional engineers with a combined work history of more than 55 years in this field, include Ron Saunders, marketing and sales; Ron Har-

John Verlis (left) and Ab Nightingale stand beside a scale model of a special 450-foot self-supporting tower developed for Ontario Hydro. Photos of other installations are in the background. Also shown is a display sample of a Chem-Rod® sitting on the table next to the tower model.

rington, engineering; Charles O'Connor, Terry Morris, and Evan Dahl, construction; and Win Nightingale, accounting.

Utilizing the latest in business, engineering, and CAD programs, ABROYD makes the most of computer technology, including special programs for the design of guyed and self-supporting towers. This results in complete in-house capabilities for the design and building of its products.

Under the direction of John Verlis, ABROYD's installation crews, supervised by foremen with up to 30 years' experience and trained for the unique high-rigging and other special installation techniques required in this industry, install the towers and systems. To do this efficiently and professionally, ABROYD's crews use a combination of standard steel erection equipment, such as cranes and

chain hoists, and special equipment, built primarily for tower and similar construction, such as gin poles, special winches, and special rigging.

In early 1990 ABROYD will be moving out of its leased premises at 614 Colby Drive in Waterloo to its newly acquired 14,000-square-foot plant just down the road at 662 Colby Drive.

Although a relatively new company, ABROYD's history in the Kitchener-Waterloo area can be traced back to 1972, when it was established as a division of Dahmer Steel of Kitchener. In June 1984 ABROYD's principals, as key employees, purchased the assets of ABROYD and incorporated the company as ABROYD Communications Limited.

ABROYD contributes significantly to the Kitchener-Waterloo region, where it subcontracts much of its steel fabrication and purchases many finished goods and services from local manufacturers and suppliers. ABROYD Communications Limited's principals are also engaged in many community-oriented activities, including the Waterloo Chamber of Commerce, KWG Training Advisory Council, and various community associations.

Ab Nightingale, president (right), and John Verlis, vice-president, at ABROYD Communications Limited's new plant at 662 Colby Drive, Waterloo. Some tower sections are shown along the side of the building.

H&O CENTERLESS GRINDING

Capability, versatility, and a tradition of excellence form the cornerstones of a Waterloo company specializing in the custom production of precision metal parts.

H&O Centerless Grinding, at 45 Bathurst Street, represents the fulfilment of a career dream for co-founder and president Earl Hillier, who has guided the fortunes of the firm from a makeshift machine shop to state-of-the-art facilities. Today his sons and grandsons are correlating the latest advancements in equip-

The assembly of skilled technicians and machinists, combined with adherence to exacting standards, led to a growing demand for hardened and unhardened metal components. A company-built plant of 19,800 square feet on 2.7 acres was occupied at 809 Victoria Street North in 1956. Three years later Herbert Odds, who had no heirs, sold his shares to Earl Hillier to give the latter 100-percent ownership. Odds continued with the firm on a reduced scale until retiring in 1967.

Widening expertise and horizons precipitated occupancy of the present facility, a 28,000-square-foot structure on a 3.7-acre site in the Waterloo Industrial Park in 1986. There the H&O operation, which had progressed from a modest turnover of

The original H&O Centerless Grinding facility at 71 Mill Street, Waterloo.

$55,000 in its inaugural year to $2.5 million in 1988, functions in a climate-controlled environment. Computerization is well advanced in the administrative and manufacturing areas in the interests of quality, efficiency, and on-time delivery.

The president's three sons are the hands-on managers in well-defined roles—Richard as general manager and controller, Bernard as treasurer and production manager, and Terrence as vice-president. The third generation is represented by Rick Hillier, who is phasing in the computer systems, and Randy Hillier, who is assistant shop superintendent in charge of scheduling.

A current objective of H&O Centerless Grinding's management and the 60-member staff calls for penetration of European markets from a predominantly Canadian, and 10-percent U.S., customer base.

H&O's Kitchener branch at 809 Victoria Street.

ment and computerization to turn out components for a diverse clientele of more than 250 industries.

The corporate name derives from Herbert Odd, an ambitious die-maker engaged in ammunition work at Waterloo Manufacturing during World War II. He converted to peacetime output in October 1945, embarking on a mutually arranged pact with Hillier, John Kerfoot, and Ed Chapman, all former CIL associates in prewar Montreal. By 1952 Kerfoot and Chapman were gone, but the enterprise was thriving with 25 employees and expanded quarters at the original 71 Mill Street site.

H&O occupied its present state-of-the-art headquarters in the Waterloo Industrial Park in 1986.

ZEPF TECHNOLOGIES INCORPORATED

A model family corporation built on dedication, daring, and a mastery of innovative production and processes occupies a special niche in the Waterloo corner of Canada's Technology Triangle.

Zepf Technologies Incorporated stands acclaimed by the community, an international clientele, and exponents of computer applications in industry as an exceptional Canadian business success.

The modest-size (50 employees) but widely known company derives from the aspirations of Lawrence Zepf, a Yugoslavian-born mechanic-supervisor with Joseph E. Seagram's Distillery in the city for 28 years. During this time he pioneered the development of change parts to handle new shapes of liquor bottles. Ultimately, his work led to a Waterloo bottling plant to service Seagram's requirements worldwide.

The inception of Zepf Technologies occurred on December 11, 1972, as a partnership with eldest son Paul, a graduate engineer. For five years the venture was located in a small machine shop attached to the Zepf family home on Caroline Street, where the firm excelled in designing quality change parts for the automatic packaging field.

As its reputation spread from the Toronto-St. Catharines axis to national scope, the company doubled in size with space in the Weber-Parkside Industrial Mall in April 1978; within six months two more units were added to a facility that finally utilized 15,000 square feet. Then, in the fall of 1987, the operation moved into a 28,500-square-foot, custom-designed plant at 70 Rankin Street

near King and Northland. On that site, with access to an array of computer-assisted design and manufacturing equipment, advances continue in the areas of technology, creativity, and quick response.

Zepf Technologies today trains its sights on new horizons from a solid foundation as a world-class producer of components and equipment for the automatic bottling and packaged goods industries. Everything that ZTI makes is a one-of-a-kind product within four main categories: changeover parts, timing screws, high-precision cams, and OEM (Original Equipment Manufacture) packaging machines and systems. Customers of distinction such as Procter and Gamble, Lever Brothers, and Corby Distiller add to the stature of the Waterloo enterprise while contribut-

ing to annual sales approaching $4 million.

The underlying assets of ZTI are abundant: an early commitment to CAD/CAM (Computer-Aided Design/Computer-Aided Manufacturing) back in 1978, when it was still

Family-owned Zepf Technologies Incorporated occupies a special niche in the Waterloo corner of Canada's Technology Triangle.

LEFT & OPPOSITE PAGE: A world-class producer of components and equipment for the automatic bottling and packaged goods industries, ZTI committed early to CAD/CAM (Computer-Aided Design/Computer-Aided Manufacturing).

Business Excellence, Small Business Category, in 1989. To date, principal markets are the United States, Canada, Europe, and South America—with 70 percent of sales to export—and approaches have been received from Asia, Africa, and Australia.

As the Zepf organization gears for progress in the 1990s, father Lawrence serves as honorary chairman and his six sons in active roles: Larry Zepf is chief executive officer, while William, Stephen, Frank, James, and Peter Zepf, with their brothers-in-law, Herb Friederich and Yuichi Fukudome, bring managerial and technical expertise to specific facets of the business as certified journeymen and tradesmen in their own right. (The family of Lawrence and Ann Zepf also includes five daughters: Nancy, Joanne, Pauline, Janet, and Helen.)

Company leadership will continue a strong community and educational relationship in the form of lectures by staff at the secondary and university levels, the dissemination of high-tech and export expertise, and the encouragement of skilled worker training. Close ties are maintained with the K-W Industrial Training Committee, the Ontario CAD/CAM Centre, and such institutions as the University of Waterloo as expressions of ZTI's enthusiasm to share formulas for success.

The entire thrust is associated with a five-year plan for gains across the board: a threefold increase in sales, personnel development, enhanced quality and diversity of product, and an overall showcasing of Zepf Technologies Incorporated as a company on the move.

experimental, and subsequently upgrading to an investment exceeding $700,000; adherence to an above-average research and development budget, untouchable even in recessionary times; and a flair for complete problem solving in the packaging line sector. In-house teamwork and hands-on approaches have paid dividends, too, in the form of design and assembly of unique machinery on the shop floor. An average of four new machine concepts per year is maintained in support of the firm's world leadership in high-speed combiner technology.

Along this venturesome route, Zepf Technologies has also carried out extensive software development, built its own six-axis lathe, and won a host of awards for productivity and industrial design. Zepf Technologies won the "Gold" in the Canada Awards for

BAUER INDUSTRIES LIMITED

A distinguished Waterloo corporation with roots deep in the community and the national fabric is advancing into its second century on the same site in the downtown core.

Bauer Industries Limited is a consummate family enterprise, owned and managed since 1888 by founder Aloyes Bauer and his heirs. Their success may be measured by a lasting and high-profile presence in the Canadian automobile industry, international hockey, and civic contribution.

The company's principal manufacturing activity, then and now, parallels the transition to mass vehicular travel in this country. At the outset, Aloyes Bauer operated a carriage business on the 2.5-acre site at King and Allen streets. The ensuing years saw the introduction of upholstering felts for furniture companies and then, at the dawn of the twentieth century, a timely move to long-run prosperity as a major auto parts supplier.

One of the first customers for Bauer floor pads, seating, and padding was another offshoot of the carriage trade, the McLaughlin Motor Car Company, founded in Oshawa in 1907. That association continued with the formation of General Motors of Canada in 1918 (one year after A. Bauer & Co. was incorporated as Bauers Limited) and

Founded at the dawn of the twentieth century, Bauer Industries Limited is still a family enterprise under the guidance of (from left) E.J. Bauer, head of sales; Lisa Bauer, vice-president; Ray Bauer, Sr., chairman of the board; and Ray Bauer, Jr., president.

prevails today. Bauer products—insulators, deadeners, absorbers, and barriers—are found throughout GM vehicles as well as in the door panels, dashboards, and seats from other prominent car makers.

The Waterloo firm has kept pace with technological development, too, switching from the original jute to foam rubber to synthetic materials while spending in excess of $5 million recently on new equipment, additional capacity, and computer-assisted design and manufacturing. In addition to the main plant and head office comprising 180,000 square feet at 187 King Street South, the company has fully occupied a 60,000-square-foot plant built on 17 acres at 518 Dutton Drive in 1966.

As a leading manufacturer of nonwoven fibre padding for applications in the automotive field, Bauer Industries credits the workmanship and loyalty of a staff of 250 for such achievements as a 500-percent

increase in sales since 1972. Its unbroken commitment to quality has also derived from successive presidents: Aloyes' sons Edgar J. Bauer I (1926) and Henry A. Bauer (1955), and grandsons Jerome F. Bauer (1965) and Raymond A.J. Bauer (1972). In 1988 Raymond Edgar Bauer succeeded his father as president of the firm, and in August 1989 he also became the chief executive officer. Interestingly, two brothers of the chairman, Bobby and Father Dave, coached or managed five Canadian Olympic ice hockey teams. Another son, E.J. II, is head of sales, and a daughter, Lisa, is a vice-president in charge of purchasing.

MELLOUL-BLAMEY CONSTRUCTION LIMITED

A partnership blending complementary backgrounds and experience in the construction business has emerged in less than a decade with an impressive record of successful projects across southwestern Ontario.

Melloul-Blamey Construction Limited, with headquarters and strong roots in Waterloo, is a progressive, public tender contractor in the industrial-commercial-institutional (ICI) field. Owners Bernard Melloul and David Blamey, president and vice-president, respectively, who founded the firm in February 1982, manage multimillion-dollar contracts from a modern, company-owned building at 700 Rupert Street.

The partners began their association as students in the Construction Technology program at Conestoga College. After graduating in 1972, they worked together at Monteith-McGrath Construction of Waterloo, strengthening their management skills over a 10-year period.

When their employer ceased operations in Waterloo, the two partners launched their own company in the old B&W Heat Treating plant on Borden Avenue South in Kitchener. After four years the firm moved to its present 15,000-square-foot facility in the Northland Industrial Park. Starting a new company during the early 1980s posed problems, but in the long run conferred on the operation a lean and mean philosophy of lasting value.

Melloul-Blamey's first contract was to renovate a Bell Canada building in Orangeville for $145,000. After that came a succession of educational, hospital, and nursing home contracts, along with a mix of industrial, commercial, and civic work. From 1984 to 1987 the company undertook a number of custom residential projects, but this area of activity is no longer pursued.

More recently Melloul-Blamey has undertaken a number of innova-

The company's craftsmen built the K-W Oktoberfest Heritage Timeteller at King and Caroline streets in Waterloo.

tive projects. Its craftsmen built the K-W Oktoberfest Heritage Timeteller at King and Caroline streets in Waterloo. Recently the new Reuben & Wong restaurants in southern Ontario have been added to the client roster.

As the company has expanded to an area south of Georgian Bay and west of Highway 400, expertise and staff have increased. Currently, a force of 40 administrative and field personnel may be functioning at peak times. An in-house design department responds to a diversity of development, including a current acceleration of Melloul-Blamey's design-build capabilities.

In the 1990s this flourishing local firm is well fitted to enhance a reputation established by its role in landmarks such as Lincoln Heights School; Mary Johnson School; Fine Arts & Dance Facility, University of Waterloo; Shelburne Public School; Waterloo North Hydro; and Sunnyside Home for the Aged.

Melloul-Blamey Construction Limited is a progressive, public tender contractor in the industrial/commercial/institutional fields, which has gained an impressive record of successful projects such as the Belgage Medical Arts Building (shown here).

NCR CANADA LTD

A world leader in the high-speed lanes of cheque processing is building on a significant investment in people, product, and facility at its spacious Waterloo site.

NCR Canada Ltd is an increasingly important division of the parent NCR Corporation, which develops, manufactures, markets, installs, and services business transaction systems for global markets. Specifically, Waterloo is part of NCR's Financial Systems Division, which has responsibility for products such as bank computer processors and teller terminals, automated banking machines, and cheque-processing equipment.

daily commerce.

The company also serves financial institutions with refinements to speed and accuracy in the handling of documents with innovative engineering and design. The research and development function at 580 Weber Street North is one of the largest such facilities in Canada, engaging more than half of the staff in improvements to current products and development of new technologies. Waterloo also affords a close working relationship with the nearby university community as well as proximity to airports for an export volume serving some 100 countries. More than 95 percent of local output is shipped to such countries as the United States, the United Kingdom, Australia, and France.

The whole thrust of the firm's presence in Canada since 1902, and in the city since 1973, is consistent with NCR's long-standing mission: to Create Value for our Stakeholders. Within this sphere of concern are

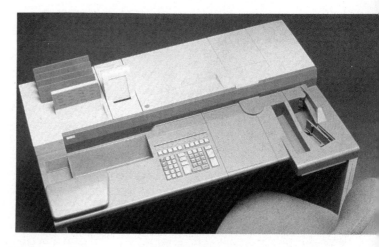

NCR Waterloo's newest product, recently released in September 1989, is this single-pocket proof and encode equipment. It is also geared to the worldwide financial/banking industry, especially the U.S. market and specifically targets large, regional offices and branches.

areas of customer satisfaction, supplier partnership, shareholder return, employee encouragement, and corporate citizenship. The latter objective has been accelerated in recent years with emphasis on employer responsibility and participation in the community. In 1987 NCR Canada Ltd was the recipient of the Employer of the Year Award from the City of Waterloo for hiring handicapped people. In 1988 and 1989 it was a repeat nominee, reflecting interaction with the March of Dimes, Kitchener-Waterloo Rehabilitation

Geared for lower-volume cheque/item processing, this in-branch, proof and encode equipment specifically targets European and Canadian banking environments. It is a modular design that is fully upgradable to an on-line proof system.

An original proof machine manufactured by National Cash Register, which carved a niche for the company in the financial/banking industry that NCR Canada Ltd would later capitalize on.

In all, NCR Waterloo stands as the world's foremost manufacturer of proof and encode equipment. The operation, employing 600 highly trained personnel and occupying nearly 300,000 square feet, indirectly touches the lives of millions of people who write the cheques, credit card vouchers, sales slips, and payment remittances flowing with the tide of

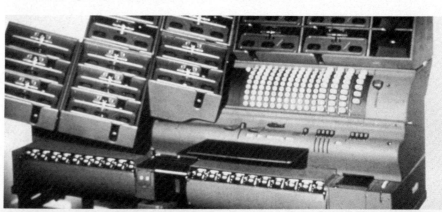

The NCR Waterloo facility at 580 Weber Street North—a popular photo subject for international customers who are from "warmer climates."

Centre, and the Waterloo Board of Education to integrate varying numbers of handicapped workers each year.

Through the years the company has been a substantial contributor to the United Way, a proponent of Junior Achievement through the Waterloo Chamber of Commerce, and a supporter of the University of Waterloo (where it endows a research chair), Sir Wilfred Laurier University, and Conestoga College. A new and successful program was the

One of NCR Waterloo's most successful products to date, multipocket proof and encode equipment for the item/cheque-processing industry is geared to the worldwide financial/banking industry. It is designed, developed, and manufactured in NCR Waterloo.

sponsorship of the invitational Slo-Pitch tournament in aid of the Waterloo branch of the Canadian Diabetes Foundation. This venture raised $12,400 in 1989 (up from $4,400 in 1988), when 32 teams and 400 people competed under the convenorship of 100 NCR volunteers.

Clearly, the NCR profile in Waterloo has widened measurably from the 70,000-square-foot plant and staff of 14 established 17 years ago. Successive additions have quadrupled the engineering, administrative, and manufacturing capacity presently within the purview of general man-

ager Dr. William Tait. Yet the 40-acre expanse offers abundant property for future expansion if the long-range perception of the company is further vindicated.

On a national plane, too, NCR Corporation has made an impact beyond leadership as an outstanding Waterloo enterprise of stature as a customer of more than 75 Canadian suppliers, of which many are located in the Waterloo region. Its product range—from small-volume counter-top units to sophisticated work stations handling tens of thousands of cheques per day—has advanced dramatically from the first imported wood cabinet cash register bought by a Toronto merchant in 1885. That item preceded by 17 years the initial one-room NCR shop in Toronto, and by well over a century the current Canadian complement of 2,400 people and 80 sales and service facilities from coast to coast.

Its strengths of dedication and commitment to excellence, and to innovation and customer satisfaction, point to an exciting and prosperous future for NCR Canada Ltd.

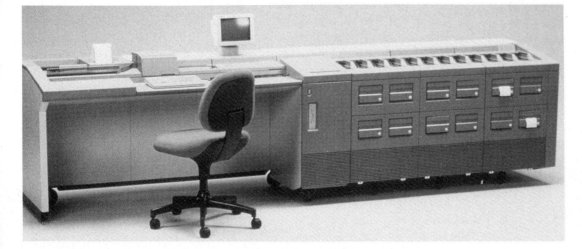

MARSLAND CENTRE LIMITED

Marsland Centre Limited is an investment property development and holding company. It is owned and operated by the third and fourth generations of the Marsland family, who settled in the area early in the century. Most of its commercial properties, comprising office and industrial buildings and luxury racquet sports clubs, are located in Waterloo.

From his 13th-floor suite in the prestigious Marsland Centre, Larry Marsland commands a view of the city and regional development that was largely orchestrated in municipal government departments located in his highrise building at Albert and

The Marsland Centre in uptown Waterloo.

Erb streets.

Just across the Kitchener skyline is the Freeport Health Care Village, which opened in 1989. It is a $46.5-million chronic-care hospital that Marsland invested a great deal of effort in helping to create.

The family business began in the 1920s, when British-born Stanley Marsland opened a radio service business called Marsland Radio.

This small Kitchener firm became Marsland Engineering Limited, and 40 years later, at its zenith, the company's 300,000-square-foot plant on Weber Street North and Columbia employed 1,400 people as Waterloo's largest industry.

During an illustrious career, Stanley Marsland advised four federal governments, served two terms as a director of the Royal Canadian Mint, and earned honors for exports and job creation. After selling his business to Leigh Instruments in 1969, he built the Marsland Centre as a retirement project at the location of the former city hall building. Marsland retired

Marsland Centre Limited built Northfield Racquet Club in 1978 to offer the first local facility for squash, racquetball, and tennis in a luxurious indoor setting.

in 1974 and moved to Bermuda. He died in 1988.

Ownership of the Marsland Centre passed in 1972 to his son, Larry, who continues as president with his wife, Margaret, as vice-president. In the course of developing and leasing commercial space in the region, the company built Northfield Racquet Club on Northfield Drive in 1978 to offer the first local facility for squash, racquetball, and tennis in a luxury, indoor setting.

The Northfield Doon club on New Dundee Road near Highway 401 was added in 1984 as a natural acquisition for the company's expertise. With Brad Marsland, an M.B.A. graduate of the University of Toronto, in charge, the combined clubs accommodate more than 3,000 members for racquet play, fitness, swimming, and social functions.

Just as the engineering business and building ventures were progressively managed, current holdings are under hands-on administration and constant improvement in keeping with the Marsland Centre Limited policy of developing and leasing only first-class properties.

WATERLOO REGIONAL CREDIT UNION

The original St. Louis Parish Credit Union entrances on George Street (LEFT) and King Street (RIGHT).

From modest beginnings in 1947, the Waterloo Regional Credit Union has developed into the largest credit union in the area with a clientele exceeding 14,000.

The handful of volunteers, who drew inspiration from founder Father Cornelius Mellen, C.R., of St. Jerome's College, has matured from identity as a part of St. Louis Parish to a multibranch commercial institution of great significance to the community.

Its 43-year rise to prominence has never wavered, however, from basic principles of sensitivity to members' needs. Encouragement of thrift and favorable loan rates were extended to the 440 first-year enrollees, just as some $46 million in assets are administered today in keeping with the credit union's mission statement, which is "to be a co-operative organization within the Region of Waterloo, dedicated to the provision of full financial and ancillary services for the social and economic benefit of all persons within the region and their families. . . to the broadest extent possible, extend our range of financial and ancillary services so that all

present and potential members within our bond of association will consider our credit union as the preferred and financially sound alternative to all other financial institutions."

The original St. Louis Parish Credit Union, chartered on December 4, 1947, grew swiftly through the 1950s to require infusions of staff, office equipment, and eventually the property at 168 King Street South, where the head office and the large Waterloo branch has been maintained since 1966. That year also saw the hiring of a full-time manager, Frank Karley, and the first one million dollars of recorded assets.

As a complete line of savings,

loan, and personal services was developed for all residents in Kitchener and Waterloo, the name was changed to Twin City Community Credit Union in 1970. Three years later an east-end Kitchener branch raised the profile another level, as did expansion of the Waterloo facility in June 1975. A third branch, in Cambridge, completed the network operating under the present name, which was adopted on December 3, 1979.

Although membership has increased dramatically since that tentative birth in the parish church basement, the spirit of sharing and helping each other prevails today in the Waterloo Regional Credit Union. Its future is positive, too, according to a five-year plan forecasting a strong performance with assets of more than $81 million by the end of 1994.

Entrance from the parking lot at 168 King Street South prior to the 1975 addition.

THE MUTUAL GROUP

The signature of one of Canada's largest—and perennially pacesetting—life insurance companies reaches from atop the skyline of Waterloo to the outports of Newfoundland and the shores of the Pacific.

Newly identified as The Mutual Group, this fully diversified financial-services organization has evolved from more than 100 years of solid growth as The Mutual Life Assurance Company of Canada to national stature as an employer, insurer, adviser, and investor. Counting early beginnings in the city and southern Ontario, The Mutual Group is well advanced into a second century of corporate progress.

A pillar of the high profile and broadly based Waterloo insurance industry, The Mutual Group enjoys distinction as the second-oldest Canadian life insurance entity, as well as current ranking in the upper echelon of its North American contemporaries. From the first policy issued to James W. Dodds of Waterloo on March 1, 1870, enrolment has swelled to more than 700,000 policyholders, while assets under administration now exceed $15 billion.

In scope of product and service, the modern-day version of Mutual Life of Canada is far expanded from

the original concept of a truly Canadian mutual insurance company put together in rented downtown offices 122 years ago. The Mutual Group includes 12 Canadian and four U.S. companies with expertise in every corner of the financial world from savings, annuities and pensions, GICs, RRSPs, and investment funds to mortgages, real estate, corporate lending, financial planning, health benefits, trust services, oil and gas, and more. This is all in addition to mainstream life insurance coverage.

From the 19th floor of The Mutual Group's imposing tower—the eighth and most impressive addition since occupancy of the head office site in 1912—a panoramic view of a bustling urban city unfolds where a tiny village and farmland existed at the inauguration of the company. Archives affirm the incorporation of the original Ontario Mutual Life Assurance Company by a special act of the Ontario Legislature on December 19, 1868, with the following four Waterloo residents as provisional directors: Isaac E. Bowman, company president from 1869 to 1897; Moses Springer, secretary; Cyrus M. Taylor, treasurer; and Dr. J.W. Walden, medical director.

All of these men were active in the community, either in politics or business. Taylor had founded The Waterloo County Mutual Fire Insurance

Jacob Winkler was one of the company's first clerical employees. An accountant, this picture was taken in 1913 on Winkler's last day at work, the 37th year to the day after he first joined the firm. He was 69 years old.

Company in 1863, while Springer contributed energy and experience as a teacher, publisher, merchant, and village reeve.

It was the aggressive Springer who led the fledgling firm to early success. By mid-1869 he had ranged as far as Seaforth and Newmarket to secure local agents in the quest for 500 charter subscribers. From Springer's office at 34 King Street North, the firm re-located to rented space downtown in the Devitt Block where it pursued business practices enunciated by Bowman toward judicious management, investment, and reserves that have redounded to the benefit of the company through the years.

On April 14, 1880, by then possessing a Dominion charter, Ontario Mutual officially opened new and larger offices in a handsome stone and red-brick building on the corner of what was then known as Waterloo Market Square at Erb and Albert

On-site recreational facilities have been a long-standing tradition at Mutual Life of Canada. This was taken at the company's field day in 1922.

The first building at the company's King and Union streets location was constructed in 1912. This photograph was taken in 1928.

streets. This site, with additions, served the company for more than 30 years and was subsequently utilized by a succession of area insurance organizations.

As life insurance in force topped the $10-million and then $20-million mark, the name was changed to The Mutual Life Assurance Company of Canada on June 14, 1900, to reflect the national arrival of the firm. Little more than a decade would elapse before continued growth would dictate the need for more spacious quarters. Accordingly, seven acres of the present site at King and Union streets were acquired, and a new head office—16,063 square feet and costing $235,000—was built. The head office staff of 38 people (2,100 today) moved in May 1912 into what was one of the most attractive office buildings in the country. When the firm occupied the original building, the general manager was heard to say, "We'll never fill it." How wrong he was.

Rapid expansions in accommodation followed, with additions in 1921 and 1928, by which time the Waterloo staff numbered 255 people. Two years later the total sales force was 1,257 full- and part-time agents nationwide, but depressed economic conditions saw the early 1930s marred by decreases in business, although conservative investment strategy had kept Mutual Life largely out of the stock market.

A third addition in 1939 and a

fourth in 1954 were required to deal with rising annuity, group life, and health insurance demand. Also, a 700-seat auditorium was provided for company and public gatherings in keeping with Mutual's long-standing philosophy of supporting a variety of local charity and arts organizations and other philanthropic activities.

In 1900 Mutual Life of Canada's staff totalled 13. These employees are working at the company's offices, which were then located at Erb and Albert streets in Waterloo.

Embarking on its second 100 years, the firm capped centennial celebrations by unveiling a completely modernized head office and a fifth addition in the spring of 1970. By that time assets aggregated $1.2 billion, insurance in force totalled $6.5 billion, and the Waterloo staff was

approaching 1,000 employees. Staff amenities such as recreational, social, and wellness programs, then as now, continued to command a high priority.

A sixth addition in 1976 and an underground computer centre in 1980 were again outdone, and in a dramatic fashion, by the erection of a 13-storey tower in 1987. The glass, steel, and concrete structure escalated from the older five floors to stand as the tallest commercial building in Kitchener-Waterloo at 300 feet.

Growth and diversification on such a grand scale would astound the founding fathers, but they would subscribe whole-heartedly to the image introduced in 1988. Underlining corporate strength expressed by The Mutual Group are the company symbol, a solid "M" composed of three human profiles, and the slogan, "Facing Tomorrow Together," both perpetuating the bond between the company and its clientele.

KRAMER+GREBE CANADA LTD.

Kramer+Grebe Canada Ltd., a high-technology manufacturer of packaging machines with sales in 70 countries has developed a substantial Canadian base in Waterloo's northern industrial park.

Located at 485 Conestogo Road, the firm was originally incorporated in Canada on November 20, 1974, as an affiliate of the parent company located in Wallau, West Germany. Early in 1975 Hubert Faulhammer left his technician's post at the University of Waterloo's engineering department to set up the venture in 2,500 square feet of leased mall space at 572 Weber Street North in Waterloo.

The assembly area on the shop floor. Each Tiromat is built to customer specifications.

The present location of Kramer+Grebe Canada Ltd. in the Northfield Industrial Park in Waterloo.

Within a year the plant area was doubled, and nine people assembled the initial 12 vacuum packaging machines. At the time approximately 80 percent of the parts were imported from Germany. Today, however, 85 percent of all components are produced locally.

By October 1977 the firm was on the move again. Eleven full-time workers occupy 12,000 square feet of manufacturing and office space in a new building on the company's present site. Expansion has continued to fill out some 15,000 square feet of shop area and 4,000 square feet of office space.

In 1989 Kramer+Grebe was acquired by the Alfa-Laval Group. Alfa-Laval AB is a Swedish-based international high-technology company whose Canadian head office is located in Scarborough, Ontario. This acquisition is a positive opportunity for Kramer+Grebe to enhance its future business potential.

Since 1985 the Waterloo operation has been fine tuning the production of intricate machinery, principally for the medical industry. It now employs a total of 47 workers who produce 60 machines per year.

Kramer+Grebe's success in Waterloo, and throughout the world, is due, in part, to its emphasis on product reliability and efficiency. More specifically, its reputation derives from developing and perfecting the Tiromat 3000—the heart of all packaging lines. Over the years the firm has added feature after feature to improve speed, performance, and flexibility in keeping with a commitment to "The Best in High Tech."

CANADIAN INDUSTRIAL INNOVATION CENTRE

The Innovation Centre helps with the commercialization of technological innovation that creates economic benefits.

The team of professionals at the Innovation Centre has evaluated more than 4,500 innovative new product ideas.

A national institution providing services of proven value to Canadian high-technology companies is phasing in new programs on the threshold of a second decade of assisting inventors, innovators, and entrepreneurs from its headquarters in the city.

The Canadian Industrial Innovation Centre/Waterloo is a not-for-profit, independent corporation with a mandate "to help commercialize technological innovation that creates economic benefits" and has a record from its founding in 1981 of fulfilling that mission on a national scale.

Presently, the 20-member staff, headed by chief executive officer Gordon Cummer, is expanding on the cornerstone inventor's assistance program, and related product and marketing analyses, to meet the needs of small- to medium-size companies. Underpinned by a renewal of federal funding of $4.6 million over five years, the centre is introducing programs of market information, innovation identification, new product opportunities, and strategic business planning. (Government financing is supplemented by centre-earned revenues, principally client fees.)

Historically, the organization has roots on the campus of the University of Waterloo. There, founder Frank Phripp, who later served as the first chief executive officer and continues as a member of the board of directors, launched an assessment service in 1976 for local inventors. As the venture took off, Phripp secured the federal government support necessary to set up the existing, stand-alone facility at 156 Columbia Street West.

In confirmation of Phripp's vision, the Innovation Centre has helped more than 20,000 inventors across the country while assessing the feasibility of more than 5,000 ideas. A broader spectrum of clientele has been targeted over the past two years, particularly in areas of market research, project management, and education. Also planned are special innovation workshops and seminars for inventors, entrepreneurs, and companies.

To amplify and inform the public of all of this activity, the centre publishes a quarterly newsletter, "Innovation Showcase," which was started in 1983, and a companion publication, *Eureka,* which began circulating to 10,000 Canadian inventors in 1987. As well, close links are maintained with the federal patent office, attorneys and trademark agents, and the National Research Council in the interests of what the Canadian Industrial Innovation Centre chairman Frank Maine characterizes as a pioneering effort to enhance the Canadian record in technology-based creativity.

JESSOP'S SPEEDY CLEANERS (1984) LIMITED

The proprietorship has changed, but by all the criteria of small-business success the dry-cleaning firm operated by June Ballak and her son David stands at the head of the class.

Jessop's Speedy Cleaners (1984) Limited—the date is a legal requirement only—continues to flourish on foundations of enterprise and industry instilled by the original partnership.

Co-founders of the company were Frank Jessop and Jack Whaley, who returned to Waterloo from wartime service with the Royal Canadian Air Force to analyze the prospects of launching their own cleaning establishment. Under the banner of Jessop and Whaley Cleaners, they opened a plant at 28 Bridgeport Road in August 1946.

The partners met with an encouraging response, soon adding a second truck for deliveries and pick-up locations in Elmira and in the Pequegnat Building at Duke and Frederick streets. They were progressive, too, as the first local cleaner to switch from petroleum-based to the safer, faster, and nonflammable perchlorethylene cleaning fluid. Services in the early days included most garments at the site, but leathers, suedes, and dyeing were contracted out. Winter storage facilities were maintained at Bridgeport Road to supplement revenue from a price list somewhat lower than today's charges. Pants were 55 to 60 cents, now it costs $4.25; a suit was $1.20, now it is $8.50; a dress was $1.00 to $1.20, now it costs $8.50; and for a tie it was 5 cents, now it is $2.25.

A member from the start of the Canadian Research Institute of Launderer and Cleaners, Jessop and Whaley were soon into drive-in accommodation at a second plant opened in the early 1950s on Ontario Street in downtown Kitchener. They installed modern synthetic equipment and expanded by buying an adjacent service station. The net effect was a volume of $1,700 per week by mid-1953, when the national *Laundry and Dry Cleaning* magazine termed the operation "the ultimate in customer convenience."

On January 31, 1961, the company announced the relocation of its Kitchener division to a modern outlet at Ontario and Duke streets, where it continues today as one of the best known cleaners in the city.

David Ballak, vice-president of Jessop's Speedy Cleaners.

In Waterloo, Jessop and Whaley moved forward in 1957 with a second division on King Street South in the former Dietrich Garage. Three years later the property was acquired by the developers of Waterloo Town Square, who have retained the cleaning business as a tenant to the present time. Originally, Jessop and Whaley was at the corner bordering Caroline and facing Erb Street, but it was shifted to the present location in 1977 when the shopping mall was enlarged.

As the founders attracted new clientele and added staff—to 22 from an original two—they also became active in civic affairs. Frank Jessop was president of the Waterloo Lions Club from 1959 to 1960 and first vice-president of the Waterloo Chamber of Commerce at the time of his death in 1972 at age 57. Jack Whaley served as president of the Eastern Canada Laundry and Dry Cleaning Association and was active in the Rotary Club and Air Force Wing. He died in 1970 at the age of 52.

Their partnership had expired earlier, however, by mutual agreement on December 31, 1963. Jessop took over the Waterloo and Kitchener plants under the signage of "Jessop's Speedy Cleaners Limited," while Whaley retained the original plant on Bridgeport Road as Whaley Cleaner Limited. Their widows managed the businesses, but Cecilia Whaley closed out her company in late 1974. Meanwhile, Betty Jessop carried on with the support of many faithful longtime employees, including Peter Ballak, plant manager, who had joined the staff in 1949.

It was a logical transition for Peter Ballak and his wife, June, to purchase the Jessop cleaning business in 1984. Tragically, Peter Ballak died in an automobile accident on April 18, 1986, leaving his widow and their son David to carry on the family enterprise.

Today they maintain the Waterloo Square branch and the main processing plant on Ontario Street in Kitchener, where Jessop's Speedy Cleaners (1984) Limited blends a professional touch with new products and equipment. The resulting high-quality workmanship and prompt service contributes to an ever-increasing patronage from appreciative customers, some of whom date to an association with the postwar start-up of the company.

GENISYS GROUP INTERNATIONAL INC.

A classic case of local business development rising from modest beginnings to national stature is credited to the Waterloo founders of Genisys Group International Inc.

Originally named Video Works Inc., this creation of Ian Forbes and Nick Czudyjowycz has carved out a substantial niche in the corporate and consumer video market over the past decade. Its thoroughly professional and high-technology capability has illuminated entertainment, commercial, and exhibition presentations while earning widespread recognition.

Two circumstances acted as catalyst for the new company in July 1980: Czudyjowycz' experience as a free-lance 16-millimetre filmmaker, and the late 1970s arrival of small-format video equipment suitable for the business community. From the outset Czudyjowycz worked around the clock, and Forbes worked part time at night until the company progressed to a permanent home on Regina Street in 1982. A year later Czudyjowycz' brother Emil (now a full partner) joined the rapidly expanding enterprise.

By 1986 the firm was well advanced in the provision of production, equipment, and related services across the whole spectrum of the fast-moving video market, including light-sound-video-laser environments for nightclubs and security packages for retail and industrial applications, as well as full field service.

The formation of Video Works London Inc. with new associate Kevin Suzuki broadened the operation to London, Ontario, in 1986. Two years later VWI opened a Toronto sales office to service a growing national clientele and also introduced a multiscreen "videowall" product line. Among its first major sales was a million-dollar system consisting of 256, 28-inch monitors for the new Erin Mills Town Centre, representing, at the time, the largest single permanent videowall installa-

Genisys Group International partners (from left) Emil Czudyjowycz, Ian Forbes, and Nick Czudyjowycz.

Genisys, a wholly owned video production, sales, service, and warehouse centre, is headquartered at 100 Lodge Street, Waterloo.

tion in the world.

As the company enters its second decade, the restructured Genisys Group International Inc. occupies modern offices, studios, warehouse, and shops at 100 Lodge Street in Waterloo, from which eight operating divisions are deployed:

—Video Works Production Services, for corporate and videowall programming;

—AV Ontario, for rentals, staging, and meeting services;

—Corporate Multimedia, for hardware sales to the corporate and institutional market;

—Upfront FX, supplying the hospitality industry with innovative entertainment systems;

—Video Works Satellite Entertainment, serving the consumer and commercial market;

—Canadian Satellite Network, for national videoconference and VSAT communications services;

—Wall to Wall FX, serving the retail and trade show markets with large-format visual-display technologies and advertising programs; and

—MasterTech Electronic Services, the service and installation division.

VAN DRESSER LIMITED

A resilient and creative auto-parts maker has adapted to sweeping changes over nearly three decades to emerge as a leading industry in the city of Waterloo.

Van Dresser Limited has progressed from modest beginnings as a supplier of automotive seat components to stand-alone capability in the production of sophisticated vehicle interiors. The firm got its start in a tiny shop on Phillip Street in 1961; it is currently housed in a 135,000-square-foot facility (plus leased storage) at 139 Northfield Drive. The original work force of 12 people has grown to 300, while sales have soared from a first-year $100,000 to $40 million annually.

At the outset the company supplied automotive seat insulators and wires to General Spring Products, now Lear Siegler, in Kitchener. With the advent of the United States-Canada Auto Pact in 1965, the plant was more than doubled to 3,000 square feet to handle the increased volume. Business increased dramatically to require the initial 30,000 square feet at the present site by June 1967. Soon new products were under development and specialized wire-bending equipment and presses installed for door locking linkages, U bolts, and a variety of other wire parts.

A major advance of long-term benefit to the company occurred in 1971 with the manufacture of formed automotive hard-board headliners (roof interiors) for General Motors' Vega cars. Until then Van Dresser parts had been hidden, but now it progressed to producing visible, tactile, and cosmetic interior components. New technology for fitting, finishing, and processing was supplemented by testing apparatus in the first phase of a complete laboratory. The firm moved confidently into such areas as

A world-class auto-parts manufacturer, Van Dresser Limited is a leading industry in Waterloo.

interior fibreboard door foundations for Cadillacs and away from wire products, which were succeeded by extruded styrene foams.

Consequently, the Van Dresser operation was poised to win major contracts, again from GM, for formable styrene laminate (FSL) headliners in 1977. By the following year the Waterloo plant was functioning in an additional 105,000 square feet of much-needed administrative and warehousing space. A unique plastic extrusion line was installed to

make FSL sheets from raw material as the company advanced toward vertical integration in many areas.

Headliner contracts multiplied in the early 1980s, first for American-built cars and trucks and then for Volkswagen Golf and Jetta vehicles. In 1983 Van Dresser Limited added glass-fibre headliners in addition to styrene and eventually signed a licence for urethane headliners under the Tramivex trademark.

Presently the Waterloo firm, as part of the private Van Dresser Corporation of Troy, Michigan, enjoys status as a world-class auto-parts manufacturer with a strong accent on quality deriving from in-house technologies.

WATERLOO BEDDING COMPANY LIMITED

Dave Sandrock (center) purchased Waterloo Bedding Company Limited in 1970 and served as president until recently as a new era began when Bill Muirhead (left) and Michael Sandrock (right), son-in-law and son, respectively, took over ownership of the business.

An upgraded manufacturing plant, new product lines, and a buoyant market blend in a thriving family-run enterprise behind the facade of a landmark industry near the downtown core.

Waterloo Bedding Company Limited, at 21 Allen Street West, is completing 80 years of operation in the Twin Cities and two decades under present management. In recent years the firm has emerged as a major supplier to the health care, institutional, and hotel fields. Its output has widened from basic mattresses to a complete range of pillows, draperies and curtains, and flotation therapy products. Waterloo Bedding is presently the only mattress company that ships coast to coast from one manufacturing facility.

The business was founded November 10, 1910, by partners Michael H. Montag and Alexander L. Dantzer as the Quality Mattress Company. It was launched in rented premises on King Street in Kitchener with three employees making felt mattresses. In 1913 the main building was erected on the present site, where Waterloo Bedding was incorporated in 1921 with Montag as president and Alfred I. Fehrenbach, secretary/treasurer. Management

increased plant and warehouse area to 40,000 square feet and installed modern machinery as the company gained renown as a manufacturer to the retail trade in peacetime and a

The early days of Quality Mattress Company, forerunner of Waterloo Bedding Company Limited.

key supplier to the military during the first and second world wars.

The signature of Dave Sandrock as president has been associated with the rising fortunes and changing profile of Waterloo Bedding since he bought the business in 1970. A former Kitchener funeral director, he took the firm into the institutional field and beyond provincial bound-

aries by selling the company's reputation for quality on a national plane.

Waterloo Bedding is now entering into a new era as the ownership of the company has been taken over by Michael Sandrock and Bill Muirhead, Dave's son and son-in-law respectively. Michael, who has considerable experience in the business joined the firm in 1981 as the production manager, while Bill, a chartered accountant, joined in 1988. Dave will continue to be involved in the company as he uses his experience in a consulting and advisory role.

With a full-time staff of 30 people, the city's oldest and largest mattress factory is frequently flat out to meet the demand from hospitals, nursing homes, universities, homes for the aged, and the hospitality sector. Waterloo Bedding's success is the result of its ability to adapt and to diversify, as evidenced by its history of continually searching for and introducing new products into the marketplace.

ENASCO LIMITED

Its installations are largely out of view and its business is tucked away on a rural road, but a father-and-son partnership in electrical contracting has completed an impressive roster of vital municipal services over a quarter-century.

The establishment of Engineering Associates Company Limited dates from June 15, 1966, when Eldon Muegge brought 20 years of experi-

affect the city, such as traffic light hookups, the road lighting at the University of Waterloo, and the wiring for utilities, television, and cable connections to new subdivisions.

The firm also dispatches its 25 to 40 employees to towns and cities across southwestern Ontario. Recently it installed the complete power-distribution system for Lon-

tion for the regional Municipality of Waterloo for approximately one million dollars of electrical work. This undertaking will involve the raw-water reservoir, and intake and pumping station on Hidden Valley Road just west of the new Freeport Bridge. It also entails a return to the Grand River for the firm, which installed a high-voltage power supply under the water course near Kitchener-Waterloo

ence with Sutherland-Shultz and Bennett & Wright contractors to the formation of his own firm. He set up on the present site, which is the old family farm of John and Lucinda Bierman, the parents of Muegge's wife, Gladys.

With Muegge as president and his son Edward as vice-president, ENASCO has successfully carried out a wide variety of public and private projects, both above and under ground. Some contracts directly

With offices, workshops, and equipment, including a dozen vehicles at the Erbsville Road headquarters, Enasco Limited is well fitted to handle major electrical projects.

don Airport at a cost of $750,000 and wired the Environmental Studies II building at the University of Waterloo.

Presently Enasco is bringing a wealth of experience to the master water supply project under constoc-

Airport in 1980.

With offices, workshops, and equipment, including a dozen vehicles at its Erbsville Road headquarters, Enasco Limited is well fitted to handle major jobs. President Eldon Muegge is a director of the Electrical Contractors' Association of Ontario (central district) and a former Waterloo Township school trustee and planning board member. The company is a member of the Ontario Electric League.

LABATT BREWERIES OF CANADA LIMITED

A rich heritage steeped in beer making and city development is preserved at the landmark, six-acre downtown site occupied by Labatt's Waterloo.

There, the third proprietor in 150 years is a relative newcomer, but Labatt Breweries of Canada Limited has imprinted indelibly its commitment to business, community, and historic values since acquiring the facility 13 years ago.

When the Labatt's sign went up at King and William streets on October 1, 1977, the prior site of the venerable Kuntz family brewery (established 1844), Kuntz got some welcome recognition. First, the Labatt's people secured designation of the Kuntz homestead on the property as a historic and architectural edifice. The residence today is fully restored and serves as a local meeting place, civic reception hall, and company marketing department. Recently, in another creative gesture to founder David Kuntz and his heirs, Labatt's Waterloo reissued Kuntz' German Lager, "the beer that made Waterloo famous," complete with labels and memorabilia in yellow and black city colors.

David Kuntz, who was an accomplished brewmaster, and barrel and brick mason, would have applauded

Labatt Breweries of Canada Limited has been committed to business, community, and historic values since its arrival in Waterloo in 1977.

such ingenuity. So would his son, Louis, who succeeded him in 1870, and grandsons David (a namesake), William, and Herbert, who with guidance from uncle Aloyes Bauer, managed the company through the early 1900s. Like Labatt's of London, Ontario (established 1847), the Kuntz Brewery survived Prohibition, but family control ended shortly thereafter with sale to the E.P. Taylor

interests in 1929. Interestingly Herbert Kuntz served on the executive board of the new corporation until his death in 1945, although the family name was supplanted by Carling O'Keefe in 1940.

Rising demand for Labatt's brands in Ontario and the United States led to the Waterloo acquisition. Since then the plant has been equipped with the latest packaging equipment and computerization to assist 226 personnel in the production of 500,000-plus hectolitres of beer per year. In addition, the firm has implemented employee involvement and social and recreational programs while contributing to civic betterment on a broad scale.

Labatt's Waterloo has set its sights for the 1990s and beyond on a continuing role as a responsible employer, community builder, and custodian of an important part of local history.

The original Kuntz homestead on Labatt's property, which serves as a local meeting place, civic reception hall, and company marketing department, has been designated a historic and architectural edifice.

SWENCO LIMITED

Creative and resilient responses to market swings have produced a positive future for a family-managed Waterloo industry. Although relatively small compared with other manufacturers, Swenco Limited, with 25 employees, is widely known for manufacturing an extensive line of metal and plastic components.

From a modest start on February 1, 1962, in a rented New Hamburg building, the firm has matured into a self-contained, 20,000-square-foot plant at 560 Conestogo Road, where skilled craftsmen and high-technology equipment turn out an ever-increasing stream of precision-made products.

Founders Dermot and Una Sweeny (president and secretary/treasurer, respectively) launched the business as a stamping and assembly supplier to area electronics firms such as Electrohome and General Instruments. By the mid-1960s the firm had branched into steel shanks for the footwear industry and then hardware items, as the electronics industry reeled from Japanese competition.

The late 1960s saw Swenco established in Waterloo and surviving with innovation at a time of great turmoil for small manufacturers. A major city fire destroyed the Swenco factory on Lucan Street in January 1972, but the Sweenys were able to continue in a small Kitchener die company they had purchased.

Acquisition of the present property in 1973 marked an upward course for the owners. Son Brian joined the firm in sales and after 12 successful years, established his own sales agency handling among other lines, Swenco Footwear Products. Son Paul, a Conestoga College graduate, joined the firm in the late 1970s and is now plant manager. A mid-1970s venture into footwear components saw Swenco make the first premoulded insole in North America, but again a flood of imports wrought havoc in this sector. However, a move to the

The Swenco team—proud to be part of Waterloo's past and future.

work-boot field proved profitable in the early 1980s, catapulting the Sweeny interest to North American leadership in the production of protective sole plates and to export clientele worldwide.

Currently new lines of company-developed and -patented products are moving to the building products and hardware markets. These include Extend-A-Bit® screw gun extensions, High Reach tape applicators for drywall installation, Torcholder™ safety propane bottle stands, Monoloc™ exhaust ventilation couplings, Reel Easy® fence wire dispensers, Holdster™ wall brackets, and Handigrip™ plastic bag holders. Many more new projects are on the drawing board. Most are being sold throughout North America and Europe.

Swenco Limited executives are also contributing time and effort to community, educational, and trade association activities, which they regard as essential adjuncts to corporate achievement in the 1990s and beyond.

B.F.GOODRICH CANADA INC.

A leader in quality, service, and technical innovation, BFGoodrich serves Canada's vinyl, specialty polymers, and chemical markets.

Before Kitchener-Waterloo had a skyline, the BFGoodrich company's water-storage tower, built around 1928, punctuated the horizon. It was to become symbolic of the company's high profile in rubber and engineered products and, in recent years, as a leader in the Canadian plastics industry.

BFGoodrich Canada's success began in Kitchener in 1922, producing tires under an agreement with the Ames Holden Company. Three years later BFG bought controlling interest, and the Canadian Goodrich Company Ltd. was born.

By 1930 BFGoodrich Canada offered a diverse line of tube, hose, and rubber goods. Over the next 30 years the firm continued to expand and grow, achieving many "firsts" in the rubber industry. In 1962 BFG opened one of the country's largest tire plants in Kitchener, the same year the city was named Canada's rubber capital. BFG Canada earned further industry distinction in 1969, producing Canada's first radial passenger tires.

As the company prospered it shared its success with the community through numerous philanthropic contributions, such as its pioneering sponsorship of the Oktoberfest festival and parade.

The firm was also a regular sponsor and contributor to Kitchener's Labor Day parades, the Western Ontario Newspaper awards, area chambers of commerce, and Kitchener-Waterloo's Federated Charities.

Employees were also active in the community, highlighted by University of Waterloo founding father Ira Needles, a former BFGoodrich president, and the 1958 appointment of Dr. J.F. Hagey, BFG Canada's national advertising director as the university's founding president.

In 1957 BFGoodrich had taken the initial step toward achieving its future business focus, constructing a $3.5-million chemical plant near Niagara Falls, Ontario. The company supplemented its vinyl resin manufacturing capacity by acquiring a polyvinyl chloride (PVC) plant in Shawinigan, Quebec, in 1972.

Strong market conditions led to a major expansion at the Niagara facility in 1979-1980. The project doubled capacity and made the plant a world-class facility. In 1985 BFG Canada purchased a modern mass vinyl resin plant in Scotford, Alberta. The focus on chemical operations was solidified in 1983 when the firm relocated its head office to Waterloo.

The office is a showcase for vinyl applications, incorporating vinyl windows, flooring, wall coverings, and vertical blinds. More than 120 highly trained employees (part of the company's 700 employees nationwide) direct administration, marketing, and provide extensive customer service from an in-house development laboratory.

Strategically positioned to concentrate on the Canadian vinyl and specialty chemicals markets, the firm moved to consolidate operations by divesting its engineered products division in 1983 and its tire group three years later.

BFG Canada continues to contribute extensively to the local community through such community programs as United Way, the Waterloo Chamber of Commerce, hospital building funds, and many other valuable community organizations.

BFGoodrich continues to lead the plastics industry in technological advances in polymer technology and new processing and manufacturing techniques for traditional and new markets. As an industry leader, B.F.Goodrich Canada Inc. is proud to be part of, and contribute to, one of the country's leading communities.

B.F.Goodrich Canada Inc. headquarters in Waterloo—a solid corporate citizen in the Twin Cities for more than 65 years.

RAYTHEON CANADA LIMITED

A Waterloo-based specialist in surface radar technology is moving forward on new frontiers as a valued local industry of rising national and international distinction.

Raytheon Canada Limited designs, develops, and manufactures air traffic control (ATC) and communications systems for civil and military applications for the world market. It functions in a 195,000-square-foot facility at 400 Phillip Street enclosing laboratories, a Tempest shielded security area, and computer-assisted design equipment. The production area features automated assembly and inventory controlled stores, quality control, and extensive testing mechanisms. Among the 720 personnel is a unique blend of highly qualified and trained engineering, program management, and manufacturing expertise dedicated to excellence.

The company was established under federal charter in 1956 to undertake production and installation of ATC radar for Canada's Department of Transport in the creation of the world's first national civil ATC radar network. That initial contract resulted in the emplacement of 15 radar at a cost of $5 million in 1957.

In its role as a developer and manufacturer of state-of-the-art systems, Raytheon Canada enjoys the full technical and managerial support of its parent, Raytheon Company of Lexington, Massachusetts, a $9-billion corporation with more than 78,000 employees. The Canadian company's product base includes a broad range of ATC equipment, including primary surveillance radar for terminal and en route applications, and ground-controlled approach radar systems (mobile and fixed base).

Since the original Department of Transport assignment, which was followed by a secondary surveillance radar contract in 1963, Raytheon Canada has flourished in a global market stretching from Europe to the Pacific Rim. ATC systems have been provided to southeast Asia, France, Italy, Africa, and the Caribbean. Along the way, the firm has developed profitable sidelines in the assembly of power supplies, single-board computers, and specialized control consoles for export, as well as lines of manufacturing under license agreement.

An outstanding achievement currently well advanced toward a 1992 completion date is the Radar Modernization Project (RAMP), repre-

Raytheon Canada equipment for Transport Canada's RAMP program, which is being installed at the Ottawa (BELOW) and Hamilton (FACING PAGE) airports.

senting a $390-million Canadian government contract won by Raytheon Canada in 1984. This Transport Canada program entails the design, development, manufacture, supply, installation, and testing of 41 radar sites at terminal and en route locations, culminating in a more efficient national radar system well into the next century.

In conjunction with upgrading the service, the company's long-term research and development of enhanced radar have produced the world's first solid-state civil ATC radar, the ASR-9000 series. The range, sensitivity, and operational superiority of successive ASR (Airport Surveillance Radar) configurations has attracted interest in the form of sales to Trinidad and Tobago. Apart from increased area of radar coverage, the main benefit of RAMP is improved performance—more precise information on air traffic and on hazardous weather conditions, as well as lower maintenance costs.

The stringent standards demanded of a modern air traffic system are built in by Raytheon's highly skilled staff who also conduct rigid testing beyond normal extremes of pressure and temperature. In the field, work stations and their components attain an amazing average of one failure in seven months, while the mean time for repair is 30 minutes.

Raytheon Canada's location is a major asset to the mainstream of ATC systems and the spinoff of custom design and manufacture of a wide range of communications equipment for sales at home or abroad. The nearby University of Waterloo affords direct access to a prestigious engineering and computer research institution. The Waterloo region is also emerging as a major centre of applied research in computer-aided design and manufacturing, and in micro-electronics, making for a high-technology centre. In addition, the firm is centrally situated for dealings with its suppliers—more than 70 for the RAMP program alone, plus hundreds of others—whose participation creates valuable exposure for Canadian expertise.

Management at Raytheon, which is headed by president and general manager John M. Stewart, also finds advantageous the prosperous and stable environment of the area, the wealth of local cultural and recreational facilities, and the proximity to metropolitan centres. Among the key people responsible to the president are G.R. Beaumont, director of marketing; R.D. Kerr, manager of manufacturing; and J.D. Collis, manager of contracts.

UNIVERSITY OF WATERLOO

Cornerstones of creative educational programming and response to technological challenge anchor the spectacular development of the University of Waterloo.

From a pioneering role in co-operative curriculums to mastery of the microchip, the 33-year-old institution has advanced to the first flight of Canadian universities by virtue of a broadening range of academic avenues. Enrolment has increased from a handful of engineering aspirants to more than 25,000 students, some 16,000 who attend full time. Approximately 800 permanent faculty members and close to 2,000 support staff are included in the campus community. It is the fourth-largest university in Ontario, even though Kitchener and Waterloo together are smaller than several other urban sites, and despite the presence of nearby Wilfrid

The scenic, wooded campus leads into modern facilities such as Dana Porter Arts Library.

lege (a small Lutheran Church-owned affiliate of the University of Western Ontario, which has since become Wilfrid Laurier). They were entering a new university-level engineering program, the first in Canada

The School of Optometry is one of several professional schools added to the original engineering core.

Laurier University.

The founding of the University of Waterloo traces to July 3, 1957, when 75 students assembled on the campus of what was then Waterloo Col-

on the co-operative principle, where students alternate between campus studies and work-related jobs.

Looking back, that fledgling school of engineering was superbly timed to meet the Twin Cities' build-up of a diversified industrial structure comprising the electronics, plastics, and rubber industries. As well, the 1950s was an era of new

interests in space, solid-state physics, and atomic energy-generating plants. Thus the University of Waterloo was launched in a climate of hope and optimism. Founding president J.G. "Gerry" Hagey (at the time president of Waterloo College) shared a spirit of progress with community leaders supporting the venture, and their objectives were soon surpassed by students flocking to enrol in the "co-op" system.

Before long the new program threatened to swamp the small 400-student college that had spawned it, leading to the first phase of independence early in 1958. A 235-acre tract, principally the Schweitzer family farm, was acquired for a completely separate institution—today's University of Waterloo—and by the end of the year the building known as Engineering One was occupied.

To the faculty of engineering were added the faculty of science in 1959 and the faculty of arts the following year. As buildings were erected, funds were raised, and the pace of growth quickened. In 1962 purchase of the 750-acre north campus quadrupled the physical size of the university. Meanwhile, Renison College (Anglican) and St. Jerome's College (Roman Catholic) had joined with the new university in 1960, followed by St. Paul's College (United Church) three years later and Conrad Grebel College in 1964. The church colleges provided the first student residences prior to university-backed student housing.

Rapid expansion generated an undergraduate population of 5,000, plus 750 graduate students, and 384 faculty members by 1967. That same year the faculty of mathematics was formed, followed shortly by the faculty of applied health sciences, which emerged from the School of Physical and Health Education, and in 1970 the faculty of environmental studies. In addition to academic extension, research activity was fostered by the faculties to cover a wide spectrum of science, health and humanities, the arts, and environment.

A single source of Waterloo's success is the appeal, from inception, of the co-operative system. Today more

The newest addition to the 900-acre campus is the William G. Davis Computer Research Centre.

Hagey Hall of the Humanities recognizes the contribution of founder J.G. "Gerry" Hagey.

than 9,500 co-operative students represent global leadership in a concept widely applied by other universities, community colleges, and high schools across Canada.

Another major reason for success ensues from an early decision by innovative Waterloo professors to equip students to work directly with computers. This decision, in the dawn of computer application, introduced thousands of students to programming into a mainframe computer on campus and ultimately to the creation of computer software. The university's now-vaunted reputation for mathematics and computer research is well established through-

out the academic world and in business, industry, and government. Total research at UW was more than $40 million in 1988-1989, including more than $4.5 million for contract research in support of industry.

Somewhat overshadowed by computer science and engineering are the faculties of arts, science, environmental studies, and applied health sciences. The university is increasingly becoming known for the excellence of all its programs, so much so that it admits more Ontario scholars for its size than any university in Ontario.

Since the early 1970s the University of Waterloo has continued to mature by adding dimensions to teaching, research, and the co-operative concept. The most recent addition to the campus was the $50-million William G. Davis Computer Research Centre in 1988.

At Waterloo, it is recognized that Canadians can no longer rely for their economic well-being on their country's rich resources. Increasingly, Canada's future will depend on how successfully its young people can meet social and technological challenges. The University of Waterloo has played a leading role in convincing business and government leaders, and the public, of the need to deal with this reality.

ONTARIO SEED COMPANY LTD.

Deep community roots in seed and hardware merchandising form a solid foundation for the flourishing enterprise of Ontario Seed, administered by the Uffelman family at their new headquarters facility. The heirs of founder Jacob Uffelman build on holdings under the banner of the Ontario Seed Company, comprising the second-largest seed wholesaler in Canada and two Home Hardware stores in Ontario.

A trio of Uffelmans representing the third and fourth generations in the business oversee the flower and vegetable seed imports from 40 countries for resale to about 5,000 Canadian grocery, general, and hardware stores annually. Seeds from North and South America, Africa, Europe, and Asia are marketed in millions of packets sold from coast to coast across Canada and in response to yearly circulation of the firm's seed catalogues.

Six generations of Uffelmans have lived in the area, but it was Jacob who first entered retailing as a general store clerk in 1874. He bought the business in 1891 and converted it to a Waterloo institution; the family's flagship Home Hardware is at 16 King

Vice-president Scott, president Jim Uffelman, and secretary/treasurer Bill "Buck" in front of Ontario Seed's Waterloo head office and seed distribution centre, (BELOW) located at 330 Phillip Street. The Uffelman family has been in the retail business in Waterloo since before the turn of the century.

cant was the founder's acquisition of Ontario Seed in 1911. The company had been launched in 1907 by two seed experts, C.H. Kustermann and Otto Herold, but they went bankrupt with Jacob Uffelman holding the chattel mortgage.

Eventually the original Pioneer Seed Farm widened to 100 acres in a now-urbanized area south of Bridgeport Road and west of Devitt Avenue. At one point Ontario Seed grew the biggest cabbage patch in town to supply its Silverthread Sauerkraut factory. That industry, the surrounding land, and the old Hogg Fuel property and CN station, once part of the Uffelman interests, have since been sold.

Today the grandsons and great-grandson of former Mayor Jacob Uffelman run Ontario Seed Company from their 60,000-square-foot office, plant, and warehouse at 330 Phillip Street where they relocated in 1988.

Street South. His son, Orley, took over in 1922 and died in 1963. Orley's sons, Jim and Bill, succeeded him, being joined by the latter's son, Scott, in 1972.

Numerous changes in assets have occurred during 116 years of Uffelman proprietorship, the most signifi-

The firm employs a staff of 120 people, evenly divided between the seed operation, which includes a 150-acre farm with test plots in Woolwich Township, and the hardware division, which has grown to a second outlet, Glenbriar Home Hardware on Weber Street North.

THE EQUITABLE LIFE INSURANCE COMPANY OF CANADA

"Achieving profitable growth at a steady pace with a strong commitment to the safety and quality of investments continues as a guiding principle of Equitable Life of Canada," says president Ian McIntosh. Adherence to this corporate philosophy has accompanied the 70-year development of Equitable Life into a mid-size, all-Canadian, financially strong mutual life insurance company offering a full range of life insurance, annuities, and group plans for individuals and businesses.

Founded in 1920 as The Ontario Equitable Life and Accident Insurance Company, the Waterloo-based firm was the creation of Sidney C. Tweed, who served as president until 1931. He laid cornerstones of ambition, innovation, and the security and protection symbolized by the lighthouse graphic identifying the city's third-oldest life insurance entity. A rented office soon gave way to a three-storey building near King and Erb streets. During its first decade, distinguished by rapid growth, Ontario Equitable purchased Policyholders Mutual Life (1923), Reinsurance Company of Canada (1926), and Equity Life (1929).

A federal charter obtained in 1936 conferred the present name and rising national scope of Equitable Life under the direction of Mervin J. Smith, a charter employee who was appointed general manager in 1930 and served as president from 1939 to

The "Equitable Building" in Devitt Block near King and Erb streets, Waterloo, 1922.

1967. Smith was a leading proponent of mutualization in the 1950s to vest ownership with policyowners and guard against foreign takeover. Equitable Life was the first Canadian company to initiate mutualization. At Equitable Life, participating policy owners share in the company earnings from all lines of business.

Other presidents serving with distinction over the years were the Honorable Charles A. Dunning (1931-1935), who was Canadian Minister of Finance in 1935; the Honorable James L. Ralston (1935-1939), a former Canadian Minister of National Defence; Howard E. Power, successor to Smith (1967-1971); Thomas R. Suttie (1971-1980); Donald L.

Today The Equitable Life Insurance Company of Canada is headquartered at One Westmount Road North, Waterloo.

MacLeod (1980-1987); and current president H. Ian McIntosh (1987-).

Equitable Life's head office at One Westmount Road North was built in 1971 and enlarged in 1989 to accommodate 300 personnel as well as the latest computer technology. All employees share in productivity improvements through a unique gain-sharing plan.

With total assets of more than $600 million, The Equitable Life Insurance Company of Canada draws from a rich reservoir of people in all facets of its operations. In addition to 230 employees in Waterloo, the company functions with 14 career agency offices, 160 full-time career agents, and 30 general agencies across Canada.

CUMMING COCKBURN LIMITED

A full-service, professional consultant in the field of urban development and municipal engineering has established a strong presence in southwestern Ontario since opening a Waterloo office in 1974.

Cumming Cockburn Limited, Consulting Engineers and Planners, maintains a staff of 70 employees (of 192 Canadian personnel) at its regional headquarters occupying 12,000 square feet at 180 Columbia Street West. Completed projects for local, provincial, and federal governments, as well as a host of private ventures, reflects the broad multidisciplinary strength of the firm.

At inception in 1960, the partnership of D.H. Cockburn and J.D. Cumming, who continues as chairman, operated in the Toronto area. It expanded to Ottawa in 1970 and to the Kitchener-Waterloo area four years later. On the heels of regional government in 1973, the firm's incumbent regional director, R.L. Thompson, P.Eng., set up the Waterloo practice. A former town engineer for Preston, and then director of operations for Cambridge, Thompson

The reception area welcomes clients to Cumming Cockburn Limited.

assembled a diverse group of engineers, planners, and support staff. The appointment of Mel Code as chief planner in 1981 added land-use/subdivision capability as the scope of services widened. In 1989 the addition of transportation and environmental service departments in the Waterloo office further broadened its scope of local services.

From basic consulting for land,

municipal, and community purposes, Cumming Cockburn has cultivated specialists in water management, environmental studies, landscape design, marine structures, bridges, and transportation engineering. It has carried out a large volume of residential advisement in the area, while collaborating with city administrations on road and utility installations. In addition, the needs of crown corporations, conservation authorities, and industrial and commercial concerns have been accommodated.

The Waterloo complement of Cumming Cockburn Limited is the foremost planning and engineering firm in the region. Overall, the company has grown substantially in Eastern Canada, with additional offices in London, Kingston, and Hull, Quebec, and an affiliate in Pompano Beach, Florida. Its present stature evolves from a solid foundation of competence, experience, and closely supervised service, in concert with innovative and realistic solutions to client requirements.

The computer-aided design drafting centre. Computer terminals are interconnected to central plotting facilities. The firm stresses the increased use of CADD technology that enhances efficient and effective design capabilities to client benefit.

THE MANUFACTURERS LIFE INSURANCE COMPANY

The Canadian Operations headquarters of a continental leader in the life insurance field stands as a showplace of elegance and utility amid a picturesque sweep of treed landscape and a spring-fed pond in northern Waterloo. Commissioned by The Manufacturers Life Insurance Company (The Manufacturers), the low-rise edifice forms a unique landmark in the city. The 345,000-square-foot building represents an affirmation of the industry's historic association with the twin cities area as well as a valued community asset.

To some 1,100 employees, who may gaze down on a panorama of wildfowl from their offices or a spacious 450-seat cafeteria, their workplace combines modern accommodation with convenient access to King North and the Conestoga Parkway. To planners with The Manufacturers, development on the 10-acre property vindicates mid-1980s decisions to decentralize from Toronto, to purchase the Kitchener-Waterloo-based Dominion Life Assurance

Company, and to consolidate the merged interests in an ideal setting.

To the ultimate benefit of the city as a whole, the undertaking assures continued permanent employment, taxes accruing from the $36-million office facility, and inestimable generation of purchasing power. The presence of The Manufacturers also signals a direct role in civic advancement, now and in the years ahead. Significantly the official opening on October 19, 1988, was accompanied by a corporate gift of $25,000 to the regional Family & Children's Services Facilities Project. Since then The Manufacturers has supported, as patron funding for the group's entire needs, the Kitchener-Waterloo Symphony Youth Orchestra. Another local annual event, The Manufacturers Celebrity Golf Tournament, raises money for worthwhile charities.

The strength of The Manufacturers Life Insurance Com-

pany has risen markedly since the Dominion acquisition in 1985, which brought into the fold the 11th-largest Canadian life insurer. Ensuing sales increases have propelled the firm to dominance in the provision of individual and group life, and health insurance and pensions in Canada. Today the 103-year-old organization ranks among the top 12 life insurance companies in North America with assets approaching $23.8 billion from worldwide operations.

ZEHRS MARKETS

An early and prominent presence in Waterloo stands out as Zehrs Markets looks back on 40 years of impressive growth in the twin cities and beyond.

Founder Emory Zehr always had an interest in the food industry. And, after several corner grocery stores, he decided to apply his corner-store idea to a larger concept. Sons Clifford and Lester joined him in opening the first Zehrs Market in February 1950 at 100 Highland Road West in Kitchener.

After launching a second store in Kitchener, Emory expanded to Waterloo in February 1958 with a third Zehrs Market at 94 Bridgeport

An in-store bakery was a "first" at the Glenridge store.

Road. By the time of a second Waterloo store at 49 Erb Street in 1966 and another at 478 Albert Street (Parkdale Mall) in 1969, the Zehr enterprise was a major player in local food retailing.

The 1970s ushered in a dramatic escalation with a fourth outlet on

Lexington Road and then another at Waterloo Square in 1972 succeeding the Erb Street store. Zehrs was quick to automate, too, and in 1976 its newly opened Glenridge Plaza market introduced computerized scanning checkout systems. (The same store unveiled Zehrs' first in-store bakery.)

During this era Zehrs also devised the Save-A-Tape plan, whereby worthy causes across Ontario receive cash donations—some $600,000 annually—in return for grocery receipts. Also during the 1970s the firm was incorporated as Zehrs Markets, a division of Zehrmart Inc.

Expansion throughout southwestern Ontario continued in the early 1980s, including the takeover of Gordons supermarkets and new Zehrs locales to the north and south. In 1982 the group's then-largest store of 32,000 square feet was opened at the Beechwood Plaza in northwest Waterloo. With this development came the closure of the Lexington Road premises.

Conestoga Mall was the site of the

Zehrs Markets come to Waterloo.

fifth Zehrs supermarket in Waterloo, and it featured a special horse-and-buggy hook-up for nearby Mennonite customers. Subsequent closing of the Parkdale Mall store in 1988 left Waterloo with its current complement of four Zehrs Markets.

Along with 53 stores in Ontario, Zehrs also operates Double Z Uniform Rentals Inc., which originally serviced Zehrs uniforms but is now a large public cleaner.

Although Zehrs Markets has widened to a formidable supermarket chain employing more than 4,000 people, it will always portray the friendly corner-store attitude initiated by Emory Zehr.

The Bridgeport Road store, circa 1978.

ECONOMICAL MUTUAL INSURANCE COMPANY

One of the country's foremost, multi-line general insurers is functioning comfortably and efficiently in a newly acquired Waterloo head-office building.

The Economical Mutual Insurance Company is managing a portfolio of more than 900,000 policies and more than $700 million in investment assets from the spacious old Dominion Life site at 111 Westmount Road South. The firm bought the 5.9-acre property in 1987 and moved in two

ty Mutual Fire (1863). Other milestones were a 1937 agreement with Merchants Casualty leading to diversification and a friendly takeover in 1947 of Northwestern Mutual Fire Association's business in Eastern Canada. The Missisquoi & Rouville (1835) is a Quebec-based subsidiary.

Viewed against the Economical's strength and scope entering the 1990s, its inception on June 24, 1871, was incredibly small. A meeting in

home and barn at an annual premium of $36. Good luck and good management—two start-up years free of claims while Jackson and his directors practised thrift—kept the company solvent.

Early principles of personal service, fiscal responsibility, promptitude, and honesty have perpetuated well into the second century of the Economical Mutual Insurance Company. Today, as the firm responds to changes in the industry and trans-

years later with 325 personnel from offices on Erb Street and the former headquarters building on Duke Street in Kitchener.

In all, the Economical enfolds several acquisitions, operates 10 branches and nine service offices, and employs 1,000 workers nationwide. Original companies predating and now integrated with the Economical are Perth Insurance Company (1863) and Waterloo Insurance Company, formerly Waterloo Coun-

Economical Mutual Insurance Company's new head office and Kitchener-Waterloo branch building at 111 Westmount Road South, Waterloo.

the Berlin (Kitchener) Town Hall saw some 40 interested people assent to the formation of a fire insurance company. By fall, charter president Henry F.J. Jackson had issued Policy No. 1 to Israel D. Bowman of Berlin for $1,100 to insure his

acts income and expense in hundreds of millions of dollars, its best interests are served by chairman of the board P.H. Sims, Q.C., president J.T. Hill, and directors J.S. Acheson, R.A. Forbes, J.M. Harper, Q.C. (vice-chairman), G.A. Mackay, W.D. McGregor, J.H. Panabaker, B.J. Ruby, H.E. Seegmiller, and T.R. Suttie. Honorary directors are W.A. Bean (honorary chairman), R.A. Harris, K.R. MacGregor, J.A. Vila, J.H. Argue, and D.W. Brown.

MILLARD PRECISION MACHINE & TOOL LIMITED

Craftsmanship, experience, and state-of-the-art equipment contribute to the finely made products—from electronic components to heavy tooling—flowing from a high-technology environment at Millard Precision Machine & Tool Limited.

The company's 22,000-square-foot facility at 109 Randall Drive responds to an infinite variety of custom work for the metal-working industry in North America. And one assignment, for a Syracuse, New York, manufacturer, involved the Waterloo specialist in air-conditioning equipment for South America and the Pacific Rim.

Founder Herbert Millard established quality and capability at the inception of the business in 1972. Four additions, the last in 1986 doubling the size of the plant, have accompanied the installation of an array of presses, grinders, drills, saws, and lathes to meet market demand. Computer-assisted design equipment functions in the engineering department, while a computer-assisted machining centre expedites projects on the shop floor. A complete electrical discharge machining service

includes the latest computer numerical control (C.N.C.) wire, cut for any type of tooling required for production dies.

The Millard firm handles tooling and die making for a wide variety of commercial and industrial concerns, with a substantial role in the office furniture and appliance sectors, as well as some automotive. One of its largest customers during the past decade has been the metal-insulated entrance-door industry in Canada and the United States, for which the Waterloo company has provided original tooling for metal skins for intricate door designs.

From the outset, Herbert Millard and his wife, Patricia, who is secretary/treasurer, have placed a strong accent on employee development. Whether a first-year apprentice or a senior master journeyman, every member shares in the

A skilled craftsman puts finishing touches on a stretch-form tool.

company's growth through profit-sharing and incentive programs. Most of the 35 personnel have advanced through rigorous training, including co-operative ventures with area secondary schools. The average age is comparatively young for a tool and die shop, but Millard management has observed a high level of competence among co-op program graduates.

In the final analysis, Millard Precision Machine & Tool Limited has earned an enviable reputation for accuracy and superior performance in serving a clientele stretching south to Florida and west to Indiana and Alberta.

The modern Millard plant houses the company's high-technology tool- and die-making operation.

CANADIAN IMPERIAL BANK OF COMMERCE

For more than a century Canadian Imperial Bank of Commerce has provided financial services to the Waterloo area.

Waterloo's dynamic growth has created challenges and opportunities from that first day of business, December 9, 1889, when manager H.J. Grasett opened a branch of The Canadian Bank of Commerce, a predecessor of CIBC.

The first offices were in the old Zimmerman house at King and Erb

extended credit to purchase modern equipment.

Since opening, the branch has had 16 managers, of whom E.H. Sippel held the longest tenure, from 1934 to 1953. Over the years managers and their staffs have reflected the bank's stability and excellence to share in the rapid economic development of the region.

The 1961 merger of The Canadian Bank of Commerce and Imperial Bank of Canada to become Canadian

the Campus Centre Building at the University of Waterloo to accommodate students and faculty. It also reinforced CIBC's position as banker to the university and initiated many long-term relationships with students that continue beyond graduation day. Additional branches were opened in 1974 at University and Lincoln and in 1978 at Conestoga Mall, each offering a full range of services.

Today the King and Erb branch is managed by J.S. Palmer, who heads

streets, which is now the site of the Waterloo Hotel. In 1914 the bank completed a new building at 27 King Street North to handle increasing business.

The Commerce was one of three Waterloo banks serving a primarily agrarian economy at the time. Farmers and merchants relied on the bank for loans, savings, and a few financial services. As agriculture became mechanized, the bank

LEFT: Canadian Imperial Bank of Commerce's first quarters in the Zimmerman house in downtown Waterloo circa 1890.

RIGHT: The first branch office structure on King Street circa 1914.

Imperial Bank of Commerce saw the King and Erb location become the bank's main branch for Waterloo. By 1968 a second branch was opened in

a team of 24 full-time employees delivering personalized service to a diverse clientele. They have access to a global network via the branch's sophisticated electronic hookups to meet every customer need, whether a retiree, student, family, small business, or large corporation. As Waterloo continues to advance economically, so will the King and Erb facility of the Canadian Imperial Bank of Commerce.

PRIORITY ONE PACKAGING LIMITED

One of the new stars in the Waterloo industrial firmament is a rapidly expanding specialist in materials-handling systems.

Priority One Packaging Limited provides single-source simplicity to the packaging sector, including the beverage and food industries, glass manufacturing, and others, with complete turnkey or design/build service. Full mechanical and electrical installations are supplied along with complete integration of computerized line controls.

The company was founded in March 1982 by the present owners, Colin Cunningham, president, and his wife, Nita, secretary/treasurer. At first it functioned as a manufacturer's representative, selling machinery and parts from a small office. As sales rose, from an initial $250,000 to a current $8 million annually, the firm acquired a wealth of expertise in the technology and problem-solving

Priority One Packaging Limited's national headquarters at 140 Bathhurst Drive.

areas of the business.

Experience gained by Colin Cunningham with U.S. and European packaging-equipment makers and his own venture led to a major expansion in 1987, when Priority One Packaging occupied the first 13,000 square feet of its permanent facility at 140 Bathhurst Drive. Two years later a 15,000-square-foot addition was built to accommodate machining and assembly operations, while recently another 10,000 square feet was required to cope with the volume of orders.

Through understanding market needs, the Cunninghams have cultivated a long and mutually rewarding association with clients in the food-processing, brewing, distilling, soft-drink, and can-making industries. No small part of their success ensues from a seven-member, in-house engineering department with access to computer-assisted design facilities. Follow-up services ensure correct installation and product flow from equipment supplied by the Waterloo entrepreneur.

Colin M. Cunningham, president and chief executive officer.

Priority One Packaging Limited now employs a full-time staff of 40 people, including engineering and shop personnel, and is pursuing plans to manufacture new lines under license from a world-class German company. In the view of Colin Cunningham, the local plant is well positioned in terms of expertise, efficiency, and the North American market to flourish in the years ahead.

WATERLOO INN

Cordiality, comfort, and fine cuisine flow from a professional background to perpetuate traditions of exceptional hospitality at the city's flagship hotel. The Waterloo Inn blends a traditionally warm and friendly atmosphere with beautifully

The traditionally warm and friendly atmosphere at the Waterloo Inn is enhanced by beautifully appointed rooms, fine cuisine, superb service, and the latest in recreational amenities.

appointed rooms, superb service, and every amenity for the business executive or touring guest.

With the convenience of freeways connecting to its spacious complimentary parking, the 160-room structure offers swift access to surrounding Mennonite country. Nearby is a wealth of visitor attractions, shopping centres, sprawling new industries, and commercial enterprises that dot the Waterloo landscape in close proximity to the university community.

For sightseers there are the famous Farmers' Markets, Seagram Museum, Doon Pioneer Village, the Centre in the Square, and Humanities Theatres. From the inn it's a short hop to the Stratford Festival

or to the Bingeman Park entertainment centre. The latter was one of the early successes of the Bingeman family, who have been the main shareholders of the Waterloo Inn since 1978 and trace their roots to Waterloo County settlement circa 1820.

The capacity of the Inn was doubled in 1982 with the provision of

new hospitality suites, a choice of dining venues, pool, sauna, exercise room, and garden courtyard. All rooms have individual climate controls and color televisions; Prime Minister suites feature wet bars and Jacuzzi baths.

Dining experiences range from breakfast or lunch on The Terrace (a patio cafe) to a candlelight environment in the Vintage Dining Room. The Waterloo Inn also cherishes a reputation for handling the diverse requirements of groups of up to 1,200 people in its 17 modern meeting or banquet areas. The staff responds to business meetings, conferences, seminars, and exhibits, which may be expedited by direct access to elevators and parking. Its Viennese Ballroom is indicative of the establishment's capability, accommodating up to 600 people seated and 1,400 standing, or 200-plus guests in each of three salons.

In every respect the Waterloo Inn, at 475 King North, functions smoothly and efficiently to the delight of the travelling public.

UNIVERSITY OF ST. JEROME'S COLLEGE

The Village of Waterloo was in its infancy, and the church school at St. Agatha a desperate measure, 125 years ago.

However, some 12,000 Roman Catholics were resident in Waterloo County and environs without benefit of a parish classroom, and their spiritual welfare was troubling to the Diocese of Hamilton.

What transpired, to the lasting credit of pioneering priests and educators, forms a compelling chapter in local education annals. From the opening January 1, 1865, in a rude log cabin, to maturity on a great campus, the enthusiasm inherent in the University of St. Jerome's College has never waned.

The inception of the school actually traces to an early failure by St. Agatha priest Father Eugene Funcken to organize classes in his rectory

Reverend A.L. Zinger, C.R.

St. Jerome's College, Berlin, Ontario, 1866.

in the fall of 1858. It was only when his brother Louis, who was partially deaf but fiercely determined, revived the project that it made progress. A cairn erected by alumni in 1935

marks the site of the first St. Jerome's school on the old Wey homestead, about a half-mile east of St. Agatha and six miles west of Waterloo.

This rural setting was short lived, for Father Louis moved the school to Berlin (now Kitchener) in 1866. In an approach not unlike contemporary curriculi, he designed two courses of study: academic preparation for higher studies and commercial subjects leading directly to occupations. The school, in an enlarged residence at Young and Duke streets, opened with 40 male students from Ontario and the United States, plus six day scholars, including three mayors of Berlin: William Jaffray in 1882-1883, Conrad Bitzer in 1892, and Dr. G.H. Bowlby in 1901. Familiar Waterloo names such as Kuntz and Bricker appear in early enrolments; graduates John A. Rittinger and W.J. Motz together founded the *Berliner Journal,* predecessor to the *Kitchener-Waterloo Record.*

Building additions culminated in a two-storey, and then four-storey, structure by 1887, when Father Louis Funcken celebrated 25 years of priesthood. By January 30, 1890, the date of his death in Holland, an ailing Father Louis had seen his creation emerge as an established college in all respects. A bronze statue erected at Young and Duke streets honors his memory.

Alongside the founder, the Very Reverend A.L. Zinger, who was named president in 1905, stands out as a leading figure of St. Jerome's. He built the administration building on Duke Street, added a spacious gymnasium, and raised enrolment to 150 boarding and 30 day scholars. The depression years saw a decline in the stu-

dent body, but by 1940 the school marked 75 years of advancement with approval by the council of universities. In 1947 an affiliation was granted with the University of Ottawa.

The vision of a separate college facility for St. Jerome's was pursued in the late 1940s by Very Reverend Cornelius Siegfried, who has been described as the most aggressive of all the school's presidents. In 1953 Father Mike Weiler also spearheaded the move to the Kingsdale campus in east-end Kitchener. Subsequently, Father Cornelius Siegfried worked tirelessly toward federation with the University of Waterloo in July 1960, just a year after university status was conferred on St. Jerome's.

An administration and classroom facility, a men's residence, and a women's residence (conducted by the School Sisters of Notre Dame) were provided on campus by the fall of 1962. A college library in 1973 and C.L. Siegfried Hall in 1982 were

added to the complex on a spacious site at the northwest corner of the University of Waterloo property.

Father Siegfried, who was succeeded by Reverend Norman L. Choate in 1979, was named president emeritus in 1980, the only president

Reverend Louis Funcken, C.R.

Mayor Aaron Brick addresses the people at the laying of the cornerstone for the new St. Jerome's College building in Berlin, 1907.

dent so honored in the college's history. Upon the retirement of Father Choate, Dr. Douglas Letson took office July 1, 1989, as the first lay president of St. Jerome's.

From 85 students at Kingsdale in 1960, the oldest original institution of higher learning in the region has broadened to accommodate 950 full- and part-time students in the Faculties of Arts and Mathematics. In recent years the college has established an impressive number of innovative programs and institutes relating to education, family life, and theological studies.

In keeping with the founding principles espoused by Father Louis Funcken, the University of St. Jerome's College perpetuates "an enthusiasm for the truth," expressed in a love for learning, an appreciation of one's faith, and a critical mind.

DUTCH BOY FOOD MARKETS

The Dutch Boy signage spanning the twin cities represents 36 years of expansion and modernization from a single grocery outlet to a 15-store supermarket and convenience store group that far exceeds the early ambitions of its founders.

Bread was 10 cents per loaf and roast beef 45 cents per pound when young Barry Humphrey and Frank Beresford bought Bert Reccia's IGA store at 216 King Street West in Kitchener and renamed it the Dutch Boy Food Market. Within a dozen years the selling space was quadrupled, and staff increased to 52 people from 12.

In the meantime, Humphrey and

BELOW: Shown here is one of the first Dutch Boy Food Markets in the area, 351 Margaret Street. Today the chain numbers 15 supermarkets and convenience stores.

Hazelglen Drive in 1972 and the fifth at 1111 Weber Street East in 1975. Between these developments, the company was sold to The Oshawa Group, after which Beresford retired and Humphrey stayed on in his present position as general manager.

ABOVE: Dutch Girl Shopettes, such as this busy spot at 596 Lancaster Street, are popular for their full-service convenience.

East in Kitchener and at Weber and Northfield Drive in Waterloo—the firm's seventh and eighth stores. A companion credit to the Humphrey-Beresford initiative is the development since 1972 of seven Dutch Girl Shopettes, which are full-service convenience stores in the area.

Beresford were well along the acquisition trail with the purchase of Steinberg stores at 351 Margaret Street in 1962 and at 274 Highland Road West in 1964. Dutch Boy's fourth location was opened at 101

In 1983 Dutch Boy was on the move again with its first store in Waterloo at Bridgeport and Weber. Then, in 1987, one of the company's most active years, new supermarkets were opened at 720 Westmount Road

An important contributor to the chain's success has been the 1975 takeover of Longo & Co. Wholesale Produce and its continuation as Belmont Produce as a supplier of fresh fruit and vegetables from warehouse facilities at 341 Marsland Drive.

Entering the 1990s, Dutch Boy Food Markets is extending the Westmount Road market and including a new shopette. This project, overall management, and transactions affecting the efficient operation of the company by some 950 full- and part-time personnel, as well as sponsorship of the Dutch Boy Drum and Bugle Corps, are co-ordinated from the head office at 230 Regina Street North in Waterloo.

WATCON INC. GENERAL CONTRACTORS

Columbia Ice Field arena at the University of Waterloo.

The city's best-known construction company draws on a wealth of experience acquired in the completion of more than 100 area building projects during the past 20 years.

Watcon Inc. (Waterloo Construction) General Contractors has been involved in a truly diverse range of work, from a $25 door repair to the recent erection of a Kitchener plant costing in excess of $3.8 million. Owner and president Douglas F. Bender subscribes to a philosophy that even rates the door-repair job as a plus.

Bender brought credentials from a 12-year association and project superintendent role with Dunker Construction of Kitchener to the formation of Watcon in 1971. At first, the business was scattered at three sites—a rented office on University Avenue, warehouse and shop on Erb Street West, and equipment on Hallman Road. Early successes saw the firm combine operations in a 15,120-square-foot structure at the present 599 Colby Drive property in 1977. By this time subsidiary Bender Developments Ltd. was commencing to build and lease industrial space that presently occupies three sites in Waterloo and one in St. Clements.

Watcon has excelled in a variety of industrial, commercial, and institutional assignments, of which a large proportion has comprised design-build arrangements between owner and contractor. In the first year Doug Bender handled the projects alone via subcontracting. Soon he assembled a skilled crew that peaked at 45 employees and now averages 15 to 20 people. Several have been on staff since the early days.

The company has been a family affair from the outset for the president and his wife, Bernice, who is secretary/treasurer. Doug's father, Edward, was field superintendent from 1973 until his retirement in 1983. The couple's children are all active at the plant: Darryl works full time, and Dale and Lori work part time.

An impressive roster of contracts fulfilled in the region by Watcon Inc. General Contractors includes the Union Gas Administration Centre, Waterloo; Blessed Sacrament Roman Catholic Church, Kitchener; Ron Schmalz Motors, Mildmay; Kinsmen national headquarters, Cambridge; St. Clements Community Centre; Columbia Ice Field (hockey arena), University of Waterloo; Ratz-Bechtel Funeral Home addition, Kitchener; Forwell's Variety Plaza, Heidelberg; Elmira Professional Building; Mac-Donald-Westburn Ltd., Kitchener and Waterloo; and Dyck Industries, Waterloo.

Watcon Inc.'s design-build headquarters on Colby Drive.

THE HUETHER HOTEL

The stunning re-creation of original grandeur and brewing tradition at a historic city landmark forms a rising star on the region's heritage horizon.

Almost a century and a half of social and business identity attaches to The Huether Hotel and Lion Brewery and Museum at Princess and King streets in uptown Waterloo. It is truly a treasure house of lore and lager, in which the present owners have recaptured lost splendor while fashioning a contemporary environment.

The founding coopers, brewer, and hosts would applaud the industry and dedication poured into this stately edifice by proprietors Bernie and Sonia Adlys and their sons Kelly and David. Like the first innkeeper, William Rebscher, who made beer there after buying the property in 1842, and a trio of hustling Huethers, two generations of Adlys are out to eclipse past performances. And in the closing decade of the twentieth century, they are well advanced toward new dimensions of product and hospitality.

The Adlys' involvement in the hotel traces to the acquisition of the then-Hotel Kent by John Adlys, Bernie's father, from Albert C. Snyder in 1953. Adlys' hopes and aspira-

The Adlys family (from left) Bernie II, Christina, Bernie, Sonia, Kelly, and David.

tions for the venture, as well as a wealth of expertise imparted to a young son and daughter-in-law, are reflected in prevailing evidence of family pride.

Founder Rebscher, a German brewer from nearby Wilmot Township, set the tone for the site with a brewery and inn. After his death in 1856, German-born Adam Huether took over the operation and renamed it the Lion Brewery. When son Christopher Huether succeeded in 1865, the signage proclaimed "C. Huether Brewer and Maltster—C. Huether's Hotel—Lion Brewery." Production of 728 barrels per year, valued at $3,648, was advertised as the "best beer in the county."

Christopher Huether was ambitious, securing the first licence to sell

The Huether Hotel and Lion Brewery and Museum is a historic city landmark at Princess and King streets.

The history of the Lion Brewery and Museum dates back to 1856.

beer in the hotel in 1868, adding rooms and an elaborate Victorian facade and tower in 1880, and amassing some 135 acres within the community. By 1886 the four-storey hotel comprised 40 bedrooms, seven parlors, a dining room, office, and bar, while the brewery was making 10,000 barrels of beer and malting 15,000 bushels annually.

The next Huether, son Christopher Nicholas, operated the business with partner J.R. Eden from 1894 to 1899, when he left to establish the Berlin Lion Brewery at King and Victoria streets in Kitchener. This later became the Blue Top, Ranger, and, by 1953, Dow Brewery. C.N. Huether's holdings in Waterloo were bought at debt auction by Theresa Kuntz in 1899 and subsequently were operated by the local Kuntz Brewery interests as a malt storage, while the hotel was managed by a succession of proprietors.

Under the banner of Hotel Ewald, the structure and property at 59

King Street North was sold to Lincoln Stroh in 1930 and then to Albert Snyder, a well-known city hockey impressario, in 1935. Records show the latter transaction for $700, with room rental at one dollar per day, during the Depression.

Renaissance of the hotel has been a long-term objective dating approximately from 1975, when Bernie and Sonia acquired outright ownership. Initially the transformation was internal as new heating, air conditioning, fire-detection units, and a roof were installed. (An $80,000 fire had ravaged the upstairs in 1969.) In 1984 Kelly and David led a facelift of the exterior, opened up old windows, and started on main floor renovations. Meanwhile, an old cavern uncovered under the rear of the building was targeted for renewal as a brewery.

As plans escalated for the Kitchener-Waterloo area's first European-style brew pub, the lower level was rebuilt amid original stone and mortar walls as a dining lounge complete with displays of artifacts and memorabilia from the hospitality industry. Visitors can see vats brewing chemi-

cal-free Lion Lite and Lager, Lion Dry, English Ale, Adlys Ale, and Huether Premium. Upstairs they can opt for the sports bar, patio, or a well-appointed billiard room with two antique Boston tables circa 1920, and three full-size snooker surfaces.

Since the official opening of the Lion Brewery and Museum in June 1987, the Adlys family, which also includes younger children Christina and Bernie II, has earned widespread local and national publicity for its accomplishments. A 1989 Waterloo Regional Heritage Foundation Award was made in recognition of the restoration, which the previous year had received heritage designations of the cavern and exterior facade.

In a fascinating way the Adlys have tapped into a welcome scenario distinguished by a relaxed and friendly ambience and heightened by professional service, fine cuisine, and refreshing natural beer.

John Peter Adlys, father of the present proprietor, who purchased the Hotel Kent (now The Huether Hotel) in 1953.

NESBITT THOMSON DEACON, INC.

The city's leading investment firm is a relative newcomer to the Waterloo business scene, but Nesbitt Thomson Deacon, Inc., has served the Twin Cities community for 35 years.

Presently, the full-service stock, bond, and financial specialist functions from spacious, highly visible facilities in the Marsland Centre at 20 Erb Street West—its first and only Waterloo site. Prior to 1976 the business had been located in downtown Kitchener for 30 years.

The first area manager and sole salesman was Bill Meikle, who opened the branch at 38 King Street in Kitchener in 1946. His successor, in a tiny office shared with the Bank of Toronto, was Bob Learn, whose father operated the Learn Pharmacy at Erb and King in Waterloo. Donald Schaefer, who was manager from 1954 to 1957, added a second salesman to the branch, which subsequently moved into the Canada Trust building.

Re-location to Waterloo established manager David Oborne and a staff of six employees on the ninth floor of the new Marsland Centre. Interestingly, Oborne would follow both Learn and Schaefer as national sales manager of the company. In 1983 William Michael Phippen was

ABOVE: A.J. Nesbitt, founder.

appointed Waterloo branch manager. Phippen, who is also a vice-president of Nesbitt Thomson, supervises a staff of 15 people, occupying twice the original space and including a futures department on the main floor of the centre.

Nesbitt Thomson was formed in 1912 by A.J. Nesbitt and P.A. Thomson. From an early expertise in power company financing and then institutional investment, the firm has broadened in scope and size. In 1977 it acquired the Canadian investment

house Bongard, Leslie & Company, followed by the 1984 addition of Canavest with a large floor trading force, and, in 1985, control of the U.S. investment firm Fahnestock & Company. More recently, Nesbitt Thomson merged with F.H. Deacon Hodgson in September 1986.

The first of many broker/banker mergers saw the Bank of Montreal purchase 75 percent of Nesbitt Thomson in August 1987. With 34

BELOW: P.A. Thomson, founder.

offices and 1,700 employees worldwide, the company is well positioned for the future. The bank's investment in Nesbitt Thomson Deacon, Inc., certainly attests to this firm's integrity and prominence in the Canadian brokerage industry.

Back row (from left): Bill Riches; William Dahmer; Carl Kaufman; Michael Tolton; William Michael Phippen, branch manager and vice-president; Paul McCusker; Eugenia Damianakis; Alan Kneeshaw; Ed Lynch, assistant branch manager; and Mark Schram. Front row (from left): Mary Low Nauman; Denise MacLeod; Terri Simmons, operations manager; and Kerry Moore. Not shown is Paul Clarke.

QUIGLEY CONTAINERS LTD.

The efficient plant is run by skilled people committed to quality.

A foundation of quality, service, and ongoing modernization anchors the aspirations of a Waterloo specialist in custom packaging.

Quigley Containers Limited at 430 Conestogo Road is marking 25 years of progress in the development of innovative solutions for users of corrugated packaging and related products.

A pioneer and leader in the sheet-plant business, the local company was founded in 1965 by Fred Quigley, who applied a personal touch to his experience with a national corporation. His son, Paul A. Quigley, continues traditions of excellence while widening market horizons. Since acquiring the firm outright in 1981, he has added raw-material sources, new equipment, and a Toronto facility to the enterprise.

One of president Paul Quigley's early strategies involved joint action with other corrugated sheet converters to form TenCorr Packaging, Inc., in 1983. It installed a $5-million Japanese corrugator to ensure a continuous supply of paper. In 1988 Quigley also became a partner in a similar operation, Montcor of Montreal.

During 1988 and 1989 more than $500,000 has been invested to buy a sheet plant in Toronto, which now serves as a warehouse and sales office, and to upgrade the Waterloo operation, where all production has been consolidated. Output has been expedited by a computerized specification program that has been fine tuned over the past eight years in concert with strict inventory control and scheduling to meet delivery deadlines.

A well-trained staff of 31 employees functions as a team in a safe, clean environment at Waterloo, whether designing, cutting, slotting, or folding cartons for a diverse clientele of 500 across southwestern Ontario. Production spans the whole spectrum of corrugated packaging, including heavy-duty pallet packs and shipping cartons made under Canadian license.

With the capacity for additional volume and larger cartons, and the imminent participation of U.S. state-of-the-art papermaking facilities, Quigley Containers Limited is poised to double its volume over the next few years. And in that attainment, president Paul Quigley is committed to maintain unsurpassed standards of quality and service.

On-time service is provided by Quigley's own fleet of trucks.

PILLER SAUSAGES & DELICATESSENS LTD.

Old-world tradition, national prominence, and high impact on its home city contribute to an outstanding business success story on the site of Piller Sausages & Delicatessens Ltd.

Multiple expansion, modernization, and product development have accompanied the rise of this upscale meat processor from limited beginnings under three generations of Huber family proprietorship. The extensive plant and administration facility off Wismer Street represent a blend of European expertise with Canadian marketing know-how against a background of unwavering commitment to quality.

The Piller organization of the 1990s has come a long way from the

small butcher shop established in the hamlet of Rummelhart, on the west side of Waterloo, by current company president Wilhelm Huber, Sr., and his partner, George Piller. Within three months the business was re-located to the present site, and two years after starting up Piller sold his interest to Konrad Huber, Wilhelm Sr.'s father, as well as brothers Heinrich Sr. and Edward in 1959.

At that time the company's main outlets were a few local grocery stores, plus the Kitchener and Waterloo Farmers' Markets. Today the firm supplies more than 1,700 delicatessens and supermarkets from coast to coast with more than 13 million pounds of cooked and smoked meat products in 120 different lines. And, from a two-man operation, it has grown to 204 employees.

One constant in the day-to-day

Owners Edward, Wilhelm, and Heinrich Huber.

routine has not changed. Rosina Huber, mother of the founding trio, who provided meals and refreshments to employees in the early years. She views with pride the involvement of five grandsons—Willy Jr., Conrad, Gerhart, Heinrich Jr., and Robert—and the perpetuation of company concern for staff benefits and working conditions.

Longtime Waterloo residents could easily have charted Piller's fortunes by monitoring construction amid former rural countryside at the Wismer Street premises. No less than 31 separate expansions have been carried out over the past three decades, culminating in state-of-the-art processing and packaging lines and upgraded office accommodation covering some 150,000 square feet.

Time and growth, however, have not altered the family's dedication to "the finest in European meats for the Canadian palate." From inception,

The original Piller sausage-making facility in 1957.

the Waterloo enterprise has excelled from a sense of pride inherent from the founders' great-grandfather, who opened a butcher shop in his native Yugoslavia in 1880. Drawing on old-fashioned recipes and methods, the Hubers still use slow and natural

aging, curing, and smoking processes to turn out the highest-quality meats.

As a testament to its success, Piller has been awarded 13 gold medals at the International European Food Fair competition in recognition of superior ingredients, recipes, and taste. The firm has also won the Junior Achievement Award of Excellence, and is a member of the Waterloo Chamber of Commerce and the Canadian Meat Council. A further affirmation of stature is a "AAA" rating for overall quality, the only such designation of a meat-processing plant by federal authorities.

Always in the forefront of marketing skill, the company accented its identity in the late 1980s with the introduction of True Deli as the trademark for a growing line of top-grade delicatessen meats, savory sausages, hams, and salamis for retail outlets across Canada and the United States.

In keeping with a long record of consumer awareness, the Hubers

are responding to a new era of changing tastes and nutritional needs across the whole spectrum of meat preparation, technology, and content. Accordingly, Golden Valley Farms in Arthur, Ontario, opened in 1988 and is perhaps the most advanced turkey-processing facility in the world. There Piller is a full partner with P&H Foods (producer of the Butterball brand) in the output of a variety of poultry products that are low in fat and high in protein. In addition, the poultry alliance is meeting modern lifestyles with the issuance of easy-to-prepare recipes for turkey sausage, turkey rolls, and roast turkey.

Piller Sausages & Delicatessens Ltd. prizes its Waterloo setting, which offers a clean environment and nearby agricultural resources, and values its acceptance in the marketplace and standing in the industry. All of these factors contribute to a solid, progressive company for today and tomorrow.

The expanded, modern meat-processing plant today.

PEAT MARWICK THORNE

The accounting practice of Peat Marwick Thorne reflects a widely known international identity, but its Waterloo office is distinguished by a strong area presence spanning more than a half-century.

The firm was originally William Robertson & Company, founded in Kitchener by William Robertson. The original managing partner, Tom McCauley, was a student in 1949, then a graduate chartered accountant in 1955, and two years later a partner in the Robertson organization. In 1961 the firm added two partners and became McCauley Robertson Bissell and Holman. When they joined forces with Peat Marwick in 1972, the quartet had built up a sound client base, to which they soon added the newly formed Regional Municipality of Waterloo. The connection dates from 1952, when Tom McCauley became auditor for Waterloo County.

In a pivotal expansionary move,

The Peat Marwick Thorne partners in the Waterloo office are (back row, from left) Keith Holman, Bill Gladwish, Jeff Sproat, Bill Mitchell, Mike Johnston, Ted Conlin, and Paul Denomme. In the front row are (seated, from left) John Moore, Lori Brien, and Tom McCauley.

the entire operation, with a staff of 18 employees, was transferred to the Marsland Centre in Waterloo in January 1973. There the first truly national accounting firm in the city developed a large and diverse clientele. After a decade the practice occupied more spacious offices in Allen Square, where, on September 1, 1987, a merger was completed with Johnston & Sproat of Waterloo. Subsequent growth led to the leasing of 20,000 square feet on two floors of the Weibe Xerox office complex at 180 Columbia Street West.

In September 1989 Peat Marwick and Thorne Ernst & Whinney

merged to become Peat Marwick Thorne, the largest accounting firm in the Waterloo region and in Canada. Presently composed of 10 partners, the Waterloo office of Peat Marwick Thorne engages 20 additional chartered accountants and 85 personnel in all. The practice is organized in three divisions: the tax department, largest in the region with three partners and 10 staff; private business, for owner-managed businesses, comprising data-processing and microcomputing advisory services; and the audit department, for larger commercial, industrial, and governmental clients. Bill Gladwish assumed the role of partner in charge of the Waterloo office at the time of the 1989 merger.

Internationally, Peat Marwick Thorne is a part of the world's foremost public accounting and consulting organization as the result of a 1987 merger with Klynveld Main Goerdeler of Europe.

The following individuals, companies, and organizations have made a valuable commitment to the quality of this publication. Windsor Publications and The Waterloo Chamber of Commerce gratefully acknowledge their participation in *Waterloo: An Illustrated History.*

Abroyd Communications Limited
Bauer Industries Limited
Beresford Box Company Limited
B.F. Goodrich Canada Inc.
Canadian Imperial Bank of Commerce
Canadian Industrial Innovation Centre
Clemmer Industries Limited
J.L. Cortes Architect Corporation
Cumming Cockburn Limited
Dutch Boy Food Markets
Economical Mutual Insurance Company
Enasco Limited
The Equitable Life Insurance Company of Canada
Genisys Group International Inc.
H&O Centerless Grinding
The Huether Hotel
Jessop's Speedy Cleaners (1984) Limited
Kramer+Grebe Canada Ltd.
Labatt Breweries of Canada Limited
Latem Group

La-Z-Boy Canada Limited
The Manufacturers Life Insurance Company
Marsland Centre Limited
Melloul-Blamey Construction Limited
Millard Precision Machine & Tool Limited
The Mutual Group
NCR Canada Ltd
Nesbitt Thomson Deacon, Inc.
Ontario Seed Company Ltd.
Peat Marwick Thorne
Piller Sausages & Delicatessens Ltd.
Priority One Packaging Limited
Quigley Containers Ltd.
Raytheon Canada Limited
Swenco Limited
University of St. Jerome's College
University of Waterloo
Van Dresser Limited
Watcon Inc. General Contractors
Waterloo Bedding Company Limited
Waterloo Inn
Waterloo Regional Credit Union
Zehrs Markets
Zepf Technologies Incorporated

The histories of these companies and organizations appear in Chapter 7, beginning on page 146.

Guide to Further Reading

The growing importance of local history in understanding our sense of identity as Canadians is evident in the diverse range of books available to those who wish to learn more about our past. What follows is a select list of some of the more important studies and an indication as to where more extensive bibliographies may be found.

An earlier history of the city, *Welcome to Waterloo* (1982) by Marg Rowell, Ed Devitt, and Pat McKegney is mandatory reading as are the many excellent scholarly articles by Elizabeth Bloomfield arising out of her 1983 University of Guelph Ph.D. thesis, "City-Building Processes in Berlin/Kitchener and Waterloo 1870-1930" and which is now available on microfilm. Trudi E. Bunting's *Kitchener-Waterloo The Geography of Mainstreet* (Waterloo, 1984) and David F. Walker (ed) *Manufacturing in Kitchener-Waterloo: A Long-Term Perspective* (Waterloo, 1987) offer valuable insights into the city's growth. These four works contain bibliographies that could guide the reader to sources well beyond the scope of this book. A new study by E. Reginald Good, *Frontier Community to Urban Congregation* (Kitchener, 1988) offers new primary research on the early years. Paul and Hildi Tiessen's *Waterloo County Landscapes 1930-1960, A Sense of Place* (1986) and their *Waterloo Portfolio: Woldemar Neufeld's Paintings and Block Prints*

of Waterloo, (1982) relate the world of art and literature to Waterloo County Life and add important dimensions to our appreciation of the past. The paintings by Woldemar Neufeld in *Waterloo: An Illustrated History* were first published in *Waterloo Portfolio* and are reproduced courtesy of the artist and Sand Hill Books. My own histories of Kitchener (1983) and Cambridge (1987) contain detailed annotated guides to further readings. The Grace Schmidt Room at the Kitchener Public Library maintains extensive holdings in local history including an index to what is unquestionably the single most important resource—*Annual Reports* of the *Waterloo Historical Society.* The Waterloo Public Library, too, is rapidly expanding its collections in this important field as is the Dana Porter Library at the University of Waterloo and the Library at Wilfrid Laurier University. Most recently a new publication by Elizabeth MacNaughton and Pat Wagner (eds) *Guide to Historical Resources in the Regional Municipality of Waterloo* (1989) is a welcome and useful supplement to the existing bibliographies.

Index